A
SPITFIRE
GIRL

A
SPITFIRE
GIRL

ONE OF THE WORLD'S GREATEST FEMALE ATA FERRY PILOTS TELLS HER STORY

Mary Ellis

As told to Melody Foreman

Frontline Books

A SPITFIRE GIRL
One of the World's Greatest Female ATA Ferry Pilots Tells Her Story

This edition published in 2016 by Frontline Books,
an imprint of Pen & Sword Books Ltd,
47 Church Street, Barnsley, S. Yorkshire, S70 2AS

ISBN: 978-1-47389-536-2

For more information on our books, please visit
www.frontline-books.com
email info@frontline-books.com
or write to us at the above address.

Printed and bound by CPI Group (UK) Ltd, Croydon, CR0 4YY
Typeset in 10.5/12.5 point Palatino

Contents

The Reputation the Air Transport Auxiliary has always enjoyed is second to none. It was formed in 1940 to supply the Fleet Air Arm and the RAF with aircraft flown straight from factory to airfield. By the end of the war, the ATA boasted around nearly four thousand pilots and ground crew, of whom over 160 of the pilots were women.

The list of different aircraft flown by Mary Ellis is astonishing by any standards, but nothing exceptional for the ATA. The knowledge and skills with which she and her colleagues were endowed tell their own story. They were an amazing group of people.

My first contact with the ATA was at an event at Lyneham in 1990 to mark their 50th Anniversary, when I was invited by Diane Barnato- Walker – another heroine of the ATA.

Through Diana, now enhanced by this lively biography of Mary Ellis by Melody Foreman, my admiration for these ladies knows no bounds. This is an adventure story of the first quality and I salute its main character, and its author. Your readers will love it.

Acknowledgements

I would sincerely like to thank all those people who believe as passionately as I do that Mary's astounding story of courage, skill, determination and achievement, should be told.

In writing this book I have met several noble people along the way who should not be forgotten for their kindness and support. Firstly, and rightfully so, I owe an immense debt of gratitude to Mary herself for so kindly and gently sharing her invaluable and often personal memories with me throughout our many meetings at her home or on an airfield – meetings that soon developed into an inspired friendship.

I am profoundly grateful to Dr Julian Brock for a raft of support and genius wisdom in all its guises. To Dr Margaret Clotworthy, whose dreams of becoming a Spitfire pilot are bound to come true because of her passion to fly, dynamic approach to life science and for her gift of great friendship, I thank so very much.

I am obliged to HRH Prince Michael and the lovely Carolyn Grace who both wrote special forewords and tributes to Mary and the ATA for this book. I must also thank author Robin Brooks who first introduced me to Mary several years ago.

I must express gratitude to the leading aviation author, military historian and editor Andy Saunders who, when he learnt that this book was underway, introduced me to Frontline Books. Thank you to my editor, Paul Hamblin, for quietly and confidently nudging me in the right direction.

Never will I forget the kindness and hospitality of former ATA First Officer Molly Rose JP, DL, OBE, who invited me into her home to share such honest memories of flying and her life experiences during wartime. Sadly, Molly died just before this book was published but her record of knowing Mary and so many other colleagues of the ATA is there to read and will live on in the pages of this book. Thank you to

Molly's son, Graham Rose, who, in his position as Chairman of the Air Transport Auxiliary Association, introduced me to his unforgettable mother, Molly. The ATA Museum at Maidenhead, headed by Richard Poad MBE, must also be applauded.

To the Battle of Britain pilot and talented writer Wing Commander Tom Neil DFC and Bar, AE, who guided me on authentic aviation matters when needed, I thank so much. Likewise to the Spitfire pilots of today who are happy to answer my questions and share their vast knowledge of this wonderful aircraft with me.

Thanks must also go to my sisters, Madeline and Helen, my friends Bryan Simpson, of The Historic Aircraft Collection, historian Tony Parslow, and Second World War aircraft recovery specialist, Terry Parsons of the Kent Battle of Britain Museum Trust, Rosie and Richard, Christine, and, of course, the late, dear, not forgotten, RAF Warrant Officer Neville Croucher, a Second World War pilot who was always so interested in the tremendous efforts of the ATA which kept him and thousands of air crew supplied with aircraft throughout the war.

Melody Foreman

'My Friend Mary Ellis'

Spitfire Pilot
Carolyn Grace

Flying a Spitfire is undeniably an emotive experience demanding immense attention to detail, judgement and inherent skill, these attributes in combination are rare. To be flying not only Spitfires, of all different Marks, but an incredible seventy-six other types of heavy piston engine fighters and bombers demands attributes far in excess of those I have mentioned and there were only a few pilots who achieved this level of excellence and one undoubtedly is Mary Ellis.

Not only was Mary flying these aircraft to the front line squadrons she was doing so without any navigational aids other than a compass and without radio assistance of any type. Relying on her calm attitude to the situation put before her, she excelled in a manner that few achieved but would be the very last person to ever intimate in conversation that she did anything special. With encouragement Mary would captivate those fortunate enough to be in earshot of her quiet voice when, finally, she would reveal just a part of her flying career during the Second World War in the Air Transport Auxiliary. I have the honour of knowing Mary for the past twenty years during which time she has never changed, with her love of aviation remaining strong. To my great delight I took Mary flying in my Spitfire (the first time) at Sandown on 29 July 2005. Mary and I had an exhilarating time together, roaring around the cliffs of the Isle of Wight in 'our' Spitfire, and sharing the flying with her was sheer unadulterated pleasure!

The second time I flew Mary was for a documentary. On 16 June 2010 Mary and I set off in the Spitfire from Bentwaters in Suffolk flying out over the sea. Once again I flew a Victory Roll much to Mary's delight. She then flew the Spitfire with her inherent skill, but this time we were more composed as we were on film! On landing I set about cleaning the Spitfire for the next filming slot when I noticed an absence of not only my team, but the fire crew as well. I looked around and there they all were transfixed by Mary, whose exuberance about what she had just flown in, encouraged her to talk about the aircraft she had delivered in the ATA. Mary was quite unaware of the impact she was having on her incredulous listeners, which I found just wonderful.

Mary Ellis is an astounding aviator and, as one of the elite woman pilots of the ATA, formed a unique band of talented flyers delivering desperately needed aircraft to the theatre of war. Amongst many other types delivered there were the iconic Spitfires of all different Marks. They had no pre-training on the aircraft they were tasked to collect and deliver just an A5 folder being the Ferry Pilots Notes. Pilots today can only aspire to fly the aircraft Mary delivered in tumultuous times and precarious conditions without fault or failure. Pilots the like of Mary Ellis remain unique in the world of aviation.

Carolyn Grace
Spitfire pilot and owner of 'The Grace Spitfire ML407'
Autumn 2016

Prologue

On a bright spring morning in 2013 I stood on the top deck of a ferry gliding towards the Isle of Wight and watched the waters of the Solent twinkling their welcome. Tiny sailing boats speckled the scenery all around and a sense of calm I'd seldom experienced before reigned within me throughout that short but glorious journey. As the island port grew closer I sensed I was about to step into the world of a woman who had achieved more in her lifetime than any of us dare hope.

I was about to meet Mary Ellis, aviator supreme, pioneer, entrepreneur, rally driver, gardener, farmer and more latterly a television celebrity who had flown 400 Spitfires and seventy-six different varieties of aircraft including heavy bombers during the Second World War. And yet within the hour we'd be at her home sharing a simple pot of tea served in delicate cups and saucers decorated with tiny flowers and I'd be softly persuading this heroine how her experiences were so much more than what she implied merely was 'water under the bridge'.

That morning as I felt the cool sea breeze drift across me during the ferry trip I tried to imagine Mary's world of seventy years ago. So I looked up at the sky and thought I saw her roaring towards the island at 400mph in a Spitfire Mk.Vb and then I blink and she's gone – a speeding angel on a mission of great importance. Oh there she is again, I can just make her out, flying her way back towards the mainland at the controls of a Supermarine Sea Otter. This time her delivery is for the Fleet Air Arm at Portsmouth, and then she'll be collecting a new Seafire and heading swiftly for her beloved Hamble – home of the all-women's ferry pool of the Air Transport Auxiliary. She'll be watching out for the barrage balloons of course, keeping an eye out for the storm clouds gathering in the distance and any dreaded Luftwaffe looking for prey.

Mary was flying in a combat zone and there was nothing unusual for her about that.

Suddenly it's the crackling loudspeaker on the ferry instructing all passengers to return to their cars for disembarkation that jolts me back to the present, and so I make ready for the final leg of my journey to the house that Mary built more than fifty years ago. She had named it 'Leafield' after the pretty Oxfordshire hamlet in which she was born.

Once off the ferry I drove for about forty minutes along small, slow-moving roads and tidy villages so typical of an island lost in a time resonant of the 1950s – a serene time when manners and etiquette were the fabric of success and life felt more complete.

I needn't have bothered with a map to Mary's place as I could have looked to the skies and followed any light aircraft heading towards the one and only airport which throughout the 1950s and 1960s she had developed and then become known as Europe's first woman air commandant. She still lives nearby.

When I reach her village and turn into the hidden lane off the main road I note the decorative black iron gates open wide in welcome and a gravel driveway leading to her beloved 'Leafield' – a house which looks like it's made of gingerbread. The lawns are perfect and the flowerbeds fit to bloom into a parade of colour.

Mary steps out of her conservatory to greet me. She is tiny, feminine and supremely elegant in light-coloured trousers, black jumper and long arty beads that make her sparkle and chime more like Tinkerbell from Peter Pan than a devil-may-care, saucy tomboy who flew hearty Spitfires, Hurricanes, Wellington bombers and all the rest during a brutal and bloody war.

At first she was cautious and polite and then we both laughed at the ludicrousness of small talk. We agreed plain speaking is best. Soon her charm began to work its old world magic into our conversation and after three hours into our interview she asked if I would like to join her for a glass or two or three of wine. A friendship was born and I witnessed then, as I have ever since, the character of a sharp and especially astute woman whose responses to my questions were often delivered in a deliciously laconic way.

I tried desperately not to gawp like a girl at the depth of her many wartime recollections, and she's not afraid to share her opinions of today's world. Mary is an extremely youthful spirit from an age gone by. Her bright sense of fun came from an era when joy and friendship were less tarnished by a modern world obsessed with financial gain and the malice it cultivates.

Then breaking off from her memories of the war, she'd lighten the load of the conversation and exclaim what really made her really cross was how rabbits kept eating her plants in the garden, and then she giggled when I suggested she build a scarecrow to frighten them off. That day, and indeed any time I see Mary now, I realise I am in the company of a rare, resilient and extraordinary woman who despite having already lived many lives of the fullest-ever kind, has discovered in her hundredth year how fate has even more in store including Spitfire adventures, aviation anniversary events, a raft of television and media appearances, and now even this book!

Mary's significance in these times of intense political upheaval and violent threats upon world peace is as potent as ever, and needed identifying in a full biography. Her vast experiences as a wartime ferry pilot, as with those recorded and cherished by all her friends in the ATA, many of whom where loved and now gone, provide us with a deep reservoir of stories showing indomitable determination, spirit and fortitude – characteristics which Mary in her hundredth year can only hope would rise to the surface in any generation facing a threat to its very survival.

Mary Wilkins (Ellis) was born during the First World War when brave pilots in delicate but feisty Sopwith Camels and other lightweight military aircraft were in combat with the enemy German aircrews at the controls of Fokker aeroplanes over the trenches of France and Belgium. Many years later several of those young British aviators who survived that bloodiest of conflicts went on to serve with Mary in the Air Transport Auxiliary in the Second World War, and with ferry pilot colleagues she was to hear these old fighter pilots tell tales of struggle and survival like no other.

As a young woman, a diminutive Mary flew the iconic super-sleek little Spitfire during the Second World War, followed thirty or so years later by an experience in another aviation phenomenon as in 1977 she was in another cockpit shooting across the skies in the supersonic Concorde at a top speed of 1,334mph.

Today, she is often back in two-seater Spitfires and proving the darling of the twenty-first century aviation circuit. So while we pause to inhale deeply in awe at her achievements and read her memories of some truly extraordinary people and events from over the decades, please remember how a century to Mary has proved as long as she wants it to be!

But before we fly back into the past of this mercurial woman there are of course a number of checks one must do on the ground and in the cockpit before take-off. As Mary's dear friend and Air Transport Auxiliary pilot colleague Molly Rose OBE who was interviewed for this book, says: 'one spends more hours getting in and out of the cockpit than flying itself!'

Indeed, when we began this book we thought it necessary to include mention of the pioneering women aviators of yesteryear, and of course Mary's own colleagues who came and went in her life because they influenced her fate and created the layers of such a rich life story. Context may not be not all but it does give flavour to character. This may also go some way towards understanding how and why flying got so well and truly into Mary's blood but be warned as some questions have no definitive answers if fate has got anything to do with it.

It's true there were some extraordinary co-incidences that have occurred in the long life of this great female pilot. Now we'll let you decide what they were and are and as you read this book, do bring to mind the words of the great war poet Siegfried Sassoon which are carved into the ATA Memorial at St Paul's Cathedral in London: 'Remember then that also we in a moon's course are history'.

Melody Foreman
2016

Chronology

Mary Ellis' ATA/Aviation Timeline

1941   Hatfield – Training

1942
February   Posted to White Waltham – Training flight
April   White Waltham – Ferrying
June   White Waltham – Ferrying
July, 19th   Seconded to Luton – Ferrying
August, 2nd   White Waltham – Ferrying
October, 25th   Posted to No.15 Ferry Pool, Hamble – Ferrying

1943
May, 13th   Posted to Thame – twin-engine training on Oxfords
May, 20th   Back to Hamble – Ferrying
August, 18th   White Waltham – Wellington training
September, 3rd   Back to Hamble – Ferrying heavy twin-engine
                    aircraft

1944
April, 20th   White Waltham – Hudson training
May, 2nd   Back to Hamble – Ferrying heavy twin-engine
                    aircraft

1945
March, 6   Late Night Duty Pilot – receiving programme for
                    next day flights
May, 8th   VE Day

August, 15th	Hamble closed
August, 20th	Seconded to No.6 Ferry Pool, Ratcliffe
October, 6th	Ratcliffe Open Day – Demonstrated Tempest
November, 10th	Posted to 41 Group RAF, White Waltham
November, 20th	ATA disbanded
December, 3rd	White Waltham (RAFVR) – Ferrying

1946

January, 1st	White Waltham – Ferrying
February, 1st	White Waltham – Ferrying
March	Flying Meteors
March, 30th	Demobilised from the ATA/RAFVR – ceased ferrying
November, 13th	Cowes, Isle of Wight – Flying Proctor for JPS Clarke Esq.
December, 1st	Cowes – Flying Proctor

1947

August	Cowes – Flying Gemini

1948

July, 17th	Sandown – Flying Gemini

Chapter 1

My First Spitfires

Air Transport Auxiliary Ferry Pool No.15
The Operations Room
Hamble, Hampshire – 09.05 hours, 13 October 1942

As I arrived for work one brisk autumn morning I parked my old black Ford car in a space near the Ops Block as usual and noted that the weather was calm and offered up the use of a pale, clear sky in which to fly my quota of aircraft deliveries for the day. As usual none of us girls ever knew what was on the agenda, so there was often a crackle of excitement in the air. That particular morning, I picked up the chitty with my name on it as usual and looked at the information outlining my aircraft deliveries for the day. Then I spotted such a longed-for word – 'Spitfires'.

All I could do was stand silent and stunned as I revelled in a quiet, surreal ecstasy. My eyes had seen the instruction but my brain was in a swirl as I had not just one but two of these beautiful fighter aeroplanes waiting patiently for me to fly to the RAF boys who urgently needed them. My first ever Spitfires! Finally, I had my chance to pilot the aircraft everyone raved about and loved. Along with the trusty Hawker Hurricane, the graceful and super-fast Supermarine Spitfire had played a seminal role in winning the Battle of Britain in 1940, and now I was to fly one. I'll never ever forget the rush of adrenaline that hit me that morning – the excitement was overwhelming and I might even have let out a small scream when I finally realised my dream had come true. I checked my name on the chitty again … yes, sure enough it said 'Mary Wilkins'.

Many of the girls around me had already flown Spitfires, and so not wanting to lose my cool and British reserve, I pretended it was just an average day and the two Spits marked down on my list were just the

1

usual – the types of aircraft I'd already flown many times like the dear old Miles Magister, the Tiger Moth, Hurricane, Fairey Battle or a taxi Fairchild Argus.

All around me as those precious seconds of realisation sank in, the other girls at Hamble were chattering about their own delivery lists which had been organised by our efficient and stately blonde Operations Manager, Alison King.

The hubbub in the room was as it was most days, loud and friendly. Someone had been allocated a twin-engine de Havilland Mosquito bomber and she was asking if anyone had any tips on flying it. I heard her say it was her first 'Mossie'. 'Yes,' volunteered my friend First Officer Jackie Sorour, 'it's a lovely aircraft, lightweight and mostly wood and a little tricky to land. Let's check the Ferry Pilots Notes and find some more technical information to gen up on it. You'll need to spend twenty minutes clueing up in the cockpit before you start the thing.' More questions were asked. 'Anyone flown an Albacore?' and 'I've got a Barracuda, what's that like?'

Then there was a small groan from the corner of the room. Someone had a Tiger Moth to fly hundreds of miles north which was fine on a hot summer's day but in chilly weather one could expect to freeze in the open cockpit. It was also about the slowest aircraft one could find and at a top speed of 60 mph it could take a couple of days for us to reach Prestwick in Scotland.

So off we all went, pleased and proud – us women pilots of the Air Transport Auxiliary wearing our dark navy blue tunics, trousers and fur-lined boots, and parachutes slung haphazardly over our shoulders. Two of us walked towards an ATA office where we could read up on the Mosquito, and others wanted to check out the finer points of other aircraft they needed to fly that day. There were occasions when our reliable little blue books of Ferry Pilots Notes needed a spot of back-up information. The more we knew, the more we felt we could control any new variety of aircraft we encountered. We also needed to visit the 'Met' office and check for more news about any forthcoming weather conditions.

That day though, just like any other, I joined a few of the other girls and made my way to the taxi Anson as we prepared to fly to various airfields to collect the aeroplanes on our lists. As I climbed into the hardy old Anson that morning I was so happy about the Spitfires, I felt as if I was floating on air and that was before we took off! The Anson was heading for South Marston, Swindon, and that's where my Spitfires were waiting for me, Mary Wilkins. I kept to my usual quiet manner throughout the short journey, but inside my heart was beating loud and fast, I was nervous and yet thrilled all at the same time.

I had already flown a great variety of aeroplanes including the lovely Hurricane when on October 15, 1942 – a date and time etched on my memory – my allocation for that day was to deliver those two Spitfires from the factory at South Marston. I took a deep breath at this information and noted two Spitfire Mk.Vs. Spitfire AR513 was to go to RAF Lyneham and I was to then fly Spitfire AR516 to RAF Little Rissington in Gloucestershire.

I could feel my little heart beating fast with excitement. My moment at the controls of this wonderful aircraft had come! The taxi Anson dropped me off at South Marston and, putting on a brave face among a gaggle of disbelieving male ground crew, 'this little girl' walked around her first Spitfire doing essential ground checks. Satisfied that all was in order, my legs propelled themselves like magic towards the wing of the aircraft and as I was putting my parachute into the cockpit before climbing in, a voice beside me asked 'how many of these aircraft have you flown?' My reply in a quiet voice was 'none, this is the first one'. I think the men that day were more shaken than me.

Within a few seconds my excitement had calmed into a steady concentration and I realised I was really quite snug and extremely comfortable in the cockpit. I looked over the instrument panel which did indeed tally with the illustrations in my Ferry Pilots Notes. I also thought about my training and noted the sleek black coated dials which housed, behind circles of glass, such bright white numbers and indicators which were impossible not to notice. There were among forty controls to watch and be aware of including the various knobs and switches. I went through them all in my mind. They were easy to reach and to handle. I noted the red metal crowbar fixed to the side of the cockpit door on my left. It was a stark reminder of a potential emergency and I averted my eyes from it as I was determined I would never need use of it to break open the canopy. Yes, all seemed above board and so far, so good. It was strange how it took only a few seconds for me to feel completely at home in this beautiful aircraft. Everything sort of fell into place. It was wonderful. I breathed deeply and closed the canopy over my head. I saw my blonde curls faintly reflected in its Perspex.

The moment arrived soon enough for me to get the magnificent Merlin engine fired up – all twelve cylinders of it. I checked my brakes were on, the fuel on? Yes. The idle-cut-off switched to 'off''? The pre-oiler needed to be on for about two minutes and the fuel pump required a ten-second breather to allow the lines to be primed.

I was making ready to start this Spitfire and concentrating like mad so I went through my cockpit drill again; idle-cut-off to run, the propeller set to fine pitch, the throttle set, booster coil and starter buttons uncovered. I then checked all around me and shouted 'clear prop!' and in tandem I pressed the booster coil and start buttons and sure enough in front of me at the end of the long nose of the Spitfire, the propeller began to turn, and turn and then spin fast – all at my command. I switched on the magnetos. I breathed deeply and the fumes from the exhausts sparked off the excitement in me again. And then came the great symphony of engineering erupting like an overture at full blast – those twelve cylinders roared and roared, blasted out instantaneous three-second show of flames and then shuddered their virility through the cockpit and into my bones. I consulted the temperature dials and the pressures – all fine. 'Come on! Come on!' the Spitfire urged me, 'it's time to taxi out of here!'

As I closed the throttle and waved the chocks away it was time to take the brakes off and slowly, oh so gently, guide the aircraft to a take-off point on the runway. I was already in heaven before I'd taken off. I soon realised the Spitfire was no Tiger Moth, and very different to the old, steady Gloster Gladiator or the Albacore. I was in the cockpit of a thoroughbred which didn't suffer fools gladly and was preparing to test me to the maximum. 'Hold tight!' it seemed to say to me as we gently swung left to right to ensure a better view of the ground ahead. I steered the Spitfire at this point with the tailwheel.

When I reached the place on the runway for take-off I repeated my engine checks, temperature and pressure controls. Good. They were all fine. I revved up the power to 1,800 rpm. The sound of that engine filled my head and my heart as I held back the stick. The noise of the Merlin got louder and louder. I watched the temperature dial rising and knew there was no going back. It was a now or never moment in my life. 'Come on! Come on!' urged the aircraft, now impatient with me. More checks. I check the magnetos, then check the propeller again to fine pitch, try out the supercharger. The oil cooler and temperatures are still within limits and I monitor the slow run of the engine.

Suddenly, oh so suddenly, I am ready for the off. No doubt the Spitfire breathing a sigh of relief at this moment as the girl in the cockpit was being a slowcoach with her caution and safety considerations. So, automatic trim was set, the elevator was two divisions on the up, the right rudder pedal fully in the forward position. Yes, the throttle was locked and the fuel was switched on. I checked again the canopy was closed and my harness was tight around me and all of the controls were in full working order. Gently, gently, I open up the throttle and the roar of the engine fills my veins with gusto. I'd never experienced such a feeling before. I pull the control stick hard over to the right, and the full right rudder keeps us straight and level. I apply more power and with six pounds of boost I succeed in getting the tail into the air and whoosh we leave the ground.

My first thought is I'd better get the landing gear up and within seconds I hear them hit the lock and the red light comes on. All of this happens in a flash and up, up, up we soar – just me and the Spitfire reaching for that pale, white sky and still we climb quickly, swiftly.

I am flying my first Spitfire. Really and truly. I decide to pull back on the power to plus four boost and 2,400 rpm and I fly away from the airfield at around 150 mph to the delight of an enthusiastic ground crew waving in celebration at my successful take off. I soon realise the ailerons are quite weighty but very responsive and the elevators refreshingly light in pitch. I check the radiator flaps and the engine is at zero boost. I look down from the neat cockpit and for a few moments enjoy the view below. I see fields, tiny random houses and then a cluster of buildings, a small village and the lanes to and from it. I listen to the thumping hum of a happy Merlin flexing its power in the sky where it belonged. But while my heart was completely fulfilled my mind was busy in the cockpit of the fastest most beautiful fighter aircraft in the world, as I was responsible for its safe journey to the RAF pilots who needed it. I must confess the moment I had surged along the runway and felt the tail lift effortlessly off the ground any small nagging fears about flying the Spitfire had disappeared. It was a wonderful experience, the power, the speed and easy controllability. All of these aspects of the Spitfire were tremendously thrilling to me.

Of course the landing was on my mind and I thought I'd carry out a few stalls, try out the flaps and landing gear – everything seemed to go according to the commentary in my Ferry Pilots Notes. It mentioned the slight wing drop and how to run in with the wheels down all below 160 mph. When I dropped the flaps down I noted the nose bouncing a little so I trimmed off and got the speed to about 105 mph. By this time, I must have been flying at about 1,800 feet and knew the landing strip at RAF Lyneham was fast approaching. It only seemed like seconds had passed since I took off.

So I got down to 800 feet and pulled my speed back below 160 mph. I was downwind and, with the landing gear in position, I did my checks again, bringing my speed back to 85 mph. The Spitfire feels strong, sure and content with me and I touch down on the grass upon which she rolls smoothly and securely to a halt. I check the temperature gauge which must be below 115 degrees and carry out important procedures which include setting the idle-cut-off to 'off'.

The Merlin takes a rest and suddenly there is silence until the short, sharp pinging sounds creak out from cylinders now cooling down. More checks – fuel off, magnetos off, brakes off, giro caged, battery off. I was snug and warm and happy in the quiet, little cockpit. I didn't want to get out! It's fair to say I made a good landing at Lyneham and as the ATA taxi aircraft arrived to fly me back to South Marston to pick up Spitfire number two, I felt I had grown ten feet tall with pride. Not that I let it show, of course. It is never in my nature to show off but I did allow myself a little pat on the back. I only wish my father had been there to see me up there in the Spitfire and to greet me as I climbed out. I would have had so much to tell him. But I knew that would have to wait.

When I got to South Marston two hours later I was greeted by a reception party and the whole factory staff came out to wave me off in my second ever Spitfire. What a great, great day and it marked the fact that my life was one now driven by adrenaline and purpose.

The Spitfires were so easy to fly and in my first moments with this wonderful aircraft I did, of course, remain mindful of my position in the ATA. The speed and thrill of the machine didn't rule my head but I did acknowledge it was so rare to experience that feeling when everything in your life comes together and feels so very, very right. That's why I was so thrilled to skim beneath the skies in that super little aircraft. I fell so much in love with the Spitfire – if that makes any sense? My childhood dreams of flight and speed and ultimate satisfaction became a reality that day. The three patron saints of aviation – St Therese, St Joseph and Our Lady of Loreto – must have been out there as I answered my calling in life. I thanked all three, as it was proof that day I had been chosen to fly Spitfires – the most gorgeous aircraft in the world.

I can comprehend now why those men at South Marston were so keen to see me take off and make a success of it. For many RAF crews, on the ground or in the air, the war was a time when anything goes, what with life and death so interlinked at any one time and there was a pseudo-sexual freedom floating about Britain too. No one knew what the future held so, to quote an old saying, the young just made hay while the sun shone. I suppose those chaps at South Marston became more enlightened that day when a girl really did show them why she wore golden wings on her tunic.

There was a general feeling about during the war among us doing our bit, that it wasn't helpful to the spirit or the confidence to acknowledge too much death, as we were all striving to survive and put danger out of our minds. There was this inexplicable pressure to live our lives to the maximum. There was an attitude especially among young men, about getting your jollies while you could and the sight of a young woman flying the sexiest icon going, the Spitfire, then that was something to be enjoyed – absolutely. One might not get the chance again if the enemy arrived on our shores.

Although many surveys of the war years show married couples didn't indulge in sex too often, the newly independent and self-confident woman in the services was not averse to enjoying herself when the country was under great threat. Some pilots have written about the 'trysts of women' who would arrive at RAF stations longing for a liaison with any man who flew Spitfires! Apparently some girls would ditch any boyfriend if they caught sight of RAF wings on the tunic of a pilot. Flying in war was deemed sexy and alluring and everything else that might prove the ultimate distraction from the prospect of invasion or death.

An RAF mechanic named Ted Featherstone was based in Cumbria during the war and said: 'I didn't know the gender of the pilot as I marshalled the aircraft into the allotted space near the Control Tower, placed the chocks in front and behind the wheels, and then made to climb on the wing to see if I could be of any help with the straps, etc. From my ground-level viewpoint, I sometimes saw the helmet come off, (NB: I didn't wear one as there was no point and besides it didn't do wonders for my hair!) the head give a shake and the blonde hair come streaming out in the breeze. I was very impressed with what happened after that, including the swarms of young officers who seemed to come from every corner to view this ATA phenomenon. Where had they been hiding? I was right out of the scene, of course, but I would dearly like to have been part of it.'

I went on to deliver 400 Spitfires with the ATA and enjoyed every second of them. They truly are beautiful aircraft and have to be the most beautiful ever designed. A lady's aircraft? Yes, no doubt.

Squadron Leader Freddie Lister DSO, DFC and Bar was full of respect for this classic fighter aircraft. He said: 'The Spitfire was a lady in every definition of the word. And of all the World War Two aeroplanes she remains, the only lady, every line of her – the beautiful ellipse of the wings, the unmatched grace of the tail-unit, the unmistakeable sit – as she banked in a steep turn – displaying that feline waist … She was sensitive to the touch, and if you treated her right she would take care of you. And if you didn't treat her right – she gave it back to you in full measure. She let you know that she was a lady, and she would not forgive you easily if you gave her brutish treatment.'

After my first flights in the Spitfire I realised what it was to be a fully qualified ferry pilot on single-engine aircraft. Likewise, the real work had truly begun. Fighter aircraft were in great demand and played a significant part in defending our skies from German invaders. Within three days I flew five Spitfires from Hamble and Chattis Hill to destinations like Hornchurch and North Weald. By the November of 1942 I had flown Spitfires and Seafires from seven different pick up points and delivered aircraft to ten different airfields. That year my logbook reveals I had flown twenty different types of aircraft. Life really had taken off for the little blonde girl from the country lanes of Oxfordshire who was born with her eyes on the skies.

My ATA friend Betty Hayman once said: 'I was once told by a test pilot how the Spitfire was a lady in the air but a bitch on the ground! There is so much power there. Once she's flying, she's really flying. It was a beautiful aircraft and so very responsive. The Spitfire is a lady's aircraft through and through. Although I don't think the designer R.J. Mitchell had us girls in mind when he imagined who would be at the controls!'

Chapter 2

Early Inspirations

My interest in flight came to me at an early age. I must have been three or four years old when I began to wonder why the birds could reach the sky and I couldn't. What did they have that I did not? They were so carefree soaring and gliding up high beneath an ever changing canopy of colour and surprise, why couldn't I join them? I could walk and talk but when would my wings grow? 'When, when, when?' I asked my ever-patient pa. 'One day soon,' he'd reply not realising his daughter's fate had already been decided long before her baby eyes had first even twinkled at the sky and its soft white clouds.

It's hard to explain why I felt so sure about my fate. I wanted to fly and that was that. Choice is seldom allowed to interfere with true destiny. Now, when I look up to the heavens I realise I have lived through a whole century of flight and personally known the eternal and temperamental skies which hosted such an historical phenomenon. And only too graciously did I accommodate the fickleness of our friend the weather and all the challenges it presents. Indeed, I was born to be a pilot. But if you ever meet me don't call me 'amazing' and run over to check I am real. There is a lot of needless fuss made about age. I am just someone who has just been lucky to live longer than most. That at least gives one a certain gravitas and a qualification to comment on life's history. When one is advanced in years there are some advantages after all and growing into a century of such remarkable aeronautical achievements and socio-political change has left me confident about discussing aspects of aviation before, during and after both world wars.

It is inspiring, and always will be, to know so many adventurous and brave women were reaching out for the clouds long before I was even thought of, and without their exploits I may well have not been in a position to assist Britain at a time of war as a ferry pilot or indeed help create this book.

9

So, apart from the glorious sight of birds in flight, who inspired me to fly? Well, I had a very supportive family and my father was always keen to encourage my ambition but I was thrilled to learn of the great advancements made by some extraordinary women who found their metier in aviation.

Indeed, long, long before I arrived on this earth, the first woman had taken to the skies in 1784. Elizabeth Thible of Lyons, France had travelled a full mile in a hot-air balloon on a warm day in June. Wearing a lace-trimmed dress and a feathered hat the world's first woman of the sky couldn't stop singing she was so thrilled with the experience. I know that feeling so well. For once the initial exhilaration has tickled the brain into a frenzy at take-off then a crescendo of delight continues to wash over one. I suppose this feeling helps explain the concept of a natural-born something and once I was airborne, I'd argue I was a natural-born flier. And once in the air everything below appears so small, inconsequential even – the world below is moving in such slow motion and when one is up high it provides the conscience with such a lift. If there is a God, then he or she has the best view of all. Flying has a wonderful way of putting so much into a credible and spiritual perspective.

Watching a beautiful aircraft in flight can also have this effect. Indeed, the sight of a Spitfire swooping high and proud is a truly poetic experience. To fly a Spitfire is to feel so alive and of course I will talk more about my relationship with this iconic little aircraft as we go on with my story. But we really must not forget the female pioneers of flight – the trailblazers and the astonishingly adventurous – which leads to mention of the British fairground entertainer Dolly Shepherd who in 1905 ascended on a trapeze attached to a hot air balloon to 15,000 feet then parachuted down to an amazed crowd below. This type of performance was not without its hazards and she was nearly killed on several occasions. However, she indeed lived to the grand age of ninety-six and in 1983 experienced a flight with the Red Devils flying team. How I would have greatly enjoyed meeting with her. Dolly was born to fly.

Gertrude Bacon was the first Englishwoman to become airborne in a balloon in 1898. Then she broke all records as the first woman to fly in a Farman biplane in 1909 with a pilot named Roger Sommer. There is little doubt she made the subject of aeronautics fashionable.

In 1910 the French aviatrix, Elise Raymonde Delaroche, gained her pilot's licence sitting in a rickety aircraft which resembled a kite frame with two big wheels. This was also the year the American woman pilot Blanche Stuart Scott was first to fly as a solo pilot.

The prospect of women making waves in the air continued in the early part of the twentieth century. On 16 April 1912, the American aviatrix Harriet Quimby set the record as the first woman to fly solo over the English Channel to Hardelot, France. She completed the twenty-five-mile flight in fifty-nine minutes flying a Bleriot monoplane. However, her achievement was over-shadowed by the tragic sinking of the *Titanic* that same month. Some years after Quimby's death in a flying accident on 1 July 1912, her sense of style, which had included a flying suit that could be transformed into a dress, melted into the wardrobe of women pilots of the 1920s.

There was even a wing-walker by the name of Margie Hobbs, who was otherwise known as 'Ethel Dare – The Flying Witch'. Bessie Coleman, an African-American woman was determined to fly, but prejudice in the USA prevented her from gaining her pilot's licence. This situation was remedied when she travelled to France for the all-important qualification. What an achievement on all sorts of political levels.

The world was changing and so was aviation – a realm which I was eventually destined to thrive in and, without wanting to sound too boisterous, conquer.

I feel it is important to mention the achievements of the early women aviatrices because the next generation of women pilots like me reaped the benefits won by their purposeful action and determination to prove they could fly as well as men.

More than 100 years have passed, but I guess these early aviatrices all felt like I did and I still do. They were born with the instinct to fly. The fact the aircraft were rickety and precariously dangerous at the turn of the last century didn't seem to put them off at all. They knew the pitfalls involved, the cough and splutter of a whimsical engine, the structural weaknesses of the airframes, and yet still they flew on, and I have nothing but respect for their fearless attitude to getting airborne in the most precarious of ways. How they'd have loved the chance to fly a neat, super-fast sleek-lined Spitfire like me and I hope some of them lived long enough to know my generation did indeed bask in the opportunities they had helped provide.

Pilots like the Frenchwoman Marie Marvingt, who has been described as 'wedded to danger' because of the number of crashes she survived, do so deserve a mention. Did you know it was Marie who became the first woman to fly in combat? In 1915 the same adventurous Marie was dropping bombs over German-held territories and for her courage she received the French *Croix de Guerre*. Marie's achievements were rare. She experienced a life full of adventures and after the First

World War she devoted much of her time to creating a fleet of flying air ambulances and exercising considerable altruism to those in need.

There was also the first British woman recorded to have flown. Edith Maud Cook (also known as Viola Spencer-Kavanagh) had learned to fly in a Bleriot XI. Sadly, Edith died in July 1910 after a failed parachute jump. Notably, a British woman called Hilda B. Hewlett made headlines when, as a forty-seven-year-old mother-of-two, she received her Pilot's Certificate No.122 from the Royal Aero Club on 29 August 1911. Just two years before that she had been smitten with love at the sight of the first aircraft ever to take off at Britain's first international flying meeting.

Hewlett's observations of this event at Blackpool make for powerful reading: 'A great white thing was slowly pushed out of a shed, so big and strange. Paulhan (the French pilot) climbed up somehow, men twisted something round and round behind, when suddenly there was a roar which got louder and louder. The white thing moved – slowly – then faster and faster, till as it passed in front of me I saw one foot of space between it and the dirty muddy grass. That one foot of space which grew more and more made everything within me stop still. I wanted to cry, or laugh, but I could not move or think, I could only look with all my other faculties dead and useless. Something inside me felt it must burst. I had seen a reality as big as a storm at sea, or Vesuvius throwing up fire and rocks – it made more impression than either of these. There seemed to be no limit to its future. I was rooted to the spot in thick mud and wonder and did not want to move. I wanted to feel that power under my own hand and understand about why and how. The whole trend of life seemed altered, somehow, lots of important things were forgotten, a new future of vague wonder and power was opened.'

Hilda adopted the name 'Game Bird' and bought a Henri Farman aircraft. She then set up in business with a Frenchman called Gustave Blondeau at Brooklands next to the racing circuit in Surrey. She also got the licence to build Farman aircraft at the site and run a flying school. Hilda Hewlett's foray into the world of aviation proved an inspiration to many women who had also dreamed it was the life for them.

Just before I was born, a twenty-two-year-old pilot named Marjorie Stinson in the United States was the legendary female flying instructor who trained Canadian men for service with the Royal Flying Corps. I wonder how many of those boys revealed they'd been taught to fly by a woman? Most of them, one would hope.

Before the First World War broke out women had test-piloted various early aircraft. The American aviatrix Bernetta A. Miller was hired by

Alfred Moisant to demonstrate the flying machines he built. Likewise, the keen French female pilot Helene Dutrieu was taken on by Henry Farman, whose aircraft would become a main staple of the fledgling Royal Flying Corps. It was Dutrieu who came close to combat duty in the Great War. Standing alone, and with a determination to prove the cynics wrong, she did get to serve as a reconnaissance pilot. In December 1911, Jeanne Herveu opened the first flying school exclusively for women. When I question why women weren't allowed to fly and help the war effort during the 1914-1918 conflict I realise there were patriarchal prejudices against women which were embedded in western civilisation that proved too strong to ignore, especially at a time of war.

It took the male pilots of the Royal Flying Corps at least two years to persuade some narrow-minded Army generals that aerial reconnaissance over the trenches was an effective way of monitoring the movements of the enemy and its trenches and, in light of this fact, what chance did women have as airborne messengers? Men take ownership of war and talk endlessly of their duty. I can't imagine why they don't think women feel such things too.

Indeed, when I was born the First World War was raging and the ardent cause of suffrage and women's right to equality had seriously begun to challenge the socio-economic climate of the time. The menfolk of Britain may have been away fighting in the trenches, at sea, or battling the enemy in the air, but the call for women to be part of the war effort on the Home Front offered a new found freedom.

The Music Hall entertainer Vesta Tilley dressed as a soldier on stage, sang jaunty songs about the wonders of joining up and trumpeted the idea that the 'New Woman', as described by the women's theatre company manager Lena Ashwell, had truly arrived. Women were also on the verge of getting the vote in 1918, thanks to strident efforts of notable Suffragettes like Emmeline and Christabel Pankhurst.

Although forbidden to take part in military combat the women of Britain found other important ways to help the men on the Western Front. Many joined the FANY (First Aid Nursing Yeomanry) and were stationed near the trenches of France and Belgium working as nurses, drivers and couriers. In Britain there were women working as engineers, fitters and drivers at the airfields operated by the Royal Flying Corps. They wore uniforms as revealed in a photograph of a woman RFC crew member posing by a car at the Port Meadow airfield near my home in rural Oxfordshire.

Those women especially determined to be involved in military combat like Flora Sandes joined the Serbian Army and rose to the rank of Sergeant Major. In France a group of female aviators, keen to help the war effort, begged the government in Paris to allow them to join in aerial combat or ferry aircraft to and from the airfields. The answer to their plea remained a firm 'non'. This dismissal of their credibility in times of war was incomprehensible when a raft of successful flying schools in France, Germany and the USA had already been set up by women like Hilda Hewlett in 1910 and Milli Beese in 1912. (Beese was the first German woman to gain a pilot's licence).

The 1920s brought with it serious enlightenment. While over in the USA it was time to celebrate the arrival of the 'New Woman' in her carefree and positive attitude to life, there were the gutsy British girls keen to break aviation boundaries too.

In 1927 Princess Anne of Loewenstein Wertheim, hired a male pilot to fly her across the Atlantic. The trip ended in tragedy as the aircraft went down into the sea. This didn't stop Elsie Mackay, daughter of Lord Inchcape, from attempting the same trip, but sadly this proved fatal and both Elsie and her co-pilot perished in the sea.

In the Britain of the 1920s such women adventurers were regarded as 'eccentric' for believing there was a future in air travel. Those hearty aviatrices of the time spent hours waiting for repairs to be carried out to flimsy aircraft, and there was grease and dirt and all manner of unpleasantness and un-ladylike behaviour associated with aircraft, but still some persisted with this form of transport that did not have be a 'men only' experience.

We must salute Lady Mary Bailey DBE (1890-1960) – an Irishwoman and daughter of the 5th Baron Rossmore in County Monaghan – who, in March 1928, made the 8,000-mile trip from Croydon to Capetown, South Africa. The year before that she'd broken the record as the first woman to fly across the Irish Sea in a DH60 Cirrus II Moth.

Lady Bailey's aviation achievements made headlines. She did join the Air Transport Auxiliary in the spring of 1940 and became the tenth woman pilot to do so. However, she retired from the ATA the same week. Why I am not sure but it may have had something to do with the ultra-busy schedule and demands and on her time it required. She later decided to join the Women's Auxiliary Air Force and reached the rank of Section Commander.

Her friend and rival was Lady Heath, also known as Sophie Mary Elliott-Lynn (1896-1939), who was keen to earn her living as a commercial pilot. Lady Mary Heath flew a de Havilland Moth from London to Capetown and back in 1928 and was the first woman to gain her commercial pilot's licence. She was popular on the talk circuit and revealed how she thought the trip would take her three weeks when, in fact, it took three months! The world was in the grip of aviation glamour and Lady Heath was in the realms of legendary pilot Charles Lindbergh and the American aviatrix, Amelia Earhart.

In 1929 Lady Heath was badly injured in a crash at the National Air Races in Ohio, USA, and never recovered her health. She had planned to stay in the USA and promote aviation as a job to women. She divorced Sir James Heath in 1930 and married her third husband and became instrumental in the creation of the airline now known as Aer Lingus.

Lady Heath's famous 1928 trip from Capetown to Croydon was remembered by twenty-first century female pilot Tracey Curtiss Taylor, who flew a Boeing Stearman along the same route in 2014. This journey was the subject of a popular television documentary charting a raft of adventures she experienced along the way, including the time she flew across the Sudan at great risk of being shot at by militant insurgents.

In the early 1920s the International Commission for Air Navigation excluded women from gaining employment in the operating crew of aircraft engaged in public transport. In 1926, thanks to the campaigning of pioneering aviatrices, this rule was reversed, though female pilots had to be examined for efficiency every three months.

For those British women in the 1920s with no financial restrictions, it was becoming more possible to make headway in a male-dominated world. And, while it was a decade that famously 'roared' during a time of recovery from the First World War, aviatrices like Mary Russell, the Duchess of Bedford DBE, RRC, FLS (1865-1937), were taking to the skies. The Duchess had blazed a pioneering trail among the clouds for me and others like us to follow. Remarkably this grand lady didn't take to the skies until she was in her sixties. So here is yet more inspiration for those women who always want to learn to fly but think age is against them.

The Duchess made some amazing flights and broke several records in her single-engine Fokker FVIII G-EBTS. I know she was accompanied by her personal pilot, Mr C.D. Barnard but even so what an extraordinary achievement for the times.

Indeed, the adventurous Duchess did a 10,000-mile flight in 1929 from Lympne, Kent, to Karachi in Pakistan, then back to Croydon in eight days. In 1930 she flew from Lympne to Cape Town and achieved 9,000 miles in just 100 hours. The 'Flying Duchess' died in 1937, aged seventy-one, when her de Havilland GIII Moth Major G-AGUR crashed into the North Sea off Great Yarmouth.

By 1928 the celebrated American aviatrix Amelia Earhart, 'the winged legend', was roaring across the skies and in the September of that year she was flying Lady Heath's old Avian to visit the National Air Races in Los Angeles and then return to New York. She became the first woman to fly across the Atlantic from Newfoundland to Wales and went on to break several other aviation records until she went missing over the Pacific on 2 July 1937 during a flight around the world. Her disappearance has remained one of the world's greatest mysteries, but there is little doubt her dedication to aviation is worth honouring.

A heroine of mine is The Hon. Mrs Victor Bruce FRGS, also known as Mildred Mary Petre (1895-1990). I have read the memoir of this record-breaking motor-sports and aviation enthusiast, *Nine Lives Plus: Record-breaking on Land, Sea, and in the Air*, and it reveals that Mrs Bruce had a serious passion for excessive speed. This is something I had in common with her. I thought 'how marvellous'. I was impressed with her achievements. Although we never actually met, I did attend an event where she was once. Our paths just crossed that day, but I would have liked to have known her. What I do like is how she recognised she had lived many lives. I know this feeling and for an adventurous person it is a good way of describing each passage of time one survives.

It wasn't just the idea of whipping about the roads in the fastest car on the planet which The Hon. Mrs Victor Bruce had in common with me. It was her utter determination to fly too. In 1930, Mrs V.B. flew her tiny Bluebird aircraft single-handed to Japan. Then, on another momentous occasion, she took part in the first ever air-to-air re-fuelling in British skies.

The pioneering Mrs Victor Bruce was 78-years-old when she roared around Thruxton racecourse at up to 110 mph in 1974. At the age of 15¾ she was the first girl to appear before a court on a speeding charge. Records reveal she did sixty-seven mph on her brother's motorbike around the village lanes near Chelmsford, Essex. Other adventures included a rally car event which took her 200 miles north of the Arctic Circle. Incredible! Mrs V.B. and I had a lot in common – the thrill of great speed was our passion.

Chapter 3

To the Skies – Aged Eight!

These days it is heartening to know how little has changed in the particular rural Oxfordshire villages where I grew up happy and much-loved in the embrace of a wonderful family. The houses of warm yellow brick and thatched roofs, the small shops and churches still sit pretty and idyllic in an England I once knew. Only the steady traffic is a reminder of a twenty-first century world in a rush.

The long narrow lane towards our first family farm at Leafield remains surrounded on both sides by lush green fields which are spread like comforting blankets all the way into the distance to greet skies of blue-grey. The old flint walls lining the edge of the lane are still uneven in height and stretch raggedly on and on for several miles just as they did a century ago when my father Charles Wilkins was tending the sheep or supervising the work in the fields.

I remember him too so vividly, striding down the lane in his thick trousers, boots and battered dark coloured jacket to meet me and my youngest brother Edward from the little school in Shipton-under-Wychwood. My Pa always had an encouraging word for us as we walked on back towards the homestead which was our farmhouse – a place which dated back to the days of King John and had over the centuries served many royal personages and courtiers as an old hunting lodge.

I am delighted to know the house with its medieval secrets is still there today. It sits buried off the road to the left of a large farmyard and frowns upon the onlooker wearing its colours of dark grey stone all brooding and mysterious. Some might say, stoic. One can still see the old chapel at the rear of the property. Its tall round arched window reaching up to the eaves provides its ancient purpose as a place of worship. It was here those huntsmen of old knelt and prayed and maybe thanked God for the deer they'd killed and brought back for a right royal feast to humour a rancorous king. Maybe the old chapel had also seen a wedding or two? Or it had witnessed treacherous confessions of the sort to make the hair curl? Indeed, the centuries-rich history of those lives gone are embedded forever in its walls.

The land is still very much farmed and the timbers and stone buildings remain beautifully familiar and remind me of childhood games and the sounds of the wonderful noble plough horses who would come by and stand patient and serene. They'd scrape their front hooves gently on the yard floor and they'd let us know they'd like to be fed. As a child how I loved to look up into their dark brown eyes and think I could see the world beneath their long lashes. I loved living on a farm and had decided early on that's what I wanted forever. And who could blame me? Life was idyllic and nature offered us so many riches. The flowers and the trees, the hedgerows and friendly farm animals, I needed little else then, and thrived too on a strange fascination with the sky and the birds so free to fly across it. I remember thinking it's like another world up there and I hoped those birds were as happy as I was muddling through on the ground beneath them. I can't recall if I ever asked my parents just why birds could fly and we couldn't but I must have spun out this childish enquiry often enough for my father to grab the opportunity when he could to let me take a trip in an aircraft. I had so wanted to fly from an early age and when I reached the age of eight I finally did.

Not long after that and while other children were at village fairs guessing the weight of a cake, I then won a competition to 'guess the height of an aircraft'. The prize was another trip into the skies.

However, a few years before that delicious insight into my destiny was introduced across the skies of Oxfordshire, I was of course born.

On that day, 2 February 1917, Leafield and the rest of Oxfordshire was covered in deep snow. It was also the day my mother Ellen was told my face didn't measure much more than an inch-and-a-half wide. This acute, arguably unnecessary, observation was made by my grandmother who then proceeded to inform my mother how she may well have trouble 'rearing such a tiny infant'.

While such a comment may seem harsh, it was commonplace for the wise elders of a family to accommodate the prospect of child mortality in the Britain of King George V. Diseases like measles, mumps, scarlet fever, rubella, TB and polio were responsible for extinguishing the lives of many Victorian children before they reached the age of twelve. A baby like me, born on the small side, was deemed then at serious risk of such a fate.

Of course in those days nobody weighed a baby at birth and I don't know why I was so small. Perhaps I just came along too early? Perhaps

I was made to be the perfect size to fit into a Spitfire cockpit! God had a plan for me after all?

However, being born small and probably underweight proved gloriously contradictory to my grandmother's prophecy of doom. For although I did contract pneumonia as a child, I recovered and made it easily to maturity. I have no idea what my grandmother would have thought about my destiny as an aviatrix with a passion for the fast and the furious.

I sometimes wonder, too, if she and my mother ever looked to the skies in the year of my birth and heard the sound of a temperamental biplane coughing its way towards the Channel in readiness for action over the killing fields of France. They would have caught a glimpse of an aviator braced against the piercing chill of minus-fifteen degrees and he would never have guessed the baby in the cot in a farmhouse 500 feet below him would one day follow his flight path and make for the skies of war as a ferry pilot ready to meet and beat every aircraft delivery deadline thrust upon her.

I was one of five children born to Charles and Ellen Wilkins (née Clarke) who had married at Witney, Oxfordshire, in 1912. My father, Charles, was a dedicated farmer and with his team of swarthy, cheerful land-workers, in all weathers diligently ploughed the fields and managed livestock around the family home at Langley Farm, Leafield, Oxfordshire. (I often wonder if my fondness for sheep came from my days of growing up with them around the farm. Decades later when I ran Sandown Airport on the Isle of Wight I had quite a flock of these gentle intelligent creatures who proved jolly useful at keeping the grass airfield trim).

My parents, newly-married, were living a few miles from the pioneering Royal Flying Corps which was stationed at nearby Port Meadow and Bicester. That year there would certainly have been talk among the villagers about any aviation incidents, including the crash of an early-style monoplane.

In those days, with the sight of an aircraft still a rare event, the topic would be discussed with great energy at the local grocery store, the post office, the smithy, the market and in the homestead itself. The news of a crash would take top billing in area for years to come.

Two RFC pilots took off at 07.00 hours on 10 September 1912. Second Lieutenant Edward Hotchkiss, aged 30, was the pilot with 28-year-old Lieutenant Claude Albemarle Bettington, in the observer's seat. Edward Hotchkiss was from New Zealand and was the Bristol Aircraft Company's chief test pilot. Claude Bettington had been an officer in the Royal Artillery before he joined the RFC. They took off in a Bristol

Coanda Military Monoplane No.263; the ground crew at Port Meadow expected their arrival at 08.15 hours.

It was noted how the rare monoplane circled the field in a controlled dive, at which point a quick-release catch holding a strap opened, a flying wire came free, and the cable whipped back striking the starboard wing. A hole was torn in the fabric of the wing which then caused the aircraft to lose its lift. The aircraft went completely out of control and hit the ground by some trees near the toll bridge at Godstow Road on the bank of the Thames in Lower Wolvercote – just north of Port Meadow. Lieutenant Bettington was thrown from the cockpit just before it crashed and Lieutenant Hotchkiss went with it. Both men died. I understand this was the third RFC monoplane to go down in just three months. The dangers of aviation were brought home to the people of Oxfordshire that day and a fundraising appeal for a memorial to the men raised more than £31.

An emerald and pearl granite tablet bordered by Balmoral red granite was set in the wall near Wolvercote Bridge on Monday, 2 June 1913, and it still stands out on view today from the cobbled bridge wall. Beneath runs the busy River Thames and the tall weeds rooted in the riverbank bend westerly in its flow. Nearby there is a place for picnics along the grassy river bank in the summer months.

Our Langley Farm had its own special place in the history books, having been frequented by royalty ranging from King John in 1204 right through to King Charles I in 1614, but the only sense of real flight in those days was of course carried out by the birds and a swift arrow or two shot by the king's archers.

It was within the walls of this ancient royal abode that I arrived and it was from its grounds I first looked up at the glorious expanse of sky which even now still feels like a friend calling me to come visit and enjoy its highs and lows. There's nothing more seductive to me than the shimmer of a bright blue sky and spot-white bubbly clouds.

I had two elder brothers – Lewis who arrived in 1914 and Charles in 1916. My younger brother Edward was born in 1918, and in 1924 along came my sweet sister Dora, who was affectionately known as 'Tiny'.

Langley Farm is situated on the Shipton Downs and in the thirteenth century was an annexe to the Palace of Woodstock. By the time I was born, 700 years later, my father Charles was farming around 1,000 acres of its good, hearty, fertile land.

As a child growing up in such an historic property how could I not imagine the colourful days of old? The walls around me had witnessed the sights and sounds of many a royal gathering. Feasts and ribaldry most probably. In those times of Tudor extravagance there was no doubt the rich whiff of venison steaks as they hung in the parlour and, to quote Shakespeare's *Richard III*, nobles dancing 'to the lascivious pleasings of the lute'.

At this time Langley was in the Forest of Wychwood which before disafforestation in 1863 was a haven for royal deer meat and therefore much visited by the men on horseback with an ambition to hunt. I imagined King Henry VIII and his falconers arriving at Langley on their fine horses with awesome birds of prey clutching on to gauntlets held high. I'd sit on a fallen tree in a field and I'd swing my little legs and feet and kick off the rotting bark in my exuberance as I imagined those hawks – great medieval winged predators – soaring higher and higher before the fatal swoop on an unsuspecting pheasant or rabbit. When I grew up and flew Spitfires in the Second World War I became like those hawks. The only difference was instead of feathers to keep me airborne I would be wearing a sleek, dynamic military aircraft that too is capable of destroying its prey at great speeds and with admirable deftness.

Chapter 4

Those Were the Days

When the men of the Royal Flying Corps and the Royal Naval Air Service flew into action against the enemy during the First World War, a rare few British women were allowed to work on the airfields as technicians, drivers, cooks, administrators and mechanics. Some even had jobs in aircraft design workshops. More often than not, they worked in huge tents as the idea of a purpose-built hangar was a luxury. As far as we know they were never employed as military pilots despite the fact they had already proved as efficient in the aircraft cockpit as men.

As a young woman Air Transport Auxiliary pilot in the Second World War, I heard stories from several of the older pilots and ground crew who had served in France between 1914 and 1918. I am referring to chaps like Royal Flying Corps pilot and journalist Keith Stewart-Jopp who had one arm and one eye – both injuries occurred during aerial battle. Many of us girls in the ATA heard directly from him how the poor, exhausted pilots of the RFC would return back to an airfield with important sketches and photographs of German trenches, troop movements, advancements and machine-gun units only to be greeted with disdain by the Army top brass who just didn't like aviators so they ignored the information. This ludicrous attitude meant our soldiers got mowed down again and again by enemy machine-gun fire they had been warned not to encounter. It took two years for the RFC to be taken seriously as a method of intelligence-gathering. It was all too late, too late.

Of course the young male pilots of those times were often characterised as an over-confident, independent and heroic type with a swagger and a joke on their lips – but, more often than not, this kind of esprit de corps got them through a Hell unrecognised and rarely acknowledged by dismissive generals who still believed the only cavalry in war was made up of men on horseback. (Incidentally, I discovered recently that the indented step below the cockpit of the Hawker Hurricane, which helps the pilot get into the aircraft, was inherited from the early idea of the cavalry. That step in fact acts like a stirrup. So instead of riding a horse into battle a pilot rides an aircraft after 'mounting' the Hurricane and settling into the cockpit).

As an infant, of course, I was oblivious to the horrors of war over in France and Belgium. I flourished happily in the safety of a busy, yet caring homestead. My Pa was managing the large Langley Farm estate and playing his part in keeping the country fed during times of war. He was one of the few who fed the many and I am very proud of his efforts. It must have been such a difficult job and yet so far as I know he made a success of it. With so many of the younger farmers away at war there must have been a severe skills shortage. My father must have recognised how to make up for this situation and kept his promise to the government to train new land-workers as fast as possible. It seemed as if the quicker we harvested the fields of Leafield so the demand for food grew even more. There can't have been much respite at all – such is farming, but as with flying there is no other job quite as rewarding when all goes well.

But very early on in my life, and as eager young aviators flew off across the Channel towards the trenches in temperamental old aircraft, I was being pushed in my pram along the village lanes of Leafield by my devoted nanny, Amy. I suspect, with all the flying going on above and around us, there may well have been the odd whiff of burnt castor oil in the air. Was this when flying got into my blood? This heady aroma would have been generated by the fits and starts of the ancient military aircraft operating from nearby Bicester and Port Meadow.

One of my first experiences of transport was, as a toddler, being placed by my father upon the back of a large Shire horse. I still remember the wonder of this occasion as I held on to the horse's mane, and I loved being so high up on such a gentle carrier. It is a wonderful memory and I did go on to learn to ride horses as a girl. I can't say I was a brilliant rider but passably adequate. Although over the years I have heard that horse riders are like pilots – they are born and not made.

Years later, as a young woman I was asked during my initial interview with the Air Transport Auxiliary if I indeed I was an equestrian. The idea that horsewomen made good pilots had become legendary and I guess the link had something to do with co-ordination skills and how these attributes translated from stirrup and bridle bit, to aircraft rudder, balance and controls.

At the time of my birth though there really was so much going on just a few miles from my family home. Oxfordshire was awash with young aviators who were keen to learn to do their best for their country. I am proud to have been born in a county which was at the forefront of military aviation and had hosted those early heroes of flight. I believe it helped set the tone of my life.

In the 1920s, and no more than three-and-half miles from our Wilkins' family homestead, lived an extraordinary collection of characters destined to embrace fame for literature and some say, notoriety, for the connections they courted and embraced throughout their lives. This was the Mitford family which lived at Asthall Manor in Swinbrook, near Burford, until 1926, when Lord Redesdale (David Freeman-Mitford) built a new property, 'Swinbrook House', in the village.

Over the years, the Mitfords were to play host to a raft of high-octane personalities whose sound and fury went on to shape the world we know today. Little did the Mitfords know but their political cohorts of the 1920s including Winston Churchill, Anthony Eden, Adolf Hitler, Josef Goebbels, Benito Mussolini and future Luftwaffe chief Hermann Goering would greatly affect the life of the blonde-haired little Mary Wilkins who lived along the lane and dreamed often of flying above the clouds. Indeed, no one knew at the time that those visitors to the Mitford family would eventually damage the lives of millions of British people and propel my ambition to fly at a time of war. Back then of course I'd never ever have dreamed I would be wearing a uniform to carry out such destiny.

As a child I sometimes bumped into the Mitford girls. I recall a time I was walking home from school and they offered me a ride with them in their posh carriage pulled only by the finest of thoroughbred horses covered in the most beautiful livery. The Mitford sisters always seemed a lively bunch and of course they went on to do some extraordinary things with their lives. It's amazing to think of the visitors they entertained at their house – the famous writers and artists read like a *Who's Who* in European politics and culture.

My family had moved to Brize Norton in 1928 – some years before any political undesirables in Black Shirts called by Swinbrook. To us quiet, hard-working Wilkinses the Mitfords had just been our neighbours. Later, of course, Diana Mitford went on to marry the British Fascist Party Leader, Oswald Mosley in 1936. As the wife of such a devout Nazi Party zealot, Diana spent the Second World War in prison. Unity Mitford is known for her Fascist sympathies and attempted suicide when Hitler rejected her amorous advances. Such extreme behaviour is an anathema to me.

Asthall Manor became home to the aristocratic Mitford family in 1919 and Lord Redesdale (David Mitford) and his wife Sydney immediately fell in love with the Cotswolds. He wasn't alone in his great fondness for the area as his neighbour, my father, farming the land at nearby Leafield, also adored the robust rural land which grew more beautiful with every season.

Asthall Manor was a gabled Jacobean house set in a valley surrounded by hills. Stories about ghosts haunting the place were spread by Pamela and Diana Mitford and it's no surprise it caught their lively imaginations. The Manor of Swinbrook itself dated back to 1504 and was once owned in the 18th century by a highway man who was later hanged for his crimes. When the Mitford family moved in by 1919 just 150 people lived in the village which had a twelfth century church (St Mary's in which I would take my marriage vows in 1961), a school, The Swan Inn and one shop-cum-post office.

Much remains the same in Swinbrook today, and I can still recall the sight of its village green and surrounds of birch and willow trees. The sheep still graze in the fields and birdsong is ever-present.

School was in nearby Shipton-under-Wychwood. I took a liking to cooking and wanted to know how everything in the kitchen worked. After school hours and as a girl growing up in the green and pleasant lands of Oxfordshire there was every opportunity to ride horses. The Mitford family were keen riders too and they trotted through the village of Leafield and past my home on fine hunters, maybe even riding to hound.

I adored my time at Langley Farm. It was a warm country family home and I was very lucky to have had a childhood in such surroundings. I loved learning how to grow things and my father taught me a lot about farming. His lessons and advice remain with me to this day.

However, living in the countryside proved too sedate for some of the Mitford family and they were schooled at private establishments and travelled the world for their holidays. They must have got used to the high-life and the social whirl and all that goes with it.

As I mentioned earlier, by 1926 David 'Builder' Mitford had moved his family into the new 'Swinbrook House'. The old Asthall Manor was sold.

That year, aged 9, I was still studying hard at school, and during the holidays I had huge amounts of fun, playing tennis and enjoying my freedom from the classroom. I loved the outdoors then and I still do. I was a happy little soul as a child and still am and I have always seen life as an adventure. I was lucky to have been born with a gift for enjoyment and basking in the glow of optimism about most aspects of life. As a child my days were charmed and full of sparkle and enlightenment and now aged almost 100-years-old I hug those youthful memories to my heart and they help me laugh away any aches or pains.

In the late 1920s and 1930s aviation as a form of civilian transport was becoming more popular and Britain welcomed the creation of a serious new transport industry. (My ATA colleague and friend Molly Rose's father, David Marshall, was a key player in the early developments of aviation)

There are, however, a few links I discovered between the Mitfords and aircraft. Diana's and Unity's friendship with Commander-in-Chief of Hitler's Luftwaffe, and former First World War pilot, Hermann Goering, is one for sure, and although I shared a small part of the glorious Oxfordshire countryside with the Mitford family in the late 1920s and 1930s I am glad my destiny was not as emotionally ragged as theirs was to become.

I made my own mark a few years later, which, whilst dangerous and exciting, was not as politically worrisome or as notorious. When one can fly a Spitfire what else is there? Who needs love and all its tortuous, fickle entanglements when there is the ultimate thrill of speed, the sky and the orgasmic experience of piloting the best fighter aircraft in the world?

In 1936, while the Mitfords were busy with their political adventures and social whirl so my first real passion was awakened, the first prototype Supermarine Spitfire designed by the great R.J. Mitchell was taking to the skies from Eastleigh, Southampton, with Captain Joseph 'Mutt' Summers in the cockpit. This was a momentous occasion indeed – and one which took place not far from my soon-to-be home at Hamble with the ATA's No.15 Ferry Pool. (Much later in my life I was to meet and greatly enjoy the company of R.J. Mitchell's late son, Gordon).

By the end of the war, I had flown 400 Spitfires and seventy-six different types of aircraft. In 1946, I became the second woman ever to fly a Meteor jet solo. By 1950 I could claim the title of Europe's first ever female Air Commandant. Today, I may even be the oldest Spitfire pilot in the world. My friends say these achievements are not bad for a shy country girl who learned how to combine her natural joy, quietude and reserve with wisdom and vision.

Our new home in 1928 was just eight miles away from Leafield. My father had rented The Manor at Brize Norton and several hundred acres of land from Oxford University's Christ Church College. By then my little sister Dora was 3-years-old. I was now a happy pupil at Burford Secondary School and my brothers Lewis, Charles and Edward were all sent off to agricultural college. All three of them went on to live their whole lives as farmers managing the fields and livestock of Oxfordshire.

The Manor had a lot in common with Langley Farm at Leafield. It was rich in history and for the girl with her heart set on flying it was perfect for my imagination to soar and flourish. As an eleven-year-old living on a site which was once inhabited by 'The Lords of the Manor' from the eleventh century, I could once again allow my dreams to indulge in a time of knights and heraldry. How I loved the idea of valour and honour – the very essence of those early aviators I so admired. My imagination was busy as ever and life for me in Brize was all about climbing trees, making friends with my father's wonderful Shire horses, running and jumping in the fields as free as a wild hare and reading adventure books – as well as dreaming about flying of course.

That glorious family home I loved so very much is listed now as the second oldest building in the village and it is mentioned in the Doomsday Book. There is even a suggestion that ancient monks resided there and turned it into a monastery, with archaeologists dating one wall in the property going all the way back to 1400 when Henry IV was on the throne of England. By the time we had moved to The Manor in the twentieth century, its lands had been bought by Christ Church College.

I went to school at Burford in the Cotswolds, first to secondary school, then to the High School where the educational standards were very high. I really do believe it was the perfect place to grow up in and I too can remember all the farm animals who were all part of our lives and proving a comforting and constant sight in the fields around our home. We also had about a dozen Shire horses to do the work in the fields. They were wonderful, wonderful creatures and I loved them dearly. There were some unusual and quirky things about the place too. I am not sure why but my father had acquired a big American Studebaker car. He also had a Model T Ford.

In the 1920s you wouldn't see many cars around and it was all a huge fascination. I often wonder if my own serious interest with cars was sparked by my pa's extraordinary vehicles. It was all so unusual then to see and hear them along the lanes of Oxfordshire.

As a schoolgirl I had amazing energy! I had an interest in music and won a prize for playing organ recitals at the St Britius Church in Brize Norton. I must stress music study didn't come naturally to me and I had to work hard at it but we had an organ in the house and I had to practice on that before I went to church. Then I found at St Britius it was a huge old instrument and I couldn't get used to using my feet as well as my fingers. It took me some time to work out the music and figure out the keyboard then play the pedals at the same time. (That's why as a teenager I would often feel the urge to go off and fly an aeroplane!) With the organ if you don't keep everything together then the parts all play a different tune. Nobody else in the house played except my Pa on a trumpet of sorts. My mother used to sing so I guess the musical part of me came from her. All my sporting activity developed adequately and I have always, always enjoyed playing tennis.

Today, The Manor at Brize Norton is still as majestic as ever and sits behind its high wall off the road heading into the village. The old farm building at the front of the property is now converted into dwellings and the large property adjacent to the building is a Guest House.

However, the top of 'The Manor' where I spent so many happy and joyful years is still visible including the magnificent gables over the front door, the roof and chimneys. Anyone looking out of the windows at the back of the house which sits sideways off of Manor Road, would see a wonderful garden that stretches far and wide into the distance. I have been back several times to visit Brize and stay in my old home. My brothers took on the management of the farm from my father in the 1960s and so we kept it all in the family. There are a lot of happy memories there and the countryside around is so beautiful and tidy. The airfield at Brize is of course is now a major RAF base and is used by HM the Queen and the Prime Minister when they fly in and out of the UK on state visits.

My friend and former ATA colleague the late Molly Rose DL, JP, OBE remembers arriving at the barn at the farm one day ready to give a talk to the farmers' wives about her life as a ferry pilot.

We once laughed about that day, with Molly remembering turning up from her home in nearby Bampton and being surprised to see me sitting on the edge of the stage swinging my legs waiting to be entertained. Molly then reminded me in that forthright, honest way of hers, that I had had a more senior rank as a First Officer in the ATA and it should be me doing the talk. I replied with a 'no fear' and I was quite happy to let her address the crowd. Apparently Molly said I didn't heckle her and she was grateful for that. Molly refers to some of her adventures in the ATA later in this book.

Chapter 5

Going Solo

I can always, always remember a bright and lovely day, enhanced by the sound of aircraft, which heralded the arrival of Alan Cobham's Air Circus to Witney Airfield on 2 May 1925. What a wonderful sight for a teenage girl with a passion for the skies.

I looked up and saw a sweet de Havilland 60 Moth preparing to come into land like a graceful little bird and the pilot waving a hand clad in a leather flying glove. 'Over here, over here, I'm here!' I wanted to call out as the aircraft rolled to a dignified stop on the airfield. I was madly excited and wanted to run over to the aeroplane and jump straight into the cockpit and head for the skies.

I desperately wanted to have a joy flight and my good, kind Pa soon agreed, paid the five shillings for the flight and I was lifted high into the Moth. I felt very grand so propped up aloft with cushions in order for me to see out of the cockpit and then off we went. It was the most marvellous and wonderful experience of my life up until that time, and I can remember the feeling right up to this day. I simply had to learn to fly on of these wonderful machines which made me feel so free, so alive. I was bubbling with excitement about it all and no doubt talked and talked about it until my family ran for cover from the chattering girl with a bee in her bonnet about aviation. Years later I learned I was among the many, many wartime pilots who encountered their first taste of flying thanks to the amazing Royal Flying Corps pilot and pioneering aviator, Sir Alan Cobham KBE, AFC (1894-1973).

Cobham's Air Circus was in its hey-day in the 1930s, and among his 'air-minded' (a term he invented to encourage the public to appreciate aviation) crew was the Kent-born aristocrat Helen 'Naomi' Heron-Maxwell (1913-1983), an individual who ranks as one of the first women daredevil parachutists. Her legendary jumps from the wing of a biplane at 20,000 feet proved a star turn. Naomi, who went on to gain her rare

'C' licence as a glider pilot in Germany before the war, was hugely popular with thrill-seeking crowds who flocked to see her take part in a variety of hair-raising parachuting stunts which I can remember when the circus arrived at Witney Airfield in 1933.

In 1934 Naomi had joined celebrated aviatrices Lady Bailey, Amy Johnson and Joan Price to set up the Oxford Gliding Club. Around this time she had met Philip Wills who was chairman of the British Gliding Club and a top glider pilot and they were to meet again when Wills, one of the first men to join the ATA, became its Chief Operations Officer. His mission was to prove an organisation operated by civilians was highly efficient when it came to the expert delivery of military aircraft and prove it he did to the admiration of many including myself. His signature appears now and then in my ATA documentation. By 1942, Naomi, like me, had joined the Air Transport Auxiliary as a ferry pilot. Her friendship with ATA Senior Commander Pauline Gower went back several years.

(But mention gliders to me and I shudder. I only went up in a couple of times and didn't like it at all. I found it most unnerving to float about without the sound of an engine or two. It was an alarming feeling and I made sure I avoided the idea of becoming a glider pilot altogether. Not even my husband Donald, who was a brilliant glider pilot and instructor, could persuade me to get into such a silent aeroplane that was guided by thermals, a rudder and what seemed very little else! Give me some engines anytime).

Another time my Pa took me to Hendon for the annual flying display – and I think he was more than pleased that I took a great interest in it all and badgered him to take me for a pleasure flight in an Avro 504. From that moment I was well and truly hooked. The thought of anything going wrong with the aircraft never, ever occurred to me. I followed my instinct and all was well. I was young and I felt indestructible.

A few years later, and with my head still full of the wonders of my childhood flying experiences, I was now a teenager. Instead of playing hockey at school I was allowed to go to Witney aerodrome for flying lessons. My dear father, although he never learned to fly himself, was always interested in aviation, and I benefited from that. I think he was somewhat proud of my efforts.

The aircraft available to me were BA Swallows and de Havilland 60 G-Moths, and my training continued apace on them. It's correct to say I learned to fly aeroplanes at Witney Airfield.

My logbook reveals that I took my first lesson on 1 September 1937 – this being in DH60 Moth G-AAKO. Later I had the beautiful BA Swallow and, in 1938, I took up G-AELH.

Also in the logbook I note that I flew Swallow G-AFGE on 5 March 1939. It was all tremendously exciting as I got used to the minimal instrument panels and learned about the structure of the aircraft and all its characteristics on the ground and in the air. I was a fearless young woman and it wasn't long before I satisfactorily landed the aircraft smoothly and without fuss, passing all the tests to gain my coveted licence.

Little did I know, at that time, what the aviation world had in store for me, or what a great adventure it would all become. I was warned by bright instructors about the pitfalls of flying, how to stall the aircraft, the speed at which to come in to land, the correct temperature of the engine, the propeller pitch, the delicacy involved with a tail-wheel and its correct engagement, and of course from then on the weather became a source of great consideration. I learned that flying demanded a lot of planning and if this went as it should then one could take off and land satisfactorily – providing one always remembered that no two flights are the same. Knowing this always kept me on my toes. A lazy pilot who becomes complacent is a dangerous pilot.

Obviously there are many reasons why one learns to fly aeroplanes. For fun and excitement maybe, but most men do it to earn a living or because they enjoy flying. During my school holidays I spent most of my time at an airfield, and had flying lessons. Everyone learns to fly in a small aircraft, even the commercial pilots of the jumbo jets you see today at places such as Heathrow and Gatwick.

The joy of going solo for the first time was tremendous. I can remember it now – when the instructor climbed out and said: 'Off you go then, and do a couple of circuits yourself ... remember what I have told you, and report to me when you come down.'

So off I went and did just that – it was frightfully exciting. It was an experience that will live with me forever. Everything seemed to be happening at a pace I was quite comfortable with and I remember taxiing over to the take-off point, doing my pre-flight checks and then doing them again to be doubly sure, and then throttling up, taking a very deep breath and suddenly I was airborne. Surprisingly I seemed to be climbing quite quickly and within seconds I was fully aware I was in control, and alone. I looked over the side of the little two-seater biplane and saw the instructor on the ground. Yes, I was definitely flying solo and the seat in front of me was empty.

I did like the Moth. It was a practical little machine which was so named by its creator and keen lepidopterist Geoffrey de Havilland because its wings could fold upwards like a Moth and thus help with its storage.

It had a top speed of 101 mph, but I didn't thrash the little aircraft into a complete roar of speed as we were still getting to know each other on a one-to-one basis and I wanted to make sure I was keeping a close watch on the dials and rudder control. It was completely my responsibility to get the Moth from A to B safely and securely, and if I followed all my instructions and training to the hilt, I would make it. The next thing on my mind was the landing of course. From what I recall it was a smooth touch-down at Witney that day and I was now a qualified pilot! No one could stop me now. I might even have had to be torn from the cockpit I was so thrilled. I had fulfilled my long-held dream to fly solo.

It was customary after this momentous occasion to have a little celebration in the airfield clubhouse – but perhaps I was too young for this as I don't remember partaking in lemonade, tea or cake. (I was tee-total then so anything stronger was out of the question). But my main delight that day was rushing home and telling my family that I had actually flown alone – solo – as a pilot. There's little doubt I talked of nothing else to them for days and days to come.

This, of course, was only the very beginning of learning the art of flying. I was the youngest pilot in Oxfordshire. My schoolteachers and friends were delighted. It had been well worth sacrificing those hockey lessons after all.

My brothers and my sister weren't very fussed about flying. Fortunately, although my father did not want to learn to fly himself, he was very happy to pay for my lessons, and when I did get my licence we spent many a happy hour together flying in the Swallow over his fields and peering from up high at Manor Farm, waving at the workers busy in the fields and noting how tiny the animals seemed. Those memories of our time flying happily over the Oxfordshire countryside are among my most treasured.

Occasionally, I received extra flying tuition from a spirited dark-haired young woman named Jackie Sorour (Moggridge). She was the only qualified woman pilot at Witney and she would later become my colleague in the Air Transport Auxiliary and a very, very dear friend.

My first cross-country flight was from Witney to Walsall with Jackie and I remember it well, as it was one of the first of many, many times I truly felt at one with the aircraft. I felt as if I was in heaven as we flew across the countryside that day. I was so happy I wanted to wave my hands in the air and shout out loud, but I didn't of course, as I had to concentrate and not worry my instructor.

Jackie was like me and had been determined to fly from a very early age. She is in the record books for being the first female teenager in South Africa to do a parachute jump. She had left her home in Pretoria, South Africa, against her mother's wishes and travelled to Britain in the mid-1930s for flying lessons in a bid to get enough hours to qualify for an 'A' licence. She was so young, and yet had complete courage and faith in her passion.

It wasn't long after my instruction from Jackie and our colleagues at Witney Airfield that I gained my treasured pilot's licence in 1938. I was overjoyed and I knew my Pa was proud of me as he enjoyed the poetry of flying just as much as I did. He always had time to chat to me about aircraft and how much I enjoyed being airborne.

My favourite aircraft to fly at that time was a BA Swallow G-AFGE which was built by the British Aircraft Manufacturing Company (British Klemm Aircraft Company). The BA Swallows were produced from the original German Klemm L.25 design. This neat little aircraft had curved wing tips and a rudder and tailplane inherited from the Klemm original. The Swallows II were Cataract or Cirrus Minor in-line engine. The BA Swallow was a popular aircraft at flying schools – a fact successfully proven at Witney Airfield.

Within a few years of Amy Johnson's epic flight to Australia in 1930, I was a teenager about to start flying lessons at Witney Aerodrome. This airfield had served previously as a First World War fighter station. Construction had started in the autumn of that year by German prisoners-of-war and this was followed by the erection of six Belgian-designed hangars and ancillary huts made by gangs of Portuguese labourers.

At the end of the First World War the aerodrome was abandoned and most of the buildings dismantled. The airfield was returned to pasture and used as grazing land for local livestock. Some of the remaining hangar was converted into a base for the Witney Tennis Club and a tennis court was created. On the former airfield there was also room for a motorcycle race track which remained popular until 1928.

Around this time Universal Aircraft Services moved in and began a flight training school with a Bristol fighter, an Avro 504k and a DH60 Moth and the weekend five-shilling joyrides were popular with the public. Private flying was also available here, and a then new Witney College of Aeronautics, Flying and Engineering School was established with a student building made available in 1936. The following year I recall how the Willoughby Delta Company rented part of the main hangar to build an experimental aircraft which sadly crashed in 1939 killing Mr Willoughby and Witney's Chief Flying Instructor Mr Olley. Everyone at the airfield was devastated by this and I recall a quiet and remorseful atmosphere around the place for months to come.

By the start of the Second World War Witney was used by RAF Brize Norton as a forced landing practice ground and in October 1939 the de Havilland Aircraft Company became sub-lessors of the aerodrome and, during the war years, Witney became a centre of aircraft repairs for DH Queen Bees, Dominies, Tiger Moths, Hurricanes and Spitfires. The aerodrome was managed by Mr P.E. Gordon-Marshall who was assisted by Mr Ken Brown as works superintendent.

New buildings were erected at Witney as its role as an RAF base increased. Neighbouring businesses also took up residence there too, including the likes of Dents Glove Factory at Charlbury, Croft Mill, and the Blarney and Tower garages. The war had led to an expansion for these firms.

Right up until August 1945 the number of aircraft returned to service was 1,450 with 655 of them front-line Hurricanes and Spitfires. In addition, 450 aircraft were broken up, and more than 6,000 components recovered. Records show the labour force at its maximum reached 1,100 with local workers and de Havilland staff doing their best to support the war effort.

(By the end of the Second World War, de Havilland at Witney continued to repair various DH aircraft types including Mosquitoes and Doves. It is worth pointing out that the Mosquitoes were flown out of Witney with great care as the runway was slightly too short for them. By the spring of 1949, de Havilland ceased operations at Witney and closed its hangar doors for the last time).

Days before the Second World War broke out though, in 1939, I flew my last Swallow aircraft, G-AFGD, from Witney and then many decades later I was delighted when I discovered this lovely little aeroplane had been fully restored by the South Wales Swallow Group. In the 1960s I was re-united with that Swallow when it was found and acquired by my husband Donald and quite by chance it happened to be the one I'd cherished and flown as a newly qualified aviatrix in 1938! I could hardly believe the Swallow I knew as a teenage pilot had come back to me. It was as if it had emulated its namesake and migrated away to another land with a warmer climate for three decades and then it decided to fly home again. I was of course too delighted to be re-united with it and yet strangely bewildered by this extraordinary coincidence.

Chapter 6

The ATA Women's Section

On 3 September 1939, when the news that Britain had declared war on Germany was announced over the family radio, there was followed a peculiar hush of disbelief in every corner of the land. Those days of autumn were to grow dark with fear and dread as we learned how Hitler's armies had marched brutally into Poland.

At this time, I soon learned that all civil and pleasure flying had to cease in Britain. Indeed, the government stopped anyone from taking to the skies unless it was on serious military business, so there were quite a few months when I couldn't fly at all and I found myself at a loose end. My hopes and dreams of flying full time looked like they'd hit the buffers.

My Pa was busy working out how the farm would need to change to suit the country's need for food and supplies during a time of rationing. And as with many young women I wanted to do my part and help the war effort but what to do, what to do? It was a duty felt by most of us so I turned my energies to sheep-farming and helping my mother nurture the local the community and ensure the efficient running of the homestead.

Aviation at this time was now set to become an essential part of our defence system, and several popular flying clubs in the UK which had light aircraft available for both men and women to fly soon found many of their pilots with a new licence were snapped up by wartime auxiliary and reserve RAF and FAA squadrons.

The Government was keen to keep the idea of club flying alive and so the Civil Air Guard (CAG) scheme was inaugurated on 1 October 1938. This was the brainchild of Air Minister Sir Kingsley Wood. He had a plan, like my old hero Sir Alan Cobham, to make Britain an 'air-minded' nation and he was keen to subsidise pilot training. Its Chief Commissioner was the Right Honourable the Marquess of Londonderry, with Mrs Maxine 'Blossom' Miles, wife of the famous aircraft designer, Frederick Miles, selected to represent the women pilots. 'Blossom' by the way had designed the Miles Master aircraft which was most comfortable to fly and was quite the woman's aeroplane. I know many of my ATA women colleagues enjoyed flying this aircraft and praised its snug, cosy cockpit.

However, the decision to choose Blossom for the CAG post infuriated the celebrated aviatrix Amy Johnson who had been hoping for the position. Amy wondered why her pioneering flying career and vast experience wasn't enough to convince the Air Ministry she could lead a squadron of women pilots. Hadn't the fact she was the first woman to have flown solo in a Gypsy Moth from Croydon to Australia in 1930 more than qualified her for the role? And what about all the other record-breaking flights she'd undertaken since, receiving much acclaim in the press? Weren't they worth taking into account when it came to a position of note within the realms of aviation?

She wrote to her father, Will Johnson, describing how very hurt she felt at not being invited to take part in the organisation of the women's section of the CAG. The Air Minister, Sir Kingsley Wood, was also contacted by the furious Amy and she demanded an interview with him. She told her father 'maybe Sir Kingsley thinks I am not respectable enough and should merely out-stunt the stunt!'

Amy did meet with Sir Kingsley who told her that all the CAG jobs were voluntary and he hadn't contacted her because he knew she would want to be paid. He did, however, offer her the role of Junior Operations Officer – a suggestion which infuriated her. She told her father 'Sir Kingsley was made aware I had a job with the Sunday Graphic at three times the salary, with a hundredth part of the work and ten times the power. I don't know whether he liked that!'

Amy Johnson, once the darling of British aviation, had begun to wonder if Britain had forgotten her contribution. It appeared, however, that all the glitter of fame, publicity and fundraising which was her world did not sit comfortably with a country now at war and facing a national crisis.

Objections were soon raised by a variety of government officials about the validity of a Civil Aviation Authority which might spend a fortune on teaching women to fly. Men yes. Women no. Eventually the CAG turned into an organisation that carried out non-flying jobs only, and those pilots and instructors, mainly men, already trained on light aircraft, became eligible to join an organisation called The Air Transport Auxiliary.

However, one female pilot among the few who had slipped through the net and was taught to fly by the CAG in a Gypsy Moth, was my friend Eirene Banister (later Seccombe) who then went on to join the ATA. Eireen was a young widow and the mother of a young child. Sadly, her husband had drowned whilst serving as a Royal Navy Sub-Lieutenant but it didn't prevent her from wanting to do her bit. After several laborious applications to join the ATA she was eventually accepted and went on to join the all-women's ATA Ferry Pool No.15 at Hamble, which also became my stomping ground. Like many, many women who decided to help Britain in its time of need, Eirene had a sympathetic mother to take care of her baby daughter while she was delivering aircraft. She was a lovely person and someone I kept in touch after the war.

By 1939 the only female CAG commissioner, 'Blossom' Miles, had resigned to start a family and the idea of women pilots being recruited or training to help the war effort remained controversial. It was suggested by the Air Ministry that perhaps they could join the ATS (Auxiliary Territorial Service) or the WAAF (Women's Auxiliary Air Force)? This would at least put them in the bracket of 'military' and avoid any potential legal problems affecting civilians and safety. Women soon rallied against the objectors who opposed the idea of them flying to help Britain. Some even volunteered to train as fighter pilots to show the government it could get its money's worth out of them. Lord Londonderry famously answered their campaign with: 'this country has not yet accepted the principle that women should be exposed to fighting risks in so far as they can be protected from them.' Fortunately, this statement did not prevent him from agreeing that women pilots, navigators and engineers would be extremely useful during an emergency when the RAF needed aircraft ferrying to airfields.

In the August of 1939, as I ruefully came to terms with the notion I might never fly again for a long time, the plan for an Air Transport Auxiliary was well underway, thanks to the determined efforts of young director of British Airways Ltd. by the name of Gerard d'Erlanger CBE, or 'Pop' as he became known. There was no way this accomplished pilot and businessman was going to let the likes of Adolf Hitler, Hermann Goering and the rest of the Nazis conquer Britain.

'Pop' d'Erlanger (1905-1962) had trained as a chartered accountant and loved to fly. He became an airline director in 1933. Records reveal he had been working on the idea of an Air Transport Auxiliary since early 1938 and this perceptive man couldn't help but be suspicious of Hitler and the alarming growth of the Luftwaffe in Germany. He wrote to the Air Ministry expressing the urgency to create an organised and essential civilian back up ferrying service to assist the RAF and Fleet

Air Arm. D'Erlanger showed extraordinary insight into the potential horrors of the German war machine and his early actions to thwart the Luftwaffe are to be commended. Aircraft were being turned out in their hundreds but there were few pilots available to deliver them to the RAF.

By the summer of 1939 he finally had permission from the Air Ministry to set up a service which recruited efficient pilots who were either too old or disabled to join the RAF or Fleet Air Arm. A proposal outlining the recruitment of reserve pilots was put forward to the Air Ministry. That same year, and under the auspices of the British Overseas Air Corporation (BOAC), he got permission to recruit thirty male pilots. BOAC had also loaned the fledgling ATA its Airspeed Oxford.

Some of these early recruits had flown in the First World War with the Royal Flying Corps and lost limbs in aerial battle. There was W. R. Corrie – a one-armed pilot who had been working as an actor before he heard the call of the ATA. (Corrie made a huge contribution to the ATA, happily flying heavy twin-engine Hudson bombers. He also had adaptors made for any cockpit which wasn't overly friendly towards disabled pilots).

Another one-armed pilot was the Charles Dutton who brilliantly flew 541 Spitfires during his time with the ATA. He described his experience in the cockpit of this wonderful fighter aircraft: 'I trim the aircraft and set the friction nuts very tight. I open up the control column between my knees and, if I've got the friction nuts right, the throttle and boost nuts don't creep back on me. I take my only hand off the throttle block and transfer it to the stick until I am airborne. Then once again I put the stick between my legs, put up the under-carriage, throttle back to the climbing revs and boost, then take the stick back again for a climb.'

Other pilots to join the merry band of 'Ancient and Tattered Airmen' (as they were labelled by satirists of the day) were Captain F.D. Bradbrooke, a journalist from *Aeroplane* magazine who became the ATA's first Flight Leader; George Curtis who ran a furniture shop; Leo Partridge – an antique dealer; Joe Ellam who flew in the First World War with the RFC and RAF; Wal Handley who was a race-winning motorcyclist; Bill Harben, an adventurer and a shipping director, and amateur gliding expert; and Philip Wills who was eventually honoured with a CBE for his diligent work as Head of Operations with the ATA.

Famous 1930s pilots like Jim Mollinson and his ex-wife Amy Johnson also joined our organisation. I remember Jim very well and flew with a few times. I liked him and found him charming. If I remember correctly he always wore gorgeous-smelling aftershave. I was always happy to fly with Jim but, apart from sharing the odd cup of tea in a ferry pool Mess at stations across the country, I never got involved with him socially. I could see how attractive he was though and I doubt he was ever short of adoring women.

A notable incident occurred when Jim flew as a co-pilot with my ATA colleague Diana Barnato Walker. Their Anson was intercepted and shot up by Luftwaffe fighters, and although the aircraft was hit the twelve passengers and crew were unhurt. On landing Jim's only concern was apparently 'how to get a cup of tea!'

In June 1941, Jim and an ATA crew delivered Cunliffe-Owen OA-1 G-AFMB to Fort Lamy, Chad. The aircraft was fitted out as a personal transport for General de Gaulle. My friend Jim eventually received an MBE for his work with the ATA. But no, he wasn't my boyfriend, more of a friend I respected and admired for his incredible achievements and someone from my life I remember well.

Those men who joined the ATA at the beginning came from professions that included banking, law, publishing, manufacturing, engineering, journalism and administration. Each one may have been middle-aged and too old and unfit for the armed forces, but they often had hundreds of hours of flying experience in their logbooks. They dutifully turned up at Whitchurch airfield, near Bristol, for their first ferrying jobs – which mostly involved trips to and from Croydon and even France. Eventually, the ATA had three one-armed pilots on its books, and two of these chaps were once overheard arguing in the Mess about which arm it was best to use when it came to the efficient control of an aeroplane!

During the first few months of the war the RAF was so small in number that it soon became apparent that all ferrying work should be left to the newly-formed ATA, so as to free up those aircrew trained to fly in combat. By 1944 any RAF pilot who was unfit for operational service was posted to the ATA.

The headquarters of the ATA was to be No.1 Ferry Pool at White Waltham, Maidenhead, Berkshire, and by 1940 the RAF had moved out and various building work and acquisitions of desks and resources took place to enable the ATA to function. It was close to the main aircraft factories with Vickers-Armstrong at Brooklands, Hawker at Langley, and Miles at Woodley. At the height of production, the Supermarine Spitfire Factory at Castle Bromwich was building 320 aircraft per month – the Air Transport Auxiliary was about to become tremendously busy and very much in demand.

Initially the aim of the ATA was to ferry medical supplies, newspapers, mail and hospital patients about the country but by the time Pauline Mary de Peauly Gower (1910-1947) had formed the women's section at the end of 1939 the main job was to deliver military aircraft to and from needy RAF bases and Maintenance Units. The ATA motto 'Anything To Anywhere' was a true one. *Aetheris Avidi* – Eager for the Air – was our unofficial motto and an apt one it was too, as it was the enthusiasm for our work which kept the ATA alive.

But just who was Miss Pauline Gower and what qualities and experience did she possess which persuaded the Air Ministry to trust her judgement to create a women's section of the newly formed Air Transport Auxiliary? As I realised later her aviation expertise and extraordinary organisational and planning skills were to prove a great inspiration to me and my career in general. Pauline was a genuine pioneer and the very highest of achievers. She was someone who was notable to me in many ways and her brief but intense life's work in the establishment of women pilots being seen as serious and committed aviators sits in the ranks of the good and the great.

As a youth Pauline, like me and many future aviators, had taken a flight with Sir Alan Cobham and couldn't get enough of the sky. But her passion to fly turned into a serious struggle when her father, the MP Sir Robert Gower, refused to pay for her lessons.

However, by 1931 he had given in to his daughter's dream and decided to support her ambition to have a 'proper career' which just so happened to be flying. She had showed her dedication to aviation by teaching the violin to raise money for flying lessons.

Pauline and her friend, an aircraft engineer named Dorothy Spicer (1908-1946) began to run their own joy-riding and taxi-service from a field near Sevenoaks, Kent. They had successfully defied many men who had condemned their venture. Dorothy was the first woman to gain all four Air Ministry licences in engineering. In *A Harvest of Memories*, a book about the pioneering Pauline which was written by her son, Michael Fahie, it reveals how she enjoyed some of the best times of her life working with Dorothy who maintained their company's Spartan aeroplanes. When this book was published in 1995 I was invited by Michael and his publisher to a special launch event marking this story of his mother's short but fulfilling and remarkable life. What she achieved in aviation cannot be praised enough. There's a photograph of me in this book standing proudly with Michael and several other ATA girls in 1995. It was a happy day and we were all thrilled to read Michael's wonderful account of his mother – a truly remarkable woman. Without her incredible determination in the face of all sorts of prejudice and political opposition, I would never have had a chance to use my flying skills to help Britain and pilot a wealth of military aircraft including of course the Spitfire.

Pauline and Dorothy's company, Airtrips Ltd., proved highly profitable in the 1930s, albeit with the odd accident, one of which left

Pauline with injuries to her scalp and her upper body. Indeed, her left arm was always weak and during her days as Senior Commander of the ATA, although she posed for publicity photographs in twin-engine aircraft, she was unable to fly them.

Aviatrix Pauline was an enthusiastic writer and contributed articles to various newspapers and magazines of the 1930s, including the *Chatterbox* young people's annual which contains a short story called *The Flying Farrants*. With Dorothy as co-author, she wrote *Women with Wings* and her own poetry book, *Piffling Poems for Pilots*, was published in 1934. She was also the inspiration for the *Worralls of the WAAF* books written by her friend, W.E. Johns of *Biggles* fame.

A few years later, as the rumblings of war became louder, the redoubtable Pauline was appointed as the second woman Civil Air Guard Commissioner for the London and South-Eastern area. She soon became the only female in this post and in the last few months of peace became the natural choice of leader for an 'Air Force of women expert in flying and ground branches of aviation'.

This idea was supported by the President of the Women's Legion, Lady Londonderry, who was a keen supporter of Pauline's ideas and her commitment to aviation. The other vital ally was the Parliamentary Under Secretary for Air, the former Royal Flying Corps pilot Captain Harold Balfour, who had been decorated for bravery after serving gallantly with Nos 40 and 43 squadrons.

On 17 May 1939, it was announced that in a National Emergency, women were to be permitted to ferry aircraft. It was the breakthrough Pauline had been waiting for so patiently. She had reason to defy the critics when she said: 'I have heard all this talk about the futility of training women to fly, and I think that the critics are wrong. Women fliers will be very useful in an emergency. They could ferry aeroplanes. They could also act as assistant instructors, thus relieving men instructors for more combat flying.'

Pauline's political contacts would eventually become most useful in her ambition to create a women's section of the ATA. Her guile, diplomacy and knowledge of aviation was impressive and soon she had convinced the powers that be, including the Director General of Civil Aviation Sir Francis Shelmerdine and Gerard 'Pop' d'Erlanger, that women pilots had an essential role to play during war time. She also recruited the support of the Conservative politician, Lord 'Brab' Brabazon, who had been the first man to fly with a piglet in his French Voisin biplane from Eastchurch on the Isle of Sheppey in Kent in 1909. The women of the ATA were sometimes called 'Brab's Beauties' or 'Brab's Babes' by a press keen to glamorise stories for a war-weary public.

However, in the autumn of 1939, the intrepid Pauline was left to play the waiting game with the Air Ministry as there was still serious opposition to her plan to create a women's section of the ATA. How could women be seen around RAF ferry pools? When Pauline chased up the DGCA about the long delay for action she received a letter from the Director General of Civil Aviation Sir Francis Shelmerdine (1882-1945) explaining he wasn't in a position to make any definite plans to enrol experienced women pilots to the ATA. He said at that time the male ATA pilots were working as British Airways employees and were based at RAF ferry pools. 'Women', he stressed, 'were not permitted to join the Central Flying School' and the RAF would not agree to them joining the all-male ferry pools either.

It was well known that Air Chief Marshal Sir Trafford Leigh-Mallory put up opposition to women flying military aircraft. Whether this attitude came from misplaced chivalry or plain chauvinism, he made it clear there wasn't any way he would allow women to ferry aircraft across the Channel either. Although he was forced to eat his words on the first part of his argument, with the women's section becoming a fully successful part of the ATA, his ban on them flying abroad seems to have stuck until 1945. It was always of great annoyance to many aviatrices that only the men of the ATA could deliver aircraft overseas. My friend Diana Barnato-Walker, who, as we shall see later, defied this instruction, demanded to know why women pilots couldn't fly to Europe. When she complained, the senior men of the ATA explained how 'there just aren't any lavatories for women in France'.

Meanwhile, Shelmerdine's letter to Pauline concluded: 'I therefore feel I cannot really ask you, or any of the women pilots you have in mind, to continue to stand by, if there is other war work which you or they want to undertake. I still feel that if the so-called war develops into a real war, it will not be long before there will be openings for experienced women pilots. I hope I have made the position quite clear.'

Ask me today how she must have felt to have received such a dithering response and I'd say she must have been terribly irritated and wondered if the rigours of the patriarchal system had indeed sabotaged the whole idea of a women's section. All of Pauline's early hard work though had then begun to create a framework which would mean I and many other women would take our places in the history of aviation. I really can't thank her enough. She was a true inspiration and a formidable leader.

By November 1939 the war had intensified enough for Pauline to realise her plans had to get back on track. The main purpose of the ATA was the provision of a ferry service throughout the UK via a number of ferry pools which had an allocation of pilots of both sexes, and from these pools the daily taxi aircraft (often the Avro Anson) would take the pilots to the factory airfields and maintenance units to collect the various aircraft. After the ferry flights were completed the taxi aircraft would fly around and collect pilots to return them to their home pools.

This went on daily unless prevented by the weather. There were also connecting ferry flights to and fro. There was also confusion over the status of ferry pilots themselves. For example, were they to wear RAF uniform or were they working as civilians? Pauline finally got the nod from Pop d'Erlanger to call on those women she'd originally selected to take a test flight. Her considerable plans and political campaigning were about to bear the desired results.

A communication was sent on 23 September 1939 from the Director General of the Civil Aviation authority, Sir Francis Shelmerdine, to the Director of Civil Aviation Finance, which reveals in detail Pauline's proposal to head up a women's section in consultation with Gerard d'Erlanger. It pointed out that the Under Secretary of State, Harold Balfour, had arranged for women of selected flying experience to be utilised as ferry pilots and the men should join the RAF Central Flying School at Upavon for testing and classification. Finally – a real result.

Balfour authorised d'Erlanger to employ Pauline to select a dozen women for ferrying duties. This number was later reduced to eight.

The DGCA's communication revealed: 'It will be necessary, for obvious reasons, to keep the women's section separate from the men's section of the ATA, and to have a woman in administrative charge of it. In agreement with Mr d'Erlanger I have selected Miss Pauline Gower for this post. She herself is a very experienced pilot holding "A" and "B" pilots' licences, navigator's licences, etc. and she earned her living for a considerable time in the hard school of joy-riding. She has never been a stunt pilot with all the publicity which is attached to that role. Miss Gower is willing to undertake the work.'

The missive also included the details of flying instruction for women to be the same as that of the men. On a chilly 1 December 1939, a message finally arrived for Pauline from the Air Ministry informing her she had been posted to the ATA's No.5 Ferry Pool at Hatfield. Here she satisfactorily completed the ten-minute flight test in a Tiger Moth and was promoted to First Officer – and made Officer in Charge of Women. Her salary was to be £400 per year. The women's section was born and within months I was to be part of it.

Pauline's guile and political contacts were top drawer and she'd learned the art of skilful negotiation while assisting her father Sir Robert

Gower, Conservative MP for Gillingham in Kent from 1924 to 1945, in the rough and tumble of parliamentary duties. She had also made many very valuable and powerful contacts with her straight-forward and yet diplomatic approach to men who could help fight her corner.

Chapter 7

'New Eves of the Air'

When the news was finally announced that women would be flying with the Air Transport Auxiliary it brought forward a flood of reporters and photographers keen to feed their readers a heady mix of adventure, drama and glamour. These eager pressmen flocked to Hatfield in the early weeks of 1940 to capture images of the 'First Eight' women pilots in their Sidcot flying suits.

I recall the newspapers' cheesy headlines, like 'New Eves of the Air', which screamed out from front pages, along with pictures of the aviatrices smiling desperately at their leader Pauline Gower – someone not that unused to dealing with the press in her long experience running her company, Airtrips Ltd. Pauline also held the honour of being only the third woman in the UK to ever hold a commercial pilot's licence. Women pilots were a novelty then.

In 1940, as I worked in and around the farm still missing my days in the sky, I learned from my Pa that some of his land had been requisitioned to extend the airfield. This made sure I was really weaned on aeroplanes.

I vividly remember 16 August 1940, during the Battle of Britain, when my sister Dora and I were in the garden and we saw a Luftwaffe bomber dive out of the low clouds to drop bombs – which resulted in all this fire and smoke pouring up into the sky. The Luftwaffe crew scored a direct hit and then disappeared way up beyond the clouds as soon as they had committed their dastardly act.

Brize Norton was home to one of the RAF's new airfields and at wartime it was mostly used as an instruction base for No.2 Flying Training School. From there pilots flew a variety of Hawker biplanes, Harts, Audaxes and Furies.

When the bombs cascaded down on RAF Brize Norton in 1940 I realised the order to launch an air attack on Britain had been given by the large German chap who had once supped cocktails with the Mitford sisters just a few hundred yards from my childhood home. His name was Hermann Goering and his actions changed my life forever.

When the Luftwaffe struck Brize during the Battle of Britain they had managed to destroy thirty-two twin-engine Airspeed Oxford trainers and eleven Hurricane fighter aircraft, whilst two hangars were gutted by fire. Poor Brize Norton. It was an essential training base for Bomber Command crews and now it was a smouldering heap. Three petrol bowsers were damaged in the raid and water and electricity supplies were affected. One 250 kilo bomb landed close to the ammunition dump. It was fortunate it failed to explode. But those bombs that did their worst on Brize Norton succeeded in wrecking ten buildings and ten people were taken to the sick bay. It was extraordinary no-one was killed during the raid especially as many RAF personnel were going about their business outside as the bombs dropped.

It seemed as if poor old Brize underwent a battering for several minutes but in fact it took the Luftwaffe only seconds to do their damage. I shall not forget the sights and sounds of that day. Certainly the loss of so many Oxfords of No.2 FTS and the eleven Hurricanes of No.6 MU (Maintenance Unit) meant the other aircraft on Brize were quickly dispersed to the landing grounds at Southrop and Akeman Street. There was no doubt the enemy had made a mess of RAF Brize Norton. The smoke from the burning hangar and its contents seemed to hang around for days despite the efforts of the fire crews, both military and civil.

In his book *Oxfordshire Airfields in the Second World War* historian Robin Brooks writes: 'Mangled metal, wood and rubble lay everywhere with parts of aircraft still smouldering. Yet despite the intense damage, the airfield was only out of operation for a short time. Once most of the damage had been cleared, it was back to the training routine. The remainder of 1940 and 1941 saw no further raids. There were sadly, however, many accidents due to the nature of the training with a considerable loss of life.'

A few weeks before Brize had been reduced to a smouldering heap the first eight women pilots of the ATA were making headlines as subjects of great criticism from some less enlightened quarters. C.G. Grey, the editor and founder of *Aeroplane* magazine, revealed his shock at their recruitment to the war effort. He wrote: 'There are millions of women in the country who could do useful jobs in war. But the trouble is that so many of them insist on wanting to do jobs which they are quite incapable of doing. The menace is the woman who thinks that she ought to be flying in a high-speed bomber when she really has not the intelligence to scrub the floor of a hospital properly, or who wants to nose around as an Air Raid Warden and yet can't cook her husband's dinner.'

Alarming isn't it? Today these words come over as dismissive, contemptuous and completely misguided. Even more disturbing were the comments from various housewives and mature women who wrote to the newspapers complaining about 'the fairer sex' flying aircraft. Heaven forbid!

Senior Commander Pauline Gower (who after the war was awarded an MBE) had more than 2,000 flying hours to her credit and had carried 33,000 passengers during her career. Achievements not to be sniffed at. C.G. Grey and his fellow doubters had got it all wrong and Pauline's organisational skills were in great demand. Pauline was the first woman ever permitted by the RAF to fly a military aeroplane. By the beginning of 1940 she had already flown the taxi Anson and made 102 separate flights. She was leading from the front and no doubt contributed many more flying hours to her licence. However, as her son Michael Fahie points out: 'After 1940 my mother's logbooks were lost and there are little details of her flying history with the ATA.'

What is on record, though, is Pauline's retort to a male cynic writing in the press about the women's section. She wrote: 'We are called the ATA "Always Terrified Airwomen" – but we're going to answer that by just quickly going on with the job. So far we have delivered 150 aeroplanes from factory to base without a hitch. We are not allowed to lose our way as we get shot at by anti-aircraft guns!'

On 10 January 1940, and fighting the chill of winter, she dressed in a flying suit and was pictured by an eager press at Hatfield aerodrome with her first recruits. Their salaries at the rank of Second Officer (my first rank) were £230 per year with £8 extra each month for flight pay. These figures were twenty per cent less than for the men who were doing the same dangerous job. All other conditions were the same as those of the male pilots and Pauline no doubt put on her 'to do' list how she would get us women equal pay, which of course she did some eighteen months later.

The first eight women of the ATA who must be mentioned were: Winifred Crossley (Fair) (1906-1984) a doctor's daughter who had flying experience towing banners for advertising companies and working as an aerial acrobatics pilot for a circus. After the war she married airline captain Peter Fair, head of BOAC-owned Bahamas Airways in Nassau.

Margaret Cunnison (Ebbage) (1914-2004) was an instructor before the war and successfully continued in this role until she left the ATA in 1943 after bouts of illness. She married in 1944. The Rt. Hon. Margaret Fairweather (1901-1944) was the daughter of Lord Runicman and the sister of Mr W.L. Runciman who was Director General of the British Overseas Airways Corporation. Margaret was already an experienced pilot and had been flying her own single-engine de Havilland Puss Moth since 1937. She married Douglas 'Poppa' Fairweather, another ATA pilot. Douglas Fairweather was nicknamed 'Foulweather' because of his advanced skills meant he took on all sorts of climates and conditions. As an avid smoker he was known to navigate and time his journeys by the number of cigarettes he puffed on his way to a destination. For instance, if one cigarette lasted seven minutes and he chain-smoked four then he'd come into land in twenty-eight minutes!

Douglas had often flown British secret agents into France. Among his many ATA missions was ambulance work and on 3 April 1944, he flew a nursing sister named Mary Kershaw from White Waltham to pick up a seriously wounded Canadian soldier from Prestwick in the north, taking him to the Royal Canadian Hospital at Taplow, when Anson N4875 went down in the sea killing them all. Douglas was just 53-years-old.

Sadly, both of the Flight Captain Fairweathers lost their lives within months of each other, carrying out vital ATA missions. What happened to Douglas' wife, and our ATA colleague 'Margie', was equally as tragic. She was a brilliant pilot but on 8 August 1944, when the Percival Proctor she was flying over Cheshire, that with the serial number LZ801, had engine problems, she had no choice but to force land in a field. This was second nature to a pilot of Margie's prowess and all went to plan until the aircraft hit a hidden ditch and it flipped over. Margie had two passengers with her including a Mr L. Hendricks from the Aircraft Production Department of the Air Ministry, and her sister Kitty Farrer who was Pauline Gower's adjutant. Mr Hendricks escaped with just a broken thumb but Kitty suffered a broken leg and was unwell for two years afterwards. Margie, who had recently returned to work after giving birth, was so badly injured she died in hospital the next day. An investigation into the crash showed the vent pipe of the port fuel tank was completely blocked up and caused it to collapse.

Douglas and Margaret Fairweather are the only married ATA couple to share a Commonwealth War Graves Commission headstone. They are buried in Dunure Cemetery, Ayshire, Scotland. The deaths of such lovely people, as with all our ATA friends who lost their lives, made me realise just how dangerous it could be working as a ferry pilot.

Mona Friedlander (1914-1994) was an ice-hockey international who was recruited to the women's section of the ATA for her experience as a pilot and navigator, flying as a target in front of anti-aircraft batteries to assist with gun aiming and searchlight accuracy. In the publicity photographs of the first eight Mona is the one in her trademark white leather flying helmet and had taken part in the Folkestone Air Trophy race in 1939. Joan Hughes MBE (1918-1993) of Loughton, Essex, had been flying since the age of fifteen, secured a licence at seventeen, and had been an instructor with the Civil Air Guard before she joined the ATA. Gabrielle Patterson (1905-1968) of Romford, Essex was the first woman to have obtained a flight instructor's licence in 1935 and was also a key member of the National Women's Air Guard. Gabrielle had met Pauline Gower at various aviation events before the war. Rosemary Rees MBE (Later Lady Du Cros) (1901-1994) was a former ballet dancer and acrobat and had worked as a flying instructor before the war.

Finally, Marion Wilberforce (1902-1996) was the daughter of Mr Ogilvie-Forbes and had notched up 900 flying hours by 1940 when she joined the ATA. Marion would later become Commanding Officer at Cosford, the second all-women's Ferry Pool. At first they were charged to deliver light aircraft like de Havilland Gypsy Moths and Tiger Moths from the factory at Hatfield to RAF bases in the north of England and Scotland. There was constant pressure on Senior Commander Gower to ensure aircraft ferried under her supervision were not damaged. It was believed at first that women should only fly small, light aeroplanes that could be fixed easily in case the girls broke them. It wasn't long before this rule changed dramatically as the need arose for women pilots to fly every variety of military aircraft including four-engine bombers.

I got to know Flight Captain Joan Hughes MBE who said the first eight women were like experiments, as the RAF just did not expect women to be able to fly aeroplanes. She said: 'It did place a burden on us and it was a case of "for Godsake don't break an aeroplane".'

This attitude prompted us aviatrices to continually prove our worth, and a tactful Pauline, soon to be promoted to Senior Commander, then persuaded the RAF to allow her women pilots to take advanced training at the Central Flying School at Upavon, near Devizes in Wiltshire.

In January 1940, Pauline told the BBC programme *The World Goes By*: 'When I started flying ten years ago I did not believe that any of us would take part in another Great War. I looked at flying as one of those things which help to unite the nations of the world. The men and women pilots of my own generation really believed that we were increasing the world's happiness. Even the words we used – words like joy-riding and aerial circus – suggested gaiety. It seemed the most natural thing in the world that I should take up joy-riding and then take part in an aerial circus.

'Soon of course, the gaiety of civil aviation gave place to more serious things. Careful planning was going on all around. New routes were being opened up. Commercial aeroplanes were flying regularly to various parts of the world. Joyrides and aerial circuses were becoming things of the past. I was doing more serious work – like running a service across the Wash from Hunstanton to Skegness. And now I can claim to have carried over 30,000 passengers in the air.

'Flying had become serious, but it was still an instrument of Peace. What was I to do when the war broke out? That question naturally worried every woman in the land. Many of us had our homes to care for, and we knew that as soon as the war began, our duty was to look after our homes. But others had no home ties. A woman who had flown for ten years or longer had to seriously ask herself whether she ought to let her flying go rusty, when it might be of real use to the nation. Could a woman pilot help to win this war without robbing a man of his job?

'The question was soon answered. As the war approached, the volume of aircraft production rapidly increased. A great deal of time was spent in ferrying the new aircraft from the factory where it was built to the RAF aerodrome where it might be wanted, or where it could be stored for use later on. This time cannot be very well spared by the RAF and Fleet Air Arm pilots, who were wanted for other duties. Eventually, British Airways launched the Air Transport Auxiliary service – better known as the ATA. Its members were civilian pilots who undertook all the ferry work from the factory to the aerodrome. Soon after the outbreak of war, it was realised that the pressure of work was becoming heavy, even for the civilian pilots. And so I was asked to take charge of a special women's section of the ATA. Today I saw a woman pilot set off on her first delivery flight. I cannot tell you how proud I felt. We are a small group of women pilots with a job to do. We are just helping, along with others, to win the war. Our job will not be obtrusive. But it is going to be well and efficiently done.'

I think this wonderful address to the nation gives a clear impression of what the women's section of the ATA was all about. Pauline instilled in us a sense of duty and I don't think I would have wanted to join any of the other services. As I loved farming and gardening I reckon I might have heard the call of the Land Army but as I was a pilot first and foremost, so the question of what type of war work I would do never really arose. The answer for me was plain as day.

Those first women to join the ATA were asked to fly a circuit and carry out various manoeuvres. Only if they were satisfactorily performed would they be considered for a job. Before any pilot would be considered she needed to have 250 flying hours on her licence. Obviously, as the ATA grew this rule was lowered to 150, then to 100 and eventually full training was offered and *ab initio* (a Latin phrase meaning 'from the beginning') pilots were recruited.

Meanwhile, as the first few women were settling into their role as ferry pilots, the Battle of France was raging and the Germans were driving back British troops and the RAF to Dunkirk. Some of the men of the ATA were asked to urgently deliver Fairey Battle aircraft to France in the spring of 1940 only to be met by anxious RAF squadrons feeling harassed by constant bombing and strafing inflicted by the Luftwaffe. The ATA pilots who had volunteered to take part in these early and dangerous missions were left to find their own way back to Britain. One of them was a Sussex farmer called Peter Mursell, who later became the Head of Flying Training with the ATA.

Peter told me that after flying to France on one occasion, he and two other ATA pilots were presented with three broken Hurricanes which had working engines but very little else! So without any brakes or flap controls, and on an aircraft he had never flown before, Peter managed to limp a broken Hurricane to White Waltham, where eventually it was repaired for action in the forthcoming Battle of Britain.

Such dramatic ATA ferrying trips to France were halted in the early summer of 1940 as the Germans completely occupied much of the country. The ATA would not arrive in France again until 6 September 1944, when our first pilot to land there was quite rightly one of our five French aviators – Maurice Harle – who flew a Spitfire that day.

In January 1940, and as the Phoney War dragged on, ATA Captain Rosemary Rees met the press and appeared in a photograph at Hatfield with the 'first eight' women of the ATA – all in their Sidcot flying suits as mentioned earlier. These heavy fur-lined suits were also worn by the RAF and Fleet Air Arm aircrews, but, more often than not, they removed the big thick collars. They did this to ensure that when they swivelled their heads every five seconds looking out for the enemy they could actually see beyond a face full of furry lining.

Rosemary Rees recalled this event: 'That day the press arrived they all asked if we could run towards them carrying our parachutes which weighed about thirty pounds. Then they wanted us to do it again and again! It was exhausting. We laughed because they had wanted us to "scramble" to the slow old trainer aircraft like the Tiger Moth! We were not allowed to talk to the pressmen on our own. Only Pauline (Gower) had permission to do that. We had to remember that although we were civilian pilots we were under RAF discipline'.

The headlines to come out of that day said '8 Girls Show the RAF' or 'Our Women Air Aces'. One article carried a few quotes from Winnie Crossley. She is described as having five years of flying experience and she'd done a lot of 'stunting' (circus work). Winnie said: 'My husband is out in France so I've closed down our home until the war is finished. He is in the army and not the RAF. He prefers to leave the flying to me!'

Mona Friedlander told journalists she drives home after a hard day of flying and if she's not too tired will go to a party. The women's restroom was described as having its own armchair and it was a place where they could smoke and apply make-up. Not all at once I hope.

The head of the ATA, Air Commodore 'Pop d'Erlanger, is quoted in the same article as saying the women pilots flew as 'neatly and as precisely as the men'. Whilst this comment was encouraging and commendable, and much needed at the time, there was a suggestion that various heavyweights in the Air Ministry were terrified about the German High Command discovering that Britain had a shortage of male pilots. It seems the publicity attracted by the women's section of the ATA was not welcomed in all quarters.

Rosemary Rees also said: 'Life was hard at the beginning for us first eight girls. More often than not we'd fly a Tiger Moth far into the Midlands and even Scotland and then if the RAF couldn't return us to Hatfield we'd have to get a train back. One night Joan Hughes and I were walking back to our billet somewhere in the ice and freezing cold carrying our parachute and overnight bags which were always with us when we asked each other if we could take much more of it.'

The first eight women of the ATA were required to fly in formation at first, as suggested by the RAF. But this, they soon realised, was not practicable; as Rosemary explained, it was impossible to keep your eye on the ground for landmarks and follow the aircraft in front.

She added: 'Of course the RAF aircrew were taught to fly just one or two types of aircraft. Later on for us Jacks of all trades in the ATA we had to rely heavily on our skills to fly solo. In the ATA we weren't really used to taking orders. The only discipline in the ATA was the sack! We first eight women all got on jolly well. We were all adults and not silly things. There was no jealousy just a little joshing about what aircraft types we'd been given, that's all really.'

Any pilot caught 'lifting the elbow' (boozing) too often and then setting out to fly was asked to leave the ATA. There were indeed a few of these individuals who thankfully got caught out.

When the CO (Margot Gore) was off duty Rosemary took charge of Hamble and her many responsibilities included visiting injured pilots in hospital or sorting out arrangements for those who had been killed. The ATA Benevolent Fund had already been set up at White Waltham (ATA Headquarters) to financially assist the families of those killed in service.

I spent many of my weekends off visiting injured servicemen in hospital – a lot of us did this and we were asked to try and cheer up these poor chaps who were suffering from all sorts of ailments inflicted upon them during combat.

One day I recall Rosemary had to collect the watch and other personal effects belonging to a female pilot who had died after crashing into a hill. 'I had to make sure I did what I could for the families at times of tragedy and need. In the ATA we knew how dangerous the job could be but we also knew we had to get on with our work,' she said.

Flying the taxi Anson meant we had to concentrate hard as we were often carrying eight passengers. There were times as a taxi pilot when there'd be a shriek or two and I would ask what was going on, and was told someone had told a joke. When Rosemary was taxi pilot she would tell us all to share the laugh when she'd landed safely, as she needed to focus on flying the aircraft and its precious cargo of pilots.

Chapter 8

Fighter Girls

One of Pauline Gower's oldest friends from the bright, breezy days of 1930s' aviation was the celebrated aviatrix Amy Johnson. Photographs from those carefree days show them together with groups of happy pilots having snowball fights and laughing. Indeed, in this particular decade the social whirl at many local flying clubs embraced anyone with a passion for aircraft. It was a halcyon time for aviators who had fun, and record-breaking achievements were at the top of the sky-bound agenda.

I believe Pauline always felt Amy had been by-passed for the Civil Air Guard job, and even command of the women's section of the ATA, rather unfairly. Maybe Pauline even felt guilty too that she had the top role in the ATA instead of Amy who had, after all, such an impressive reputation and had been among the first women to conquer the longest flights across the world. For some months Pauline did everything possible to convince Amy that becoming an ATA pilot would be a fine thing and she could be of enormous help to the organisation.

It took a few weeks for Amy to accept Pauline might be right, and there was a chance she would enjoy assisting Britain in its hour of need. In 1940 there was little doubt Amy's aviation career was flagging and no one in a time of war was in a position to offer her the dream job as a private airline pilot. She had also recently divorced playboy pilot Jim Mollison and was still recovering from such a personal blow.

If she wondered why it was Pauline who landed the top post with the ATA women's section, then she had to accept how at a time of war the ideals of fame and glamour were not the best credentials for a taking on such a highly responsible position. The realities of war demanded serious dedication and vital leadership skills that brought results. Flying was no longer all about fun. The jolly days when one could hire an aircraft from a green field in Sussex and fly without a licence to

Budapest in Hungary for a picnic disappeared when Hitler's armies marched into Poland and Britain declared war on Germany.

The famous 'Budapest' picnic had been a social event enjoyed by several of my ATA colleagues and friends, including Flight Captain Philippa Bennett (Booth). She is recorded as saying how, in the 1930s, one could hire an aircraft and fly anywhere without papers. In those days, aviation was all about enjoyment. It was on a par with a hobby like skiing. It was completely unregulated; nobody asked any questions. Philippa was absolutely right. My early days flying my Swallow across the skies of Oxfordshire were delightful and unhindered. It was a super time.

By the summer of 1941, and after much hard work, Pauline achieved another significant breakthrough. She had persuaded ATA Commodore d'Erlanger to permit ATA women to fly fighter aircraft including the Hurricane and Spitfire. Can you imagine? Pauline had finally persuaded the men in power this is what women could achieve. Brilliant. What a wonderful piece of politics, sexual chemistry, call it what you like.

So, the first woman to fly a Hurricane that month was Flight Captain Winifred Crossley (Fair). That first Hurricane had been flown from ATA headquarters at White Waltham to Hatfield on 19 July 1941. Standing ready to fly it, by turn, were: Winnie Crossley, Margaret Fairweather, Joan Hughes and Rosemary Rees. The next day it was the turn of Philippa Bennett and a few other women who soon realised this lovely fighter aircraft was a joy in the air and such a well behaved machine.

In the first real-life book about the ATA, *Brief Glory*, E.C. Cheesman wrote: 'It was a red letter day for the girls at Hatfield. Captain Henderson, the Headquarters Test Pilot, brought over a Hurricane, and the first flight ever made by a woman in an RAF fighter took place. Flight Captain Crossley climbed into the machine, buckled on her parachute harness, and taxied down the field to get into position for the take-off. Open mouthed, the little group of onlookers kept their eyes glued to the plane as it roared into the air.

'It was a proud moment for Pauline Gower, at long last, one of her girls was flying an operational machine. When Flight Captain Crossley landed she described the Hurricane as a "lovely little aircraft". Four women in all including Rosemary Rees, Margie Fairweather, Joan Hughes were checked out that day on the Hurricane, and from that moment the Women's Section of the ATA began to take its place alongside that of the men pilots and to share fully their work.'

However, ATA First Officer Lettice Curtis, who climbed into her first Hurricane a few weeks later, admitted she was nervous and could feel the pressure to fly the aircraft successfully and maintain the good reputation of the women's section. She was asked to pick up an old Hurricane Mk.I at Dumfries and fly it on to Prestwick. In her book *Forgotten Pilots*, she revealed:

'What was I to do? Much as I disliked the thought of it, I saw no alternative to accepting the task, feeling as ever that any excuse I made to get out of it would reflect badly on women pilots generally. And anyway, what excuse could I make? I was not allowed to fly a Hurricane and though I would have much preferred a little more time to think about it, to have been with someone of whom I could ask questions, fly it I must or forever lose face!'

All went well for the cautious Curtis, who described the take off as easy, but it was landing the Hurricane she dreaded the most. She need not have worried as once again she made a successful delivery and the following week she flew a Hurricane Mk.II.

When it came to the Hurricane and Spitfire, First Officer Curtis did feel the women of the Hatfield ferry pool had been thrown in at the deep end and there was not the helpful banter of the men around to compare notes and chat about the first fighter aircraft flights.

At the all-male ferry pools, more often than not the Commander carried out essential training. Curtis pointed out that owing to an organisational workload and administration duties, and through no fault of her own, Senior Commander Pauline Gower did not fly Hurricanes and so the women's section was left at times to rely on the 'little blue book – Ferry Pilots Notes' and learn from each other's experiences. No one wanted to admit they were nervous of an aircraft. The ATA motto of 'Anything to Anywhere' ran deep in their veins.

Some months before I joined the ATA there were casualties in the ATA, with the most famous being that of the legendary aviatrix Amy Johnson who went missing on 5 January 1941. Amy was ferrying an Airspeed Oxford from Blackpool to Kidlington, Oxfordshire and is believed to have run out of fuel and gone down into the Thames Estuary near Herne Bay, Kent.

Amy appears to have had got lost in fog and baled out into the freezing waters, and stoic attempts by the crew of the HMS *Haselmere* to rescue her from the icy Estuary failed. The ship's own Commander, Lieutenant Walter Fletcher, dived into save the drowning pilot but not long after he had reached her she was swept away beneath the ship. Amy Johnson's body was never found and Lieutenant Fletcher died a few days later from the intense cold he had suffered in the water.

I know there is a lot of different theories about what happened to Amy Johnson, with some saying that she was shot down by our anti-aircraft guns because she didn't give the right signal when passing over the coast. The thing is we didn't have any radios in the aircraft to do such a thing. Others suggest Amy was carrying a German spy on board and was on a special mission which was all very hush-hush. This notion came about because at one time she had a Dutch boyfriend. I think, in reality, the accident was caused by the cloud and as she flew on and on there was no break for her to see through to bring the aircraft down to check her whereabouts. She ran out of fuel and lost her life that day.

However, ATA women's section Operations Manager, Alison King, always believed Amy was on a secret mission. Alison had flown with Amy and described her as a good person to know. Although I never met Amy Johnson I heard she was a helpful person and was especially kind to the younger pilots seeking advice.

Alison King told an Imperial War Museum researcher the following during an interview in 1985: 'Pauline (Gower) came to see me the day before Amy's death and asked if I could give Amy an Oxford to fly to Scotland. I thought this was unusual and when I asked Pauline why, she didn't reply and left the room. When I look back I wondered if Amy had a secret job to carry out. I wonder if she had to pick up a German. I then got to know the captain of a ship who told me Amy had been shot down by his gunners because the Oxford looked like an enemy aircraft. I asked him why he didn't see the roundels on the Oxford.'

Alison's theory is unusual and if Amy was carrying a passenger I wondered if it could have been a boyfriend on board? The conjecture Amy was flying with a German passenger may well have gained momentum because one of the crew of the HMS *Haslemere* reported seeing two people in the water on the day the Oxford went down. A pigskin bag belonging to Johnson was picked up. The unmissable initials A.J. confirmed its rightful owner. Perhaps the sailor mistook the bag for a body?

Alison said: 'I think Amy picked up a German from Germany or Holland and was bringing him to England. Pauline had been very secretive about Amy's flight that day and didn't say much about it after Amy's death either.'

ATA Senior Commander Pauline was no doubt saddened by the death of her friend and colleague. Amy's career with the ATA had been brief and after persuasion by Pauline she had eventually joined as a Second Officer on 20 May 1940. Within seven months she had lost her life, a time which left the women's section in shock for some days to come but, as with the men of the RAF who suffered the loss of so many friends in action, the war continued and so must the duty to carry out the grand plan to defeat the enemy.

Chapter 9

Reporting for Duty

I am often asked how I came to join the ATA. Well, in the early autumn of 1941, I heard a BBC radio appeal for women pilots to contact the recently formed Air Transport Auxiliary. I remember I was terribly excited when I wrote off, telling them that I loved flying, how I only had a few hours on my licence and yet was dying to get back into the air. I soon received a reply and was asked to go to Hatfield for an interview. With my very limited experience I rated my chances of being accepted as very slight indeed.

Although I was nervous it went well and I was asked to have a flying test at Hatfield. I was overjoyed and thrilled too when I got that letter confirming I had been accepted for further training. It was a wonderful feeling to know I might be able to not only fly but help the country too.

Of course I had to get my parents' permission, but I need not have worried, they gave me their blessing. So off I went to Hatfield Airfield on 1 October 1941 and was signed on. I remember that bright, chilly autumn morning so well. As my brothers had wanted to be sure I arrived at Hatfield safe and sound, they volunteered to drive me there. They were all very supportive of me. I recall having to report at Hatfield before noon.

It had been quite some time of course since I had last flown, and I was more than a little concerned as to what would happen. However, I muttered a few prayers and hoped that I would not make a mess of the flight. The Tiger Moth was quite unfamiliar to me, and my fears increased, but once I had settled into the cockpit and discovered all the knobs and handles, I began to enjoy myself.

I was proud I had remembered all my pre-flight checks and how the aircraft should behave before, during and after take-off. I adapted well to the Tiger Moth on that first day, which suited me fine as I needed to make an impression on the instructor who was seated, hopefully not too nervously, in the seat in front of me. I was in the cockpit of an aircraft which has no starter, no nose wheel, no stall-warners, no flaps, no brakes and no roof.

I had remembered, of course, to climb into the cockpit good and steady whilst knowing all the time the aircraft was made of wood and fabric, so no bouncing on the wing. The Tiger Moth was a tidy, neat and straightforward simple aircraft and I soon understood why its no-nonsense attributes lent to its status as a trainer aircraft.

As I strapped myself in tight that day I looked at the dashboard, which was made of thin wood and reminiscent of something from a toy aircraft. There were four dials with indicators and the large compass at the bottom. The memory of flying its relative – the DH60 Moth – then came back to me in a rush as it too had a tail-wheel and two big wheels beneath the wings.

I held back the stick on starting the Tiger Moth to stop it from tipping over on its propeller and then we began to slowly taxi forward. I managed to reach the pedals and the rudders ok and I made my way over to the take off point, slowly but surely. I remembered it was important to think ahead and to make sure the nose of the Tiger Moth didn't go forward on take-off. Within seconds I had the aircraft off the ground and flew the required pattern, then the instructor said 'do a tight turn then a practice forced landing, and go back to the airfield and land'.

The wind was now snatching at my hair as I made to climb higher and, sure enough, I felt as if I was in control. Phew. I was back in the air again, back where I belonged. The months without flying didn't seem to have affected me too much at all.

I was gentle on the stick and put the aircraft in trim, so I could head for the horizon which appeared straight and level. The trim on the Tiger Moth can be difficult to set as it requires co-ordination of various rods and cables by the careful pulling back of a knob on the dashboard. It has been said the accurate and successful setting of the trim on the Tiger Moth can sort out the real pilots from the fakers.

I don't recall having much time to look at the Hertfordshire countryside below me. I was busy keeping my focus on the aircraft and making sure it wasn't going to expose me as a faker. I climbed higher but remained mindful of the need to keep below 1,000 feet. I flew on for a short while and then turned back towards the airfield, fully aware I had to get the landing just right.

As I came down towards the airstrip I remembered to keep the nose high so I could make a successful three-point landing, which meant the big wheels must touch the ground together at the same time. I said to myself 'careful, easy does it Mary', and I landed light as a feather and came to a stop. I turned the engine off, checked the cockpit dashboard dials and then listened to the brief sound of creaks and moans from the cables.

I was rather pleased I'd made such a good landing – but I did concentrate hard to ensure my flight was a success. I also realised the old Tiger Moth isn't always easy to handle, but if you concentrate then absolute control can be achieved. I climbed out of the cockpit and was told by the instructor: 'That's fine. You don't seem to have forgotten much, even though you haven't flown for some time'.

On day four, the wintery weather had set in so it was Ground School. This consisted of adjusting to aircraft instruments, learning some Morse Code, navigation and plotting numerous courses on maps for use on cross country flights. Maps were four miles to an inch and very detailed, roads, woods, lakes, golf courses, mansions and castles, churches and railways. We had no radio.

I was then informed I would be interviewed by the head of the Women's Section of the ATA, Senior Commander Pauline Gower. I was quite nervous about that.

She sat behind a desk and seemed quite formal but when she started talking I realised she was most pleasant with a wonderful sense of humour. I knew she was the sort of person who would have my every respect and of course she had achieved so much in aviation throughout the whole of the 1930s. I guess I was a little in awe of the big white chief.

After we'd chatted for some while about flying, and I'd answered her questions satisfactorily, it was to my utter amazement she suddenly asked: 'Can you join us straight away?'

I was very excited, but underneath a little apprehensive; it was a huge step for any young woman to take. With my very limited experience of flying I had rated my chance of being accepted as very slight indeed, and couldn't quite believe I had finally been accepted as a candidate for training.

I wasn't worried about the flying, though, and never stopped to wonder if it would be dangerous. I was young and fearless and the idea anything bad might happen never occurred to me.

That day when I was accepted into the ATA I was aware my Pa would need to find a replacement for me on the farm, so I asked for two weeks' grace before I returned to report to Hatfield. That year my Pa was managing around 670 acres of land and 2,000 livestock and, to give some idea of the scale of his workload, the 1941 Ministry of Agriculture records show that Manor Farm at Brize Norton managed twenty-two acres divided up into the cultivation of sprouts, cabbages, savoys, kale, sprouting broccoli, cauliflowers, turnips, swedes, runner beans and peas for market. Each June there were ten tons of hay and twenty tons of straw. There were two Fordson tractors parked in our farmyard each night and a dozen Shire horses to care for. The Manor must have been the busiest farm in the county.

My Pa managed to get a few German prisoners-of-war to help him farm the land, so that must have been a huge help to have this free labour on tap. There were also Land Army girls about the place. I remember I came home one day and wondered if the farm had been taken over by strangers! All three of my brothers were essential to the farm and chose to work solidly throughout the war to feed the country. Farming was a reserved occupation and what they did along with my Pa was no less than anyone who joined the armed services.

In October 1941, I became a fully signed-up civilian member of the Air Transport Auxiliary – Second Officer Mary Wilkins, No.56.

It was a huge step for me but I was overjoyed to drive along the wet roads spotted with autumn leaves to report to Hatfield ready for training and instruction. Six other girls joined me at Hatfield that same day. While we were on ATA training courses we had accommodation in a big house at Brookmans Park, being billeted with a Mr and Mrs Hambling, who were a pleasant couple and related to the sisters Joy Gough and Yvonne Macdonald, otherwise known as the 'Gough Girls' who would later join the ATA. Both sisters were successfully trained from scratch as *ab initio* pilots, with Joy later based at Hamble with me, and her sister, Yvonne, posted to the second all-women's pool at Cosford.

The ATA training was very comprehensive and I soon became accustomed to a) flying with no aids like radio, and only compass between you and your destination b) battling with the elements and c) map-reading. For three months solid we attended lectures between flying training, and more lectures and classroom tests. It was the most arduous time of my life. Imagine – a three-year training programme condensed into three months. It really was hard going, and many gave up and departed to become nurses or to join another service, or plainly some found they were not suitable people to become ferry pilots.

I soon realised I had so much to learn, but it made sense for pilots to know the technology of an aircraft as it helped breed confidence on the ground and in the air. I would describe the ATA training as immensely good and the organisation was excellent. There was always, always opportunity to learn more, ask questions, talk to the instructors and of course get accustomed to our ever trusty Ferry Pilots Notebooks which went everywhere with us. It really was an essential survival guide.

After being signed in at Hatfield I was posted to the ATA's headquarters at White Waltham (No.1 Ferry Pool) for my flying training on Moths and 'Maggies' (the Miles Magister), Hawker Harts and Hinds, and the lovely Avro Tutor, then weeks later the next step on to Harvards before we were let loose on fighters like the Hurricane. (I had flown twenty Hurricanes before I took off in my first Spitfire).

The training enabled me and other pilots to fly and deliver aeroplanes across Great Britain without the use of radio or other aids to navigation. We relied on maps, the compass and a watch and were finally pronounced efficient to fly all small types with the emphasis on getting the aircraft safely to its destination which, after all, was the reason why the ATA was formed.

I was, like many of the girls, accepted into the ATA with very limited flying experience. Provided one could pass the simple flying and navigation test, the next step was conversion courses.

These began with ground training on a variety of practical subjects such as hydraulics, automatic boost, controls, carburettors, constant speed units, mixture controls, etc. and of course the gas analyser. We had a saying to remember the all-important cockpit drill – Hot Tempered MP Fancies Girls', or HTTMPFGG. This stood for Hydraulics, Trim, Tension, Mixture, Pitch, Petrol, Flaps, Gills, Gauges. Then there was my checklist – Gyro, Fuel boosters, Un-lock controls, Supercharger, Tailwheel unlock.

This pre-flight check I repeated every time I got into an aircraft. Should anything NOT be okay, then a snag sheet was made out and the fault corrected, if not, then the aircraft was made U/S (unserviceable). If a fault occurred in flight, then a Snag sheet was made out and given to the person receiving the aircraft.

There was a certain amount of 'Met' to be studied too. This was not only for the purposes of en-route navigation, but to make us aware of the actions we should take in the case of deteriorating weather, and this helped us enormously until we had built up enough experience and subsequent ability.

Coping with the weather was quite different from present practice, as never at any time did we use radio and we had no radio navigational aids. Ours was all visual map-reading and of course good old *Bradshaw's Monthly Railway Guide* – that was until the track disappeared in a tunnel.

Our biggest worry of course was the weather and the balloons. Considering the small number of Met observation stations that were available in war time beyond our shores, the Met men did an excellent job. The balloons were something else, you could be happily flying along, particularly around my ferry pool at Hamble, when up would go the Southampton balloons in a trice. This was alright in good weather, but when the visibility was poor or it was raining it was sometimes quite frightening.

Following ground instruction, we were sent off in Moths or Harts or an Avro Tutor aircraft on long and longer cross-country flights to get to know the countryside. Hopefully all this information would be retained for later. And then came the real ferry work. All the aircraft that ATA ferried were divided into one of six classes, and likewise pilots were upgraded on to a higher Class as experience was gained.

The Class I licence qualified a pilot to fly a light single-engine aircraft like a Swordfish, Albacore and Fairchilds, with the latter being used for taxi work. There was no dual-control training in any of these types before flying them. After a while ferrying these aircraft, pilots were called to a Training Pool and upgraded to Class II, which meant they took a conversion course on to faster and heavier single-engine Hurricanes, Defiants, Battles and Spitfires, etc. Then came Class III; pilots with this licence could fly light twin-engine types including Blenheims and Airspeed Oxfords. I was taught asymmetric flying and in plain language what to do, apart from pray, when one engine failed.

Next came the Class IV conversion to fly heavy twin-engines like the Wellington, Beaufighter, Whitley and Mosquito bombers. The Lockheed Hudson was considered to be a tricky aircraft to manage and the tricycle aircraft like the Mitchell and Boston were classified as Class IV plus.

The Class V was the licence to fly four-engine aircraft including Lancasters, Stirlings and the Halifax. Among the few ATA women who qualified to fly the four-engine bombers were: Marion Wilberforce, Joan Hughes, Philippa Bennett, Margot Gore, Lettice Curtis, Ruth Lambton, Rosemary Rees, The Rt. Hon. Margaret Fairweather, Winnie Crossley, The Hon, Elizabeth Francis May and Cassandra 'Fay' Bradford MBE. I was a co-pilot in Lancasters, Short Stirlings and Liberators and was about to take the Class V licence but the war and the ATA came to an end.

The grand Class VI licence was only available to the men, as this was needed for the huge Sunderland flying boats and the men kept them for themselves. The excuse given as to why we shouldn't fly them was the feeble one – that a woman pilot might get stuck out overnight with a male crew, as if we would have minded anyway!

By the time I joined the ATA the work for the girl ferry pilots was increasing rapidly and had fast moved beyond those tentative early days when we were only allowed to deliver Tiger Moths. We worked long hours taking it in turns to be Operations Officer, obtaining the latest information on the whereabouts of balloon barrages, prohibited areas, etc. and obtain weather reports from the nearest RAF station. There was an awful lot of hard work to be done in the lecture rooms, too.

Most evenings I just needed to get back to the digs for a good hot meal, a bath and then a decent night's sleep. My brain had been busy and hard at work for hours.

But this training was all very necessary and our chief instructor was on loan to us from BOAC. His name was Mr A.R.O. Macmillan – and he was excellent at his job. After all, we needed the best if we were going to fly many types of fast fighter aircraft and great monster-sized bombers too. Whereas the RAF boys usually stuck to the same type of aircraft, we civilians had to be prepared to pilot up to 140 varieties.

We had to know what was happening in dozens of types of engines and to be able to interpret all sorts of different indicators and instructions. Our very lives depended on the training as flying military aircraft was a highly specialised job.

So all this intensive training in the classrooms and in the air was of the utmost importance. There was of course the navigation to really get to grips with. We had to know how to get from factory to every RAF station by maps alone. We were not allowed to use the radio because of blocking the RAF channels.

Weather! Oh dear the weather! The English weather is a constant worry in every aviator's life. We simple had to know about Met conditions and what to expect.

The physical effort of flying Tiger Moths with their open cockpit was often made worse by the intense cold in the winter months and I was very glad to progress to the cabin types.

Captain Rosemary Rees described the Tiger Moth as a ghastly little aircraft that was slow and so icy cold in winter. Rosemary was always telling me and the rest of the girls how cold she was and it was not unusual to see her fly the taxi Anson bundled up in two thick coats, scarves and gloves. In the Mess she always wanted the windows shut tight to keep the draughts out. For those gymnastic girls like Jackie Sorour who liked to do headstands and cartwheels to keep fit and warm up, the window opening and closing routine was like something out of a West End farce. Rosemary wanted it shut but the athletic types wanted the fresh air.

The learning went on at a great pace and I used to wonder when it must end. But that is one of the most fascinating things about aviation, one is always, always learning.

The ATA pilots' success was down to the instruction we received coupled with the Pilots' Aircraft Handling Notes which were produced by the ATA Technical Library. These were written by aviators and engineers who had flown the aircraft and managed to write down their findings in very understandable language so that if one hadn't seen a particular type of aeroplane before one would go off with the handling notes, sit in the cockpit, have a look at all the knobs and see what was what, and having got the aircraft started would taxi out. The notes were so comprehensive that it would tell one about the brakes and how to use them, and the same for take-off, if the aircraft would swing, which way and how viciously and what to watch out for. Or the notes might reveal it was a docile machine. I know that without these notes it would not have been possible to do what we did. Indeed, we managed to fly all types that we had never even seen before even on the ground.

Mr Macmillan devised our training programme as well as compiling our life-saving Ferry Pilots Notes – that small blue book which contained everything we needed to know about every aircraft ever built. We were then instructed in the classroom by a Mr Bill Gribble before we graduated on to the Hurricane fighter. Mr Gribble was a good teacher but every now and then he would weary of us when we lost concentration in the classroom. He would try and catch us out by suddenly saying something unrelated to the lesson.

As the training was comprehensive I quickly became accustomed to flying a great variety of aircraft, battling with the elements, honing my map-reading skills and generally learning to survive in a dangerous occupation.

On 15 December 1941, I was posted to White Waltham to prepare to do a cross country flight and the ATA found me digs in a large house in Cookham Dean, near Marlow, Buckinghamshire where there were already three male ATA pilots ensconced.

After I had enjoyed two days' leave with my family at Brize Norton, I travelled to White Waltham, Berkshire in my own car which was a big black Ford with a canopy roof. Driving myself around certainly did make life a little easier in all sorts of ways although I was always aware of the petrol rationing so there were few long journeys. I was always happy though to offer people lifts if it was convenient.

On 17 December, I flew a cross-country flight test from White Waltham and did rather well. I was proud of myself for achieving this success and I was also mingling with the likes of famous pilots like Jim

Mollinson. By this time too my ATA uniform was about to arrive from Austin Reed and I was officially deemed a civilian pilot. My salary and expenses (apart from my uniform) would be financed by British Airways. The ATA uniform was a darker navy blue than that of the RAF and the number of gold bars, thicker and thinner on the shoulders would indicate rank. The cadet/trainee rank was one thin gold stripe called 'the blonde hair'.

When it came to our lovely uniforms then we had a choice. We could either get them made by a local military tailor or get them made to measure in London. Most of us, including me, got measured up at Austin Reed in London although one or two of the ATA women who went to the official military outfitters found it funny when the male tailors faffed about getting the measurements.

To ascertain an idea of the chest size the nominated, red faced tailor would look away as he flung the tape measure around the giggling woman and then make several embarrassing attempts to catch the other end of it. Of course these chaps nearly had a nervous breakdown when they had to take women's inside leg measurements!

When the new uniform arrived those women who'd chosen to use the military outfitters were bitterly disappointed as they'd find the crotch of the trousers was far too low and the chest size was all wrong! The giggling could be heard all around when they tried on their uniforms – and then followed the wail of disappointment because they had wait again to get the whole uniform re-made. The guesswork by those embarrassed military tailors had not paid off and after that we were advised to record our own sizes, write them down on a piece of paper and take them to the shop to ensure an eventual good fit!

The ATA uniform was, I admit, terribly smart and afforded us a few privileges. As my friend Molly (Rose) once said, 'all young people look dashing in uniform'. I certainly felt quite the ticket, proud too. The uniform certainly made us stand out and we were often asked what service we were in. I think the golden wings stitched on to our tunics above the top left pocket helped and many ATA women got priority tables in restaurants, boxes at the theatre and decent treatment in shops.

In the early days of the ATA the chief, 'Pop' d'Erlanger, wanted the women to fly in navy uniform skirts. It was a surprisingly ludicrous suggestion to come from this intelligent, charming, sophisticated man. The women's section commander, Pauline, protested quite adamantly and said that it would be jolly cold and draughty to fly in a skirt in an open cockpit, and so a compromise was reached. Pop suggested the girls change into trousers to fly and then after landing and leaving the aircraft they could change back into a skirt. But within weeks every woman in the ATA just stuck together on the issue and steadfastly wore the trousers and big furry boots – most of the time.

Rosemary Rees, the daughter of the Member of Parliament Sir John Rees, who later became second in command at Hamble, and after the war, as Lady Du Cros, was honoured with an MBE, was no stranger to the delights of the uniform and all its accessories. She said her saucy furry flying boots were so comfortable that she wore them so often the heels were completely worn down. Rosemary went on to fly ninety-one different varieties of aircraft during her years with the ATA.

It was a great relief that the wearing of trousers in and around the airfields became the norm. Imagine parachuting out of an aircraft in skirt let alone fly in one. When we were off duty and went into the nearest town we were supposed to wear skirts and black silk stockings. Our dramatic RAF flying boots were tremendously comfortable unless one wanted to walk far in them. However, these big boots were very handy to tuck maps into during flying.

It was a grand day for me when I first put on that blue shirt, black tie, golden wings, trousers (there was also a skirt) and the golden strap to put on the shoulders to denote rank. I felt wonderful and by wearing that uniform I realised all the hard work had been worth it, as I was now a qualified ATA ferry pilot and I had those glorious wings on my tunic to prove it. I was now heading towards my dream aircraft – the Spitfire and all the wonderful exciting chemistry that went with that. How I'd admired those beautiful, sleek little fighter aircraft when I saw them on the airfields. One day, one day, that would be me flying one, I told myself as I chugged around in the Tiger Moth doing my best to please my instructor. But all the time it was the Spitfire in my dreams and in my heart.

But whilst I basked in the warmth of my new-found profession and my glorious new uniform the weather of Christmas of 1941 wasn't so cheery. The country was wreathed in fog and the climate was sinisterly mild at around two-degrees Fahrenheit. Yet compared to the bitter and freezing winter of 1940, it could, I suppose, be classified as an improvement until Boxing Day brought in a sharp frost and icy winds. Towards the end of the month, and well into January 1942, there was rainfall and icy wet conditions. None of this was exactly conducive for flying. I spent Christmas with my family at home in Brize Norton knowing I'd soon be back to the ATA and my flying would continue at its rapid pace. I think everyone at home was proud I was flying to help the war effort and if my parents were worried about me they didn't let on. It was still a time when none of us really knew what was going on.

In early 1942 the day came at last when I was told I had completed my training successfully. You are 'A Ferry Pilot' and will be posted to your station tomorrow. How did I feel? I was delighted of course. I'd worked tremendously hard and now all of it had paid off. I was qualified to fly to help the war effort and make sure those brave aircrew fighting the foe had the aircraft they needed to do it. (Did I mention the ATA had forage caps to go with the uniform? Well these were worn at all different angles. I suspect the day I was told I had passed all the tests may well have been the moment I'd thrown this cap into the air in exhilaration, although in the photographs of me when I got my golden ATA wings, the cap is sitting at quite a sensible angle. The dreams of a three-year-old girl had turned into a serious occupation. I was a pilot and we were at war with Germany).

Life was often difficult and nerve-wracking and there was little of the glamour that the public sometimes imagined surrounding the life and work of a female ferry pilot. Many girls did not survive the rigours of the life and the intensive training and left the ATA. However, for those of us who stayed, we were all urged on by two desires, to help England, and the great need to fly. After about a year I was among the members of an efficient and highly organised group, and it meant a lot that the girl ferry pilot venture was a success; and literally for the first time were now doing EXACTLY the same job as the men, and I am happy to say, we got the same pay too. This salary worked out at about £6 per week. It was adequate and much appreciated. It was our Senior Commander Pauline who ensured we received equal salaries to that of the men. This was a first, and a milestone for equality and a great achievement for women. At last we were being recognised for our work even though we went about it quietly without fuss. We were just as committed as the men of the ATA and risking our lives just as much as them.

All it takes to fly is determination, an independent spirit and a certain amount of good judgement and common sense. In return one gets pleasure and excitement. When women pilots cease to become news, the battle of equality will have been won.

Chapter 10

Ferry Girl

All too often I felt the bitterness of an icy weather and the grey and dreariness of winter would threaten to seep into my bones. There were occasions when the temperatures fell so low, and were therefore so hazardous, that I would be left with no choice but to be away with an aircraft for three or four days. Flying the Tiger Moth anywhere was a slow business and we always had to stop a lot to re-fuel. The Tiger Moth only reached about 60 mph and in the winter months it was freezing in the open cockpit.

However, we tried not to complain too much. I think now about how bone-chillingly cold it must have been for the Russian women flying in combat against the Luftwaffe. Apparently the metal sides of the Polikarpov PO-2 they flew would ice up so badly that if they touched the sides of the aircraft the skin would be torn from their hands, resulting in great pain and distress.

In the ATA the only way back south from Prestwick Airfield in Scotland might be the night train which was dreadful and especially so in the winter. Indeed, I think the longest flight I ever did was in the early days from Hatfield to Prestwick in a Tiger Moth and that included two or three nights to stay over. This was the norm with this little aircraft as it speed only reached around 60 mph and then there would be the stopping and starting to re-fuel. I came back on the night-train after these trips which wasn't so good as it could be crowded. I know one of the girls, Lettice Curtis, would often curl up and sleep in the luggage rack as there were rarely any seats left.

There was one time on my way back from Prestwick that I found myself alone in London for the night and had no option but to stay in the Underground with a crowd of strangers. Everyone else seemed to be sleeping down there for the night so I decided to join them. I didn't have much choice. There were no heroes or villains that night. All of us down there had been thrown into a world of chaos – all of us were surrounded and united in our battles with a myriad of fear. Oddly enough I felt safe even though I was in uniform. So I lay down and curled up like everyone else and rested my head on my parachute and I was fine and safe from the bombing. When I awoke I got on the early morning train heading towards my ferry pool.

After those long intensive months of training, by the spring of 1942 I was posted to the all-women's ferry pool (No.15) at Hamble, near Southampton. The ATA adjutant told me I would be living with the Westmacott family in Bursledon. The ATA was wonderful about organising our digs for us. We didn't have to worry about anything like that. The adjutant took me to meet the family and they were most friendly. My friend Dora Lang was already in a room opposite mine. Everything was great and I met up with all my friends – Doreen Williams, Betty Grant, Mary Fuller-Hall, Jackie Moggridge, Vera Strodl and a little later Veronica Volkersz.

All these girls were great to be with. There is a photograph of me with Mary (Rosemary) Fuller Hall dining out in the ATA Mess at Hamble. We're also reading what looks like a newspaper. It's a never-seen-before picture of the 'two Marys'. Mary was 22 when she joined the ATA on 2 December 1941, not long after me. She had thirty hours flying experience at the time, and from 1938 to 1939 she'd worked as a stenographer (shorthand/typist) with the ATS. She married a flying instructor named Peter Pennington-Leigh and left the ATA a year or so before me. I was sad not to hear much from her again as our lives took different turns over the decades.

We had all learned to find aerodromes which were quite unrecognisable to the uninitiated as they were so well camouflaged during the war, and since the weather plays a very important part in flying we had passed exams in this also. My most difficult subject proved to be the Morse code; it took me simply ages and ages to be able to make any sense of it at all but in the end I was able to operate it and send and read messages.

Well, after completing successfully this training course in the summer of 1942, I was posted to back to Hamble which is just across the water from the Isle of Wight. Our unit comprised of: one Commander (Miss Margot Gore), one Deputy Commander (Miss Rosemary Rees), fifteen pilots including me, four engineers, four Operations officials, and two weather forecasters. The ferry pool itself comprised of a number of rooms – signals and maps, parachute, locker, rest, dining and kitchen rooms. There were also various offices around the site. I think the good atmosphere at our ferry pool was all down to Margot who was such a good leader and kept us all motivated in one way or another. Of course the discipline wasn't strict like the armed forces and we didn't salute or anything like that, but we did have seniority to respect and that suited most of us well. Remember, we were civilian pilots who wore a uniform because we were required to visit RAF stations. Out of work we were not required to wear it. We lived in our ATA slacks (trousers) most of the time and the summer season was long and busy. We finished our day when we'd delivered the last aircraft on our chitties and so, more often than not in fine weather, I'd fly back to Hamble around the dusk.

During the time I was welcomed into the heart of the Hamble gang, the ATA had already proved itself a vital organisation, having delivered Spitfires from Supermarine's Chattis Hill factory to RAF Maintenance Units at Brize Norton and Colerne, where they would be fitted with radios and guns. From there, these Spits, now ready for action, would, for example, be ferried to the north of Britain and placed on an aircraft-carrier bound for the Mediterranean. Once Malta was sighted in the distance these aircraft would take off and make for an island in great need of their help in what became known as the Siege of Malta in the spring of 1942. Two of the several ATA women to be part of the great Spitfire rush at this time were my colleagues Lettice Curtis and Ann Welch. An American aircraft carrier known as *Wasp* was lent to Britain by President Roosevelt and on its first trip to Malta it had forty-seven Spitfires parked on its decks. *Wasp* did its duty steadfastly until the Germans bombed the island and rendered many of the aircraft unserviceable. After a second delivery trip of sixty-four Spitfires to Malta, *Wasp* was torpedoed by the Japanese and sunk. Churchill told the American president, 'Who says a Wasp never stings twice?'.

At the time of the great Spitfire rush I was still at Hatfield getting to grips with my training, but I do recall the weather of February 1942. On one occasion Ann Welch was sitting in a draughty hut at Chattis Hill watching the snow as the ice prevented her taking off in a new Spitfire resplendent in its desert camouflage of blue and tan. It was just the slushy grim winter weather that had grounded Ann and two other women ATA pilots, but the House of Commons remained uneasy about the delay in getting Spitfires to Malta.

If those grumbling MPs had visited Chattis Hill at this time they too would have seen the blinding snow which had hidden the treetops and blocked any straightforward view towards the airfield of RAF Colerne in the Cotswolds.

Ann described in her autobiography, *Happy to Fly*, how the only way to be sure of reaching Colerne was to carefully plan a route so that she could follow the roads and railways all the way, and then stick to it rigidly, even round a double loop in the Savernake Forest railway line.

When everything was ready she watched for the promised improvement as the trees at the end of the field appeared and disappeared in veils of light snow. Then they reappeared for a little longer. Visibility was now up to 700 yards and the cloud-base, if you called the amorphous weeping greyness a base, about 300 feet, perhaps 400 feet. Now was the moment to go. Her Merlin started with its comforting rumble and she taxied out at once, doing checks on the way, to take off uphill towards the trees which were still just visible. A minute later the second Spitfire roared into the air, but the trees disappeared again for the third, so it was taxied back to the hangar.

Ann wrote: 'My plan worked. I flew as sharply as possible, flaps down. It was not possible to fly with the wheels down on a Spitfire for extra drag as the undercarriage left down obscured the oil cooler. The weather did not improve, but neither did it worsen and I picked my way along the roads and railways tracks at 140 mph, flying the last mile along a lane uphill to the aerodrome. At Colerne they did not seem to have heard about any parliamentary panic but this was now their problem. About twenty minutes later I was astonished to see our collecting taxi Puss Moth edge out of the murk, flown by a junior pilot called Bridget Hill. As stooge she asked if I wanted to fly back but she deserved something for coming to get me in such awful weather. She had even brought some newspapers for the trip so I sat in the back with my feet up on the front seat and read them. After a while I thought I had better check to see how we were getting on, and was horrified to see just underneath a hedge with a cow on one side and an Oxford on the other. "Where the hell are we?", I asked. "Don't worry," replied Bridget. "My parents live here, I know it well." Quickly I averted my eyes from any more undesirable revelations and read about the war; it seemed much safer!'

Hamble itself though was very much like a 'sisterhood' and life had its pleasantries. Off duty too I was never without an escort from the either the Marines, the RAF or the Fleet Air Arm.

Indeed, I recall a funny day when a few of us went for a day out with a few Marines and we were having a paddle in some river somewhere. Anyway after some larking about we decided to leave the water and get some lunch. Well when I got to the place where I'd left my shoes they were gone. I said 'who's taken my shoes? Where are they?' Then I saw them floating along down the river. Fortunately, they were retrieved and I didn't have to walk about in my socks for the rest of the day.

Rooms and accommodation were rented to us girls in Hamble-le-Rice village itself, such as Sydney Cottages, Mere House, or the Southern

Yacht Club. There were also properties in nearby Satchell Lane. Hamble was picturesque and, pre-war, it was inhabited mostly by yachtsmen and their families. I remember then, when I first saw the village from the lane at the top of a hill, it was as if I'd gone back into the fourteenth century.

It was a charming little place and it was very hard to imagine there was a war on. The village had a strange and dignified peace about it, with its little shops like Hookers the Baker, and Serpells the Grocer. There was even a butcher's shop run by 'Sparkes' where there'd always be a queue of women clutching ration books and shopping baskets.

I recall about six pubs in Hamble and some of them were set off the road. There was The Victory, The King & Queen, and The White Hart. (The latter bore the same name as the famous drinking hole at Brasted frequented by the fighter boys at RAF Biggin Hill. It was in this White Hart where a huge black-out board was signed in chalk by all the pilots who used the place. This famous artefact of the Battle of Britain now sits on show in Shoreham Museum near Sevenoaks. I often wonder what happened to the old black-out curtains in the Hamble Mess which had been signed in white paint by all the women ATA pilots).

The other pubs known to some ATA people were The Bugle and The Yacht Club. My family was tee-total so I did not drink alcohol during the war and it remained that way for me until after I was married.

I had digs in Bursledon which is a village on the River Hamble, and the lovely Westmacott family treated me just like one of their own. I was very happy there and felt very much at home as they were always kind to me, and I appreciated that, as some days with the ATA were very trying.

If I had to stay overnight anywhere away from Hamble because of the weather preventing any flying, then the ATA gave us £1 to spend on overnight accommodation. Of course, if you stayed in a cheap B&B or in a Waafery you could make quite a profit. £1 would happily cover a night in a good hotel.

Most mornings, though, I would drive to Hamble in my large old black Ford and park at the airfield. It was wonderfully convenient in the evenings to hop from the cockpit and get straight into the Ford and drive back to my digs, especially during the winter time. No one liked to trudge a few miles in the rain, ice or snow and even cycling in weather like this is pretty grim. As you can imagine I was often asked by the other girls for lifts here and there and I didn't mind. Sometimes I recall offering to help ATA pilot Yvonne Macdonald who needed a lift from the local railway station to visit her sister Joy Gough who was a Third Officer at Hamble. Yvonne was based at the second all-women's ferry pool at Cosford so I either dropped her off at Joy's billet or gave her a lift to and from the station.

The village of Bursledon where I lived has always been linked to the sea and the Elephant Boatyard at Old Bursledon goes back many centuries. In fact, Henry VIII's fleet was built there.

When it comes to famous aviators it seems I had moved to the right place, as Claude Grahame-White was born there in 1879 and had gone on to become a Royal Aero Club pilot and race winner, and he counted among his friends the great Louis Bleriot. Grahame-White established a flying school at Hendon in 1911 and before the First World War he recognised the commercial value of flight, and heartily supported the use of aviation for military effectiveness. During the First World War he flew the first night mission in 1914. By then he had created the Graham-White Aviation Company. In 1925 the RAF bought his aerodrome and he retired to Nice, having made money in the US property market.

Today at the RAF Museum in Hendoon, an original Grahame-White hangar houses the First World War collection. This pioneer aviator and aircraft manufacturer died in 1959. During my stay in Bursledon I was certainly in the right place if aviation history and uncanny connections are anything to go by.

By the time I had begun my training, though in the autumn of 1941, ten women had already been posted to the new all-women's pool at Hamble. The pressure was on to make a success of it and our boss Pauline had assured Air Commodore d'Erlanger and the Air Ministry it was the way forward if the ATA was continue to improve and develop the efficiency of its vital ferrying work.

There is evidence to suggest the huge pressure Pauline was under from the RAF, especially in the early days of the women's section. This was revealed by my ATA colleague Ann Welch who pranged a de Havilland DH82B 'Queen Bee' aircraft on landing.

Ann said she had collected this aircraft from Witney and twenty minutes into her journey the engine spluttered and stopped for good so she had to try and make it to a field and land the thing. She headed for a furrowed stretch of land and put down. The Queen Bee tipped on to its nose and within a few minutes a team of airmen ran over to see if she was okay and look over the aircraft. Ann was assured by the sergeant there was 'no damage' and so she contacted Hatfield ferry pool to report the situation.

The following morning an angry ATA Queen Bee – Senior Commander Pauline Gower – demanded to see Ann and asked her why she had reported there had been 'no damage' when in fact there were two dents in the cowling. Pauline informed Ann that pilots had been told it was foolish to land in furrows as the aircraft will tip over and the propeller will break.

'I was dismissed from Pauline's presence with a flea in my ear,' recalled Ann who had joined the ATA in December 1940. Later on, after the ticking off, she realised Pauline was having a tough time convincing the RAF and the Air Ministry that her women pilots were competent and careful and able to deliver military aircraft in one piece. 'It was no surprise she told me off,' added Ann.

We all soon realised that Pauline had a tough job to do and she was rightly held in the highest esteem. When I was well into the job I bumped into her at Hamble and she said 'you are doing very well Mary', and it was made known that 'Mary Wilkins has a wonderful enthusiasm for her work'.

Of course, I was chuffed to hear that from the big white chief! Then as I watched her walk briskly along the corridor that day I wondered how she managed to carry such a lot of responsibility and yet continue to smile so broadly and be friendly and kind to us all. Her vast experience in aviation and her good humour must have provided Pauline with a certain in-built confidence to lead and inspire. I like to think her excellent attitude, at a time of great stress brought on by the war, influenced me right through my life and career.

When I think of the times I first saw Pauline's original eight 'chosen few' women pilots of the ATA I thought they looked so old, which of course they weren't. Lois Butler was a grandmother and Gabrielle Patterson had a small son when she joined the ATA. The eldest of the first eight ATA was almost 40-years-old. This was the Rt. Hon. Margaret Fairweather, who was one of the most experienced pilots in the women's section, and she'd been flying since 1931 and had worked as an instructor at the Scottish Flying Club. I also thought my CO at Hamble was pretty ancient too – but dear Margot was just 28-years-old!

We new girls in our early twenties did, however, have great respect for the original eight aviatrices. Lord knows what they would have made of us high-spirited youths, particularly the time when some of us had to stay overnight in a hotel. It might have been during a training course somewhere. Anyway, we all thought it would be great fun to creep out of our rooms at night and swap all the boots and shoes around which had been left outside the guests' doors for cleaning. We thought that was a hoot when the man in room number five found his size ten Brogues had turned into a pair of ladies' high heels!

Chapter 11

No.15 Ferry Poole, Hamble

The ferry pool at Hamble was first introduced by the ATA in the September of 1940 as an all-male pool led by Captain Brian Wardle. However, within a year, it had become No.15 Ferry Pool and its then CO, an Australian by the name of Geoff Wikner, was transferred to another pool and women like Margot Gore, as Commanding Officer, Alison King, as Operations Manager, and pilots, including Rosemary Rees, Ann Welch, Philippa Bennett, and a former WAAF called Dora Lang who had trained to become a pilot, moved in. Also at Hamble in the early days was the brilliant Lettice Curtis (although she soon found an all-women's pool boring and familiar and, as she was desperately keen to compete with the male pilots, she soon headed off to White Waltham headquarters where she could be one of the boys in the thick of the action).

The first women at Hamble were greeted by two middle-aged ATA men, a Mr Dayton and a Mr Armstrong, who had stayed behind to help and guide the new inhabitants about the place. This cheery duo proved of enormous help to the newcomers, with Met reports and engineering assistance. However, within a few months they were transferred to other ferry pools. Our CO, Margot, was a very reliable person and was often busy with administrative duties, but when she did get a chance to fly, we'd see her revving up and preparing to deliver a four-engine bomber like the B-17 Flying Fortress – a giant of an aircraft which she had no qualms about flying.

Not far from Hamble were several local airfields which also needed aircraft, like the one at Marwell, or the camouflaged Chattis Hill next to Stockbridge. Hamble, like most of the south-east, was, of course, always in danger of falling in the sights of any Luftwaffe pilot who might be looking for the Spitfire factory at Southampton, so while we were ferrying aircraft we were, I admit, easy targets for any enemy attacks. Some ATA pilots asked to be transferred to ferry pools in the north which were not so much of an enemy attraction, but I never felt the need to do this as my ferrying duties had been a case of so far so good and not a German aircraft in sight.

Vickers also had two other factories maintaining all types of Spitfires. Airspeed produced Oxfords at Christchurch and Portsmouth, while AST at Hamble was the country's main Spitfire repair base. AST eventually worked on larger aircraft such as the American B17 Flying Fortresses.

The important airfields such as Eastleigh were surrounded by the dreaded barrage balloons for protection. At the same time, often I had to find out the secret arrangements for landing at some airfields, especially if the site was in deep camouflage. Pilots also had to avoid anti-aircraft guns and training areas, plus steer clear of bad weather. There was a lot to think about on every journey and there could often be a surprise en-route, as many of us discovered, and we did our best to be prepared for any eventuality.

We all carried a parachute, but I am glad to say I never had to use mine. The thought of such a prospect never filled me with glee and yet I must embrace the idea that I was lucky to have had the chance to even carry one. The pilots of the First World War were forbidden to fly with such a safety precaution. 'No,' the RFC high command told those brave young fliers, 'we can't have you jumping out of the aircraft at the first sign of trouble! You must do your best to protect such valuable machines to the very end'. Oh dear.

In the Second World War, of course, the RAF issued its aircrew with parachutes and Mae Wests life preservers to help them float if they had to bale out into the grim, relentlessly choppy, dark Channel. At first the colour of these Mae Wests was completely wrong because the dark green colour, as many young aviators knew, was undetectable if they baled out into a sea of the same shade. These artful young pilots remedied the problem by painting their Mae Wests bright yellow the minute they got them.

When I first joined Hamble it seemed I had only Tiger Moths to fly. Then, glory be, I suddenly was given a lovely Fairey Swordfish to pick up from White Waltham and fly back to Hamble. The Swordfish was a joy to fly (unlike the Walrus). Many of the aircraft we delivered, including the Seafire (which was a Spitfire really), were for the Fleet Air Arm pilots who were stationed at nearby Gosport, Worthy Down and Lee-on-Solent.

In 1942 I had a whole month of taxi flying which involved me transporting pilots to pick up aircraft from various airfields and collecting them again after delivery. This gave me wonderful exercise in navigation which was much appreciated when I came to fly fast and furious aircraft like the Spitfire.

It was a big day for me on 4 April 1942, as I was deemed skilled and responsible enough to take off alone at the controls of a Hawker Hector biplane. It was my first real ferrying job and I flew from Dumfries to Speke (Liverpool) and to Little Rissington (Gloucestershire). What I can't recall is whether I was nervous on this great solo experience. But I know I would have been focussing very hard on the aircraft and the journey. I felt tremendously responsible about getting that aircraft and myself from A to B in one piece.

The Hector, I learned, was to be transferred to an Auxiliary Air Force squadron. The battle history of this type of aircraft included a mission with 613 Squadron when it joined RAF Hawkinge, Kent, and flew out in support of the Allied garrison during the Siege of Calais from 22 to 30 May 1940. Six Hectors were known to have dive-bombed German positions around Calais in northern France. By this time, though, the British troops were on the retreat towards Dunkirk. Not long after 1940, the Hectors were mainly used as target-tugs or sold on to the Irish military.

I soon learned that the Hector was unpopular with the ground crews because of its complicated engines, which had twenty-four cylinders, twenty-four spark plugs and forty-eight valves. That kind of set up requires an awful lot of maintenance.

After my first ever ATA solo ferry flight I quickly became accustomed to flying a great number of aircraft, battling with the elements, honing my map reading skills and generally learning to survive in a quite dangerous occupation. In June of that same year I was sent to White Waltham to train to fly the Harvard. It was then that I got my first Hurricane – and that was quite a moment.

I could immediately understand why this lovely Hawker aircraft was popular with the RAF pilots. Trusty, fast, good at turning, it was an ideal opponent against the Luftwaffe's Me109s. For me the varieties of aircraft started to build up from then, as in the July of that year, I flew a Fairey Battle from RAF Newton to RAF Llandow.

On 19 July my task was to fly a Hurricane Mk.II from Witney to St Athan. I was delighted as it was at dear old Witney Airfield of course that my flying had begun in my early teens.

On 28 July I was at the controls of an example of the versatile Lysander (which, incidentally, was an aircraft used by the ATA to occasionally drop SOE agents in France) and I flew it from Watford to Kemble that day.

On 17 August I took a Boulton Paul Defiant from St Athan in Wales to Prestwick, with two stops en-route at Speke and Millom. I remember the Defiant was quite a slow aircraft. It was built to carry two people and had a turret to house a heavy gun and the gunner, and whilst the Defiant looked like a Spitfire it certainly didn't fly as fast. The maximum speed was listed in my Ferry Pilots Notes at 304 mph. I wondered how the gunners who had to stand in that turret so vulnerable to enemy fire could deal with the terrible noise made by their own guns. It must have been deafening and a terrible experience all round. I thought of the pilot too as he must have had a most difficult job flying in the direction of an enemy aircraft so precisely that it ensured the gunner could get good aim on the enemy.

On 19 July 1940, during the Battle of Britain, seven out of nine Defiants of 141 Squadron were wiped out by the Luftwaffe, which had attacked them from underneath – this day has become known as 'The Slaughter of the Innocents'. Boulton Paul built 1,064 Defiants, and during my ATA career I happened to have flown a few of them.

A typical day's work for me might involve the collection from a factory and the delivery of say three or four different types to widely spread destinations. Of course the really exciting time for me was on arrival at the airfield each morning when the Operations Office would open, and in due course there on the table we would soon find the day's chitties. These pieces of paper gave details of a) the pilot's name, b) the aircraft to be flown, and c) the aircraft's collection point and destination.

By the end of 1942 I had delivered 119 different single-engine aircraft. Indeed, that year I flew twenty different types of aeroplane. I know I was always kept busy and people appreciated my excellent flying skills so I had a lot to do. I enjoyed it.

Every month you had to send in your logbook to the CO, Margot Gore. In this you had listed what aircraft you had flown, and the flight details, and she would sign it off. She would be the person who said, 'Right, you must go up a class and fly other things like fast and furious aircraft' – and I liked that idea immensely. Margot was there every morning and then she might be out during the day as she did a lot of flying herself.

Of course, while I noted all my flights down in my logbook, I never realised how some 70-plus years later I would be asked so many questions about my life in the ATA. I was doing my work then and that was what mattered.

All of us girls, and of course the men, of the ATA were working flat-out to do what we could to help the war effort. That was the reality. I could fly and so I could help.

Yes, life could be grim and I've listened to lots of RAF pilots tell me about the horrors and the joys. For the men, of course, life was about combat. For me, it was all about assisting them to conquer the skies and deliver their aircraft on time and with the ultimate efficiency. At our women's ferry pool at Hamble we started with just ten pilots plus a junior taxi pilot, one Operations Officer and one driver, with five engineers to deal with the Avro Ansons and Fairchild Argus taxi aircraft.

Within months, though, Hamble's personnel had increased to thirty pilots and twenty engineers to service our Ansons and Fairchilds. Additional support staff included four drivers, three in operations, two adjutants, a map and signals officer, a resident sick bay nursing sister, plus canteen staff and typists. This required more accommodation, so a dedicated ATA one-storey building was constructed and opened in July 1942, which included a mess room, dining room and staff offices.

At Hamble we were flown in our taxi aircraft from the ferry pool to the factories to collect our ferry aircraft. Usually, that evening we would be collected from the airfield to which we had delivered the last ferry aircraft of the day and taken back to Hamble in one of the taxi aircraft.

We never got to see much of our Senior Commander, Pauline Gower, as she was deeply involved in her administrative and official duties at our headquarters at No.1 Ferry Pool, White Waltham. Hamble, in general, was a friendly place, and I can't remember any really serious competitiveness among any of us girls. It could be good fun and I made some fine friends. There was often a lot of giggling, but to be honest I was so busy flying and getting on with the work there wasn't too much time to get wrapped up in the conversations about the ferrying and aircraft.

When I had a chance, I was socialising with numerous male friends and there were plenty of them out there. I had many proposals of marriage but I wasn't prepared to commit to anyone in this way. There were several officers' messes around the Hamble area and if they were having a party or a drinks gathering then they'd always send over an invitation card and it would go up on the Hamble noticeboard.

If you wanted to go you needed to put your name down and these chaps would send a car over to pick us up and return us to our billets. There were always plenty of chaps about, but the problem was they didn't stay around for long as they were always being posted away. There wasn't that much time to really get to know any of them that well, but I was a happy little soul and enjoying my own life by making the most of every moment. Romantic encounters weren't my reason for living. Flying was my real soulmate at that time. Flying the Spitfire itself gave me plenty of mind-blowing thrills. It was breath-taking, exhilaratingly fast, reliable, dynamic and glorious to look at, and I wondered if any mere human being could ever successfully provide me with those pleasures in life.

Chapter 12

Forced Landing

It had been a whole year before I jumped into the cockpit of a Spitfire for the first time that I had broken the news to my father, in 1941, about my success in joining the ATA. Of course, he was delighted for me, but he did stress, however, that I was not to be involved in any 'fighting'. He made that quite clear and so I eagerly re-assured him I would only be delivering aircraft and not flying off into battle.

I wonder what dear Pa would have said if he'd known the ATA's taxi Ansons in the summer of 1940 often carried an air gunner in case any Luftwaffe fighter or bomber came calling. These gunners had been taken on by the ATA during the Battle of Britain and trained to use a Vickers or Lewis machine-gun. Ammunition was sent to the ferry pools. Records reveal one gunner had been sent from White Waltham to Hatfield. It is extraordinary to think this decision was made, as we were civilian pilots working under the auspices of British Airways and, according to the law, we were not allowed to carry weapons. There followed a legal debate about the status of the gunners, and, as far as I remember, the ATA top brass decided it wouldn't be necessary to employ them any more after 1940. As far as I know, no gunner on board a taxi Anson ever fired in anger.

At the time, of course, I never even thought about flying in any sort of combat. In the ATA we did sometimes fly with loaded guns, but were always advised not to go anywhere near the turret or indeed touch the gun buttons on an aircraft. After the war, one of the ATA women, my friend Freydis Sharland (Leaf), recalled how she often flew armed Spitfires and Hurricanes to the airfields where the Polish pilots of 303 (Polish) Squadron were waiting. These feisty aviators, angry their homeland had been invaded by the Germans, insisted the aircraft were ready loaded with ammunition so they could jump straight into the cockpit and go to work on the Luftwaffe. They just didn't want to hang about. The lively exploits of the Polish boys of 303 Squadron ensured they achieved in their Hurricanes the most victories during the long, hot, deadly days of the Battle of Britain.

I must point out how the British government's steadfast law against women flying in combat (a rule much supported by my Pa) was not shared by the Russian leader Joseph Stalin, who was more than happy to allow female fighter and bomber regiments to take to the skies. Stalin's belief was 'the more the merrier', to help rid the world of the enemy Luftwaffe and the German hoards.

It suited the communist ideal for both genders to share the battle against a European foe. Russia's all-women aircrews were extraordinary. The 588th Night Bomber Regiment was formed by Colonel Marina Raskova and led by Major Yevdokia Bershanskaya. The Luftwaffe labelled these determined women 'The Nightwitches' owing to their often deadly and effective sorties taking place after dark. From 1942, the Russian women flew 23,000 sorties and dropped 3,000 bombs on the enemy.

One of the most famous Russian women pilots was Lydia Litvyak (1922-1943), who was also known as 'The White Rose of Stalingrad'. She shot down the Luftwaffe ace Erwin Maier of *Jagdesgeschwader* 53. He parachuted out and when he was captured by the Russians he demanded to meet the 'man' who had destroyed his aircraft and nearly killed him. When Lydia Litvyak stood before him as the 'man', he was incensed and thought the soldiers were having a joke. It wasn't until Litvyak described the detail of their combat together that he was forced to concede she was the victor! Litvyak was just 21-years-old and had amassed several 'kills' before her own death in combat in 1943.

Back then I was so dedicated to flying and it was a major part of my life. The ATA wasn't known to that many people really, and all my Pa wanted to be sure about was that I wasn't serving in the RAF and fighting. He didn't know the Russian women went into aerial combat and neither did I. I didn't know about anything like that and none of us in the ATA did until we met some of the girls who had fled Poland to fly with us. In Britain and at home we didn't know much detail at all about the fighting, and what with all the bombing going on we didn't have time to think about anything but survival. If my Pa realised Hamble and the South Coast were prime targets for the Luftwaffe, he never said.

In her memoir, ATA Captain Rosemary Rees explained: 'We were really lucky in that no ATA pilot was shot down by the enemy. Most of our aircraft did not have their guns fitted, and when they were, I can only remember three times being warned that they were loaded. That was in Typhoons and Tempests during the D-Day period: and in any case we had no idea how to use them. As for taking evasive action any trainee fighter pilot could have made rings around us, so we were sitting ducks for an enemy; but we relied on the RAF to defend our skies against the enemy Luftwaffe.'

My friend and ATA colleague Veronica Volkersz was just finishing a training course on twin-engine aircraft at White Waltham (No.1 Ferry Pool) when she decided, with one of the Polish women pilots, Anna Leska (Daab), to visit the boys of 303 (Polish) Squadron at Northolt. Once they had landed at Northolt they were greeted warmly by the Poles, who proved to be a charming bunch. It was while they were having tea one of the male pilots had an idea Veronica and Anna should go on a 'sweep' with them. The excitable men explained there wouldn't be a problem and Veronica and Anna would be fixed up with a couple of Spitfires.

Luckily, a definite date to go looking for the Luftwaffe with the girls was never set. I fear the enemy would have added two more Spitfire kills to their list if Veronica and Anna had joined the Polish fighter boys. Before Anna had joined the ATA she had been a sports pilot in her home country, had flown with the Polish Air Force, and, by 1939, was carrying out vital liaison missions and delivering aircraft. But as the Germans advanced on her homeland, Anna decided to make her way to the United Kingdom via Romania and France. She reported being shot at by the Germans on the way; her departure from her homeland had been a perilous one. Anna was among three ATA women from Poland.

The other girls were Jadwiga Pilsudska and Barbara Wotjulanis. I counted them both as valuable colleagues – and they were very capable pilots. I recall how we were all amused by Barbara's attempts to ride a bicycle. In fact, some of the girls used to try and teach her on to ride when the weather was bad and we couldn't fly. Whilst Barbara was happy and skilful flying a multitude of different aircraft, including the Spitfire, when it came to two wheels she'd wobble away and continue to fall off. If girls like Barbara and Anna were homesick we could never guess, as they blended in with us all and carried out their fair share of the workload.

The only indication Barbara was missing her homeland was one time just before Christmas in 1941, when all flying was stopped because of snow and ice, She had gone into Winchester to do some shopping. As she walked near the cathedral the stars were out. At the same time, from an open window nearby, came the sounds of Chopin's *Revolutionary Study*.

My friend Ann Welch was with Barbara that night and recalled how our Polish friend just stopped suddenly to listen intently to the vibrant piano music which was a symbol of nationalistic hope. When the playing stopped, Barbara said nothing and simply walked on, with the crunch of the snow beneath her feet the only sound in a dark night. If there was a tear in Barbara's eye nobody saw it, but Ann had noted how our friend's mood had shifted from bright to silent in second.

I can't think of our pilots without mentioning 'Chile' – one Margot Duhalde (Sotomayer) – who had arrived by default in Britain to fly with the ATA. In her homeland of Chile, she had trained as a commercial pilot and, as the war progressed, she decided she'd like to join the Free French who later sent her to fly in combat; and often these raids took her over Africa. It seems the Russian women pilots weren't the only ones to take on this brave role during the war. 'Chile' received decorations from both France and the UK. After the war, aged eighty, she took her first parachute jump.

As the Free French were based in the UK, 'Chile' contacted ATA Senior Commander Pauline Gower who invited her to Britain for an interview. Pauline was doubtful the optimistic Miss Duhalde would pass the tests because her English language was so poor, and she had feared for the 19-year-old Chilean's ability to last the three months of intensive training.

'Chile' was a great person and a good friend. I note from my logbook for the year 1944 that I flew her in a twin-engine Bisley, that with the serial number BA156, from Wroughton in Wiltshire to Renfrew, west of Glasgow. I have a lovely photograph of 'Chile' and I in the taxi aircraft on our way somewhere.

At this point I will let my ATA colleague and friend Molly reminisce about Anna Leska and 'Chile' – they were, of course, friends of us both. Molly once recalled:

'I was stationed down at Hamble where Mary was and actually although I had been married four and a half years I thought being sent off to an all-women's pool was going to be frightfully dull but I really couldn't be more wrong about that. There about thirty pilots at Hamble and twelve different nationalities. It was a League of Nations all on its own. We had Australians, New Zealanders, South Africans, Canadians, Americans, Dutch, Irish and South Americans. You never knew what language would be spoken in the Mess, you'd have Spanish in one corner because one of our pilots was "Chile" who came over from Chile. There was also a very pretty girl called Maureen Dunlop and they went on speaking Spanish because Chile's English was rather remote.

'Mary and I both remember this interesting story about Chile who was an instructor in her home country and had a lot of hours on her licence and so she was promptly put on to ferrying. However, within a very few days she had an engine cut somewhere over Hatfield and landed in a field there whereupon the police promptly arrived and when they discovered this woman was flying one of our aircraft but couldn't speak English at all they took her off to the police station and it took the ATA and our CO Margot Gore a whole twenty-four hours to get her released.

'This was when they decided she should learn some English before she continued flying – and they put her in the hangar to work with the men who had some very interesting English language skills! But of course chaps can't trim their language because they have one female working there so whenever after the war I used the phrase "bloody hell" I always put it down to Chile because I had never ever sworn before that. I think Chile taught us all how to say "bloody hell"!

'One of the Polish girls, Anna Leska, was put in charge of eight women pilots and Chile was one of them. Well they disliked each other very much. They were always trying to put each other right over their use of English. There was one occasion when one of them said, "How many petrols did we got?" and the other one said, "It's not how many petrols did we got, it's how many petrols have we got?"

'It was terribly funny, but of course Anna, bless her heart, was quite serious. She was rather older than most of us and in Poland like Russia they were already using women in combat. She came over to England to join the ATA and she was a very nice woman.'

During the war, Anna, wearing her trademark white leather flying helmet, was photographed in the cockpit of a Spitfire by the talented female American photo-journalist Lee Miller. This wonderful picture appeared in a wartime copy of *Vogue* magazine and it was eventually used on the posters to promote the awesome Lee Miller Photographic Exhibition at the Imperial War Museum in 2016. This image of Anna was used on the front cover of a new IWM book which contained biographical details about Miss Miller.

My ATA friend Maureen Dunlop (de Popp) (1920-2012) once told reporters once that she'd have flown in combat if it was required. She said: 'I thought it was the only fair thing. Why should only the men get killed?' Many remember Maureen as the attractive dark-haired young woman who famously appeared on the front of *Picture Post*.

She became the poster-girl of daredevil women of the Second World War, and yet she always maintained the *Post* photographer snapped her that day in September 1944 without her knowing. She'd just flown a Fairey Barracuda and landed it on a hot day. She jumped out of the cockpit, pulled off her flying helmet and as her hair caught in the wind the photographer took a picture that is now legendary. Maureen always maintained it wasn't planned. I believe her. Many of the women pilots were embarrassed and irritated about press attention.

Today, because of the wartime media coverage about us girls, there are still many people who think only women flew in the ATA, and male ferry pilot colleagues seldom get any mention at all. This is why I should point out that in total there were 1,152 men flying for the ATA and the women pilots numbered 166. The number of flight engineers was 151 with four of them women, and the ground crew totalled 2,786. There were nineteen radio officers and twenty-seven cadets from the Air Training Corps and Royal Navy. The men of the ATA were of course just as dedicated as us women with most, if not all of them, committed to the idea of providing a serious and essential help to the war effort. If they couldn't fly with the RAF or Fleet Air Arm, then the ATA was the place to be.

By August 1942 – the month I made my first ever force-landing – I had already been flying aircraft like Hurricanes, Swordfishes, Defiants, Albacores and Barracudas. Well, it was a hot sunny day when I was detailed to fly a passenger from White Waltham to Reading in one of the taxi Fairchilds.

All was going well when, ten minutes into the journey, there was a tremendously loud bang and the engine stopped dead. Eek. I knew I would have to make a force-landing, which I did quite successfully thank goodness, but it was all very frightening at the time. At the sound of that bang a great rush of fear had swept over me, but all my training propelled me to take the correct action and before I knew it we were on the ground with a thump. A car was sent to pick us both up – fortunately there was no damage done to either the passenger or myself.

One day in the October of that year a film unit turned up at the ATA's headquarters in White Waltham. As usual, the director wanted a woman pilot to promote the organisation. The glamour question never went away when it came to the cameras. It turned out to be my colleague Veronica Volkersz who was asked to play a part in a documentary which John Boulting was making for the Crown Film Unit.

Veronica, who had recently married a Dutch RAF pilot, recalled: 'This involved some flying and what is laughably called "acting" at Pinewood Studios. The flying – low runs over the aerodrome – and some formation stuff, was taken at Aston Down, and there were two ground sequences, in the first of which I was shown walking along with my parachute over my shoulder, and in the second, climbing into a Hurricane. After six or seven re-takes I thanked my stars I was not a professional film actress. Things were even worse in the studio. They put me in a mock-up of a Hurricane, with a Spitfire canopy! And puffed smoke at me from a diabolical machine. I gathered that I was supposed to be flying in bad weather and registering anxiety which ought to have come easy after the winter flying experiences. All that happened was that the smoke almost choked me. I went into a fit of coughing and the next shot was quite terrible.

'The story, or my part of it, was roughly this: I am delivering a Hurricane to a fighter squadron which is urgently in need of it. I press on madly through storm and tempest, and on arrival find I cannot get the undercarriage down. Eventually, game to the last, I do a belly landing.

'Luckily I was not expected to do the actual landing, as a shot of a Hurricane coming in with its wheels up had already been taken. But another mock-up was arranged to show me stepping out of the wrecked aircraft and saying nonchalantly to the admiring ground crew: "All right boys. I don't think she'll burn." It was really too corny, and the words stuck in my throat every time. They shot the scene again and again but when I saw the finished film I was relieved to see they had cut the line out. All in all this film was one of the unit's better efforts. When I saw it I squirmed in my seat. I could not look any of my friends in the face for weeks! So ended my first and last appearance as a film star. The slice of film showing me stepping out of the Hurricane was used in another documentary called "Women at Work" but I didn't catch sight of myself in that documentary until sometime after the war.'

Chapter 13

'My' Spitfire

The late Molly Rose once described quite wonderfully the way some of our ATA friendships worked, offering up her impression of the personalities we knew and loved. She recalled: 'I was quite lucky because one of glamorous socialites or "It Girls" of the ATA – Diana Barnato Walker – had got a flat on the waterfront at Hamble on the river and as I was in digs I thought I would much rather have a lovely flat with such a beautiful view. I knew Diana was going up to London every day 'and dancing until the early hours and then coming back to Southampton on the milk train. So, I managed to pull off one of the cleverest things I have ever done, and that was to persuade Diana she would be better off staying in a big hotel in Southampton, so if she came down on the milk train at least she'd have people to look after her and give her breakfast and see she got a bit of sleep before she caught the train out to Hamble.

'Well, she fell for it! So one Thursday evening she moved out and I moved in and that was great because my greatest friend at Hamble was Phillipa Bennett (Booth) and Rosemary Rees. Rosemary had a cottage around the corner and Phillipa was there too. They had a cat called "Pushkin".

'Any sort of free time we had we would spend at their cottage or they would come around to me at the flat and that all worked very well. I recall there was an American chap called Slim who was a very tall individual. He had become quite a friend of Philippa and Rose, and if Slim was going to the cottage they'd get me. He'd arrive with terrific T-Bone steaks and we'd be faced with what you couldn't possibly eat as your appetite is much smaller when food is scarce.

'It was always amusing. Before the flat, I was in digs in Bursledon and although it was very nice, it was tiresome and I had to be picked up for work. Being in Hamble village meant I could cycle up the hill to the aerodrome. (In fact at Hamble today there is one of the memorials to the

ATA women). So was Diana happy to be in the hotel? Well, Diana did just what she liked! For example, we were meant to have our hair pinned up in the ATA but Diana merely put hers into a snood if it suited her and got away with it. Also, we were always meant to go from one aerodrome to another instead of wasting fuel on the way, but if she wanted to go somewhere else for lunch she always did and got away with it, always.

'Although I was happily married to Bernard, I mixed with everyone in the ATA. I think it helped me to fly and be part of the ATA as it concentrated my mind. Bernard was away in the Army and I missed him. I don't think there were many married women in the ATA.'

When I ferried aircraft to France towards the end of the war, I had to land and then clear out back to England pronto. Unlike Diana, for me, there was no opportunity to go shopping for stockings or chocolate or fancy goods in France or Belgium. I would just land the aircraft, get out, say hello to whoever met me and get into the taxi Anson and head back for home over the Channel.

Diana was really a law unto herself and her funny stories were legendary among us though. We were always amused by her tales of adventure especially about the time she told us she did a roll in a Spitfire and her make-up fell from her handbag and doused the entire cockpit in face powder. She thought she was in for a telling off from the RAF when she landed but apparently no one said a word. If she was covered in white face powder perhaps they thought she was a ghost pilot and were frightened to challenge her.

However, Diana's interesting attitude to making her deliveries on time sometimes meant she'd fly a Spitfire to a friends' field in Cornwall instead of taking it directly to its designated RAF base. If a friend invited her for a picnic, then she'd often do a detour. This behaviour did not amuse Senior Commander Pauline Gower and Diana was demoted to Third Officer for a few months and it was a close call as to whether she could remain with the ATA.

Mind you she wasn't the only one who might stop for lunch somewhere. On the odd occasion if the timings worked out I would put down an aircraft at an airfield near to a friend who had invited me for lunch. I did have to use the loo after all so it was a good excuse to spend a few extra minutes enjoying the company of a lovely CO before taking off again to deliver the aircraft. I've kept this occasional detour a secret for years. But of course I never did it if time was tight.

By the end of the autumn of 1942, I was nurturing my new relationship with the wonderful Spitfires and never ceased to be thrilled to arrive for work early in the morning to find them on my delivery chit. But, like all aircraft, Spitfires have their own unique qualities and operating techniques. The long upturned nose made taxiing a challenge and weaving from left to right was the norm and a somewhat exacting part of ground movement. There were four engine runs before take-off. Sometimes in windy weather at least one member of ground crew would sit on the tail to add ballast to this flighty and dynamic aircraft.

Once in the air, however, the Spitfire was a delight to fly with its instant response to the controls. The power and speed were exhilarating and the energy and excitement of being at the controls of this aircraft never, ever left me. If I am honest, it still lives in my dreams today.

The landing of a Spitfire, though, was quite different from say the Hurricane, because of the reduced visibility forward. One became used to the problem of half a view and compensated accordingly. I always enjoyed flying the Hurricane, even though it was slower when compared to the Spitfire. The Spitfire could give you a jolt in the back when it took off but I never had that with the Hurricane. If you wrote down that you felt a boot in the back, you would be told 'you're not flying it properly as you must open the throttle slowly'. You have to be careful there.

Between 20 and 29 November 1942 I flew nine Spitfires. My goodness me! I flew a Swordfish in between, so no-one can accuse me of being greedy. In 1942 I flew twenty different types of aeroplane. I find it hard to imagine now.

When Griffon-engine Spitfires had to be delivered I had some important rules to remember. These variants of the Spitfire first flew on 27 November 1941, and went on to prove an important part of the Spitfire family. There were rumours about at the time that the Griffon-engine Spits swung violently on take-off and that it was impossible to keep them straight. There was even a suggestion that they sometimes approached supersonic speeds. These notions greatly concerned my ATA colleague and friend Veronica Volkersz, but they proved to be nonsense of course.

Flying Griffon-engine Spitfires like the Mk.XII meant it was most important to remember to turn rudder full left before take-off. I once forgot this rule and the consequences scared me beyond measure, but no harm was done. I shot off the runway and into the air with an uncontrolled swing with just a moment to sort myself and the aircraft out.

Of course, the Spitfire is one of the most beautiful fighter aircraft ever designed. It has its own special noise; everyone loves the Spitfire, and pilots find it so easy to fly. The response from the control column is magic – just a gentle touch and the aircraft obeys immediately. It is so wonderful. It remains to this day a symbol of freedom. I will always love the Spitfire – it was my wings, my freedom and my joy.

In my ATA logbook I noted that the maximum speed of a 1,500 hp Merlin Rolls-Royce-engine Spitfire Mk.IX is 400 mph. The Griffon-engine Spitfire, with its 2,000 hp engine, has a maximum speed of 430 mph. During the war, Supermarine built twenty-four Marks of Spitfire, making slight changes to the wing shape in an attempt to improve the aerodynamics.

The early marks of Spitfires and Hurricanes were fitted out with small Browning machine-guns which ultimately proved no competition against the Luftwaffe's Bf 109s which were equipped with cannon. It wasn't long, though, before the later Marks of the Spitfire were equipped with comparable weapons.

I loved all Marks of the Spitfire, except, perhaps, some of the Mk.VI and Mk.VII variants which had to have the hood screwed down after I was in the cockpit. I did not enjoy that as I felt so trapped. The RAF pilots had a radio, of course, so when they landed the ground crew would run over and release the hood when the aircraft had taxied to a stop. For us ATA pilots we had to wait what seemed like ages before any one of the ground crew noticed us. I really didn't like those types of Spitfire, as one felt one could easily die shut in such a small space. There wasn't much use shouting from the cockpit to be let out as no one could hear you.

These marks of Spitfire had longer, pointier wings for higher altitude work and had these pressurised cabins. If RAF pilots needed to bale out of them they had the ability to set off little explosive charges to blow the hood off. But I didn't know any of this as we ATA girls hadn't been informed of any of this. For me personally, this information came to light recently when we talked to Battle of Britain pilot and former test pilot Wing Commander Tom Neil, the author of several excellent books including *Spitfire from the Cockpit*.

I remember once, when taking off in a Spitfire from Chattis Hill, the undercarriage refused to fully retract, and jammed in the half-way up position. Having followed the correct procedures for such an incident, I returned to land back at the airfield.

Located in Hampshire, Chattis Hill became a key landing and take-off location for ATA pilots picking up Spitfires. Following the Luftwaffe's bombing attacks on the Supermarine factory at Woolston, it was decided to move Spitfire production from there to Chattis Hill. The assembly buildings were in the woods so they were well camouflaged and heading up past the area was Spitfire Lane.

To assist with production of fighter aircraft a special assembly shed was built to the north of the aerodrome which had begun life during the First World War, being initially used by the Royal Flying Corps. The aircraft flying out of Chattis Hill in 1917 were Sopwith Pups and Sopwith Camels. The site also became home to the School of Wireless Telegraphy at this time.

When I flew in and out of Chattis Hill during the Second World War there was a fairly new airfield situated on the west of the site and the whole operation was brilliantly concealed from the roving eye of the Luftwaffe. The bosses at Supermarine were delighted with the factory's new facilities and production began in December 1940, with the first Spitfire flown out from the base in March 1941. Spitfires were assembled at Chattis Hill through until 1945 when the airfield closed, though Supermarine continued to make use of the buildings until 1948.

I also got to fly unusual and important variants of Spitfires, including the Mk.VIII – which for a while was deemed the ultimate development of the Merlin-engine variety. It appeared late in the Second World War, though, and the majority of them were supplied either to the Mediterranean or Far East war zones.

Technically, these Mk.VIIIs were more advanced than the Mk.IX which confusingly had appeared some months before the Mk.VIII. The Spitfire Mk.VIII was noted for its retractable tail-wheel and additional fuel capacity. It eventually became the fastest of all of the Spitfires when used in dive tests at Boscombe Down in Wiltshire, where they were tested to a Mach number of .92. Its Rolls-Royce Merlin engine developed 1,710 hp for take-off and in level flight the aircraft could well exceed 400 mph. Wow, how I loved that!

I recall collecting an example of this particular variant of Spitfire from the Vickers Supermarine factory at Eastleigh on 15 September 1944. Its number was MV154 – and it was my responsibility to fly this gorgeous Spitfire to the RAF's Maintenance Unit at Brize Norton. I was lucky this destination wasn't far from my parents' house and I could conveniently begin a spot of well-deserved leave.

This particular Spitfire and I bonded well. I don't know why, but somehow I fell in love with this aircraft more than any other Mark of Spitfire and distinctly sensed a connection. I know it sounds peculiar to feel united with an inanimate object, but there you are.

When I delivered MV154 to Brize Norton, I got out my flight pencil and signed my name on the inside of the cockpit, perhaps hoping some handsome pilot might see my name and track me down! Now that really would be something. Also, and I can't explain the mysteries of impulse, but I felt I wanted to know what was going to happen to this lovely aeroplane without me to look after it.

Many years later a miracle occurred when I learned Spitfire MV154 and I would be re-united again. It seems this little Spitfire had quite an adventure since that day I left it in 1944. Initially, it was packaged up at No.6 Maintenance Unit and put on a boat for operations in the Far East and Australia. All ready for action, it was delivered to No.2 Aircraft Depot in Richmond, Australia, on 28 November and, before long, she was given a RAAF (Royal Australian Air Force) serial – No.A58-671.

However, by this time the Japanese were in full surrender and this particular Spitfire was never used operationally. So there it stayed, stored away again in its crates at Richmond until, on 24 May 1948, MV154 was struck off charge by the RAAF. At the end of that year, MV154, once flown by me and never forgotten, was finally reassembled and used for systems testing.

A dozen or so years later MV154 was bought by Squadron Leader 'Titus' Oates, who was a test pilot for de Havilland. It was October 1961, and Squadron Leader Oates planned to restore MV154 as memorial to the Battle of Britain pilots. The aircraft was then transported to Bankstown Airport. When the Memorial plan fell through, MV154, with my name still pencilled on the inside of its cockpit door, was sold to Sid Marshall of Marshall Airways, being destined to be exhibited in his museum.

In 1979 Robert 'Robs' Lamplough had opportunity to buy MV154. The deal done, the Spitfire was shipped back to the UK. It duly arrived at Duxford, where it remained for a short stay, before being transported to Charfield in Gloucestershire, for restoration to airworthy condition.

In January 1980 I had a call from Robs, who introduced himself over the telephone. He then announced that, 'I've just bought a Spitfire with your name written in it!'

He wrote to me on 15 January: 'Please excuse me calling you Mary, but this is the way that you signed the wind shield lower mounting bracket on my Spitfire Mk.8 in August 1944. I cannot tell you how thrilled I am to have tracked you down and how much I am looking forward to showing you MV154 again complete with the inscription "F.O. Mary Wilkins ATA" on the left front windscreen panel lower mounting bracket.

'Nothing much has happened to the Spitfire since you last flew her and I am sure that nobody else has ever flown this aircraft apart from yourself. We have the complete service record from this country and Australia and the aircraft passed from Maintenance Unit to Maintenance Unit without ever being issued to a squadron. After shipment to Australia it was then sent north in the closing months of the war against the Japanese. However, it was never taken out of its box and wasn't assembled until 1960. At this stage it was acquired by an Australian, Mr Sid Marshall, who had the aircraft in its original box. He opened the container and assembled the aircraft whereupon he asked permission to fly the Spitfire in Australia – permission was not granted.

'With disappointment about not flying the aircraft he decided to preserve it as well as possible, fixed a wire cable around the front engine support and through the rear lifting points and had the aircraft "en bloc" and hoisted into the eaves of his hangar where nobody could touch or get into the aircraft. There it remained until his death in 1977. I was fortunate enough to acquire it from his estate and it arrived in the UK shortly before Christmas 1979.

'It was at this stage while opening up the aircraft to make an assessment of its condition that we discovered your inscription on the wind shield surround. I immediately contacted Edna Bianchi who is the widow of Doug Bianchi who flew with the ATA during the war. She then put me in touch with Freydis Sharland who told me you were married and connected with Sandown Airport. From then on I found your contact details.

'Unfortunately I am having a little problem at the moment with the Australian authorities in relation to the export of this little aircraft as in fact they had deemed the Spitfire should be part of their national heritage and decreed it should remain in Australia. However, their legislation wasn't totally watertight and through a complicated process it arrived back in this country.

'Presently the aircraft is near Bristol and naturally I would be thrilled if you could come and re-acquaint yourself with her in the near future.'

MV154's registration code then became 'G-BKMI' during its final reassembly at Filton, Bristol. It was from there that it also made its first flight back in the UK on 28 May 1994 – almost fifty years since I last stepped out its cockpit. In September that year, and to mark the fiftieth anniversary of the aircraft's maiden voyage, a special celebration was held at the ATA's former headquarters at White Waltham.

Robs and I were guests of honour and we had a bangers and mash lunch with the famous Shepherd Neame Spitfire beer served to the party. I was delighted to be re-united with this lovely Spitfire which still had my name written on the inside of the cockpit. It was unbelievable all this was happening for me. While no handsome RAF pilot came to find me it seems the loyal Spitfire did! What do you make of that? The chances of meeting up with a wartime aircraft one has flown are so remote. I'd argue there was something uncanny about it all as it was as if my initial sense of bonding with MV154 had been a sort of sign about my future.

I had a wonderful day at White Waltham with Robs and friends in 1994 and we took so many photographs to prove it. Robs told me that when he first saw 'my' Spitfire in Australia it was just hanging suspended from a roof in a hangar so he offered to buy it there and then. Perhaps my signature on the cockpit door brought it some good luck as it's remarkable it survived for more than seventy years. I recall Robs' family laughing when I told them I'd hoped my signature would bring a handsome young RAF pilot running in my direction.

While this treasured Spitfire was in Filton in the 1980s it was rebuilt over ten years by a team of Rolls-Royce and British Aerospace engineers led by John Hart.

In 2010 it was sold to the German-based Meier Brothers (Max Alpha Aviation GmbH) becoming the first German-registered Spitfire ever. Spitfire Mk.VIIIc MV154/G-BKMI now lives, ironically, at Bremgarten Airfield near Eschbach when it is not at Goodwood in Sussex. Not long after the Meier brothers bought the Spitfire. Maxi, one of the owners and pilot, visited Goodwood aerodrome and I enjoyed their company at dinner and we got on tremendously well. I have every belief he will look after the aircraft as he is most protective about it and didn't want anyone else to pilot MV154 but himself.

In 2016, I was re-united once again with MV154 when Maxi flew it into Sandown again for some filming work and I signed my name inside the cockpit again. Then on 1 October of that year I flew around Goodwood in a Cessna 172 alongside this lovely Spitfire which had Maxi at the controls. That day I recall the warm haze of autumn presented a golden glow across the skies and the hint of a halo brought a sparkle to the outline of the Spitfire. I closed my eyes and it was 1944 again.

Chapter 14

Life and Death

One particular narrow miss in a Spitfire which scared the life out of me took place in the autumn of 1942. It involved my close friend, a married woman, First Officer Dora Lang. I hadn't been flying Spitfires for very long but our chitties on this particular day required the two of us to deliver P1 (Priority 1) Spitfires to the same airfield. We had taken off from Chattis Hill near Southampton at around the same time and the visibility was absolutely atrocious – we knew this, but had both elected to fly.

I lost sight of Dora because of the terrible fog and although we were always advised to put down in adverse weather conditions I went all out to make my P1 delivery. You can imagine I was overjoyed when I spotted a hangar looming up out of the mist near Wroughton airfield close to Swindon.

Dora had also spotted it at the same time. I had just landed and was on the runway when something shot by me going in the opposite direction at the same level. Eek! Dora, flying her Spitfire, had whisked past me on the same runway. It was a miracle – an absolute miracle – that we didn't collide. The wing-tips on both aircraft must have been an inch apart. The embarrassment was caused by the very bad visibility as one of us had landed from the wrong direction. Fortunately, we had observed the first rule of landing and that is to keep the left of the runway. And that rule is what saved us. We were both lucky not to have been killed that day.

On 3 November 1942, Dora wrote in my autograph book a poem and had a drawn a picture of a Spitfire. Firstly, she wrote: 'Enjoy the sky, Possess the field of air, Cloud be your step, the west wind be your stair'. Dora then added in the corner of the page, 'And the next time we land on the same aerodrome, on the same runway, at the same moment, may we be going in the same direction!'

It was a deeply upsetting time for all of us when, on 2 March 1944, Dora and Flight Engineer Janice Harrington were killed when the Mosquito Mk.VI that they were flying crashed and burst into flames at Lasham airfield, near Alton, Hampshire.

It was hard to believe when I heard the news; all sorts of memories of Dora and little Janice flooded my mind. I recalled the conversations we'd had, the meals we'd shared. One minute they were there and now they'd gone. It was a shocking reminder that death was never far away, especially when flying aircraft. I was upset of course to lose such dear friends, especially Dora who I saw nearly every day as she was in the same billet at Bursledon. Our CO, Margot, told me to come to work but take a day off from flying.

Dora's death was a bad shock, not only for me, but our ATA colleague First Officer Anne Walker who was also a great friend of hers. When Dora's mother visited us at Hamble she said we, as Dora's friends, could take what we wanted from her locker as a memento. Of course I had my autograph book containing that lovely poem and memory of our scary moment on the runway, so I will never forget her as she was a kind and very lovely woman, a very skilled pilot and we'd shared some great times and extraordinary adventures together.

Born in London in 1914, Dora was one of the few women to be trained to fly by the Civil Air Guard Flying Scheme before the government clamped down on women learning to be pilots. When the war began she had joined the WAAF as a plotter at RAF Hornchurch. She then wrote to Lord Londonderry in 1941 in response to his appeal for pilots.

That letter from Dora has survived: 'Dear Sir, I possess a pilot's "A" licence and would very much like to qualify as a ferry pilot. I have 25 hours in my logbook and have since done some passenger flying in RAF machines (Magisters). I am studying for a navigator's licence. I would be pleased of the opportunity to fly at my own expense to complete the required number of solo hours necessary to qualify for the advanced training provided under your scheme. I will be very eager to hear if any arrangements can be made – ACW Dora Lang.'

Soon after, she received a reply to say she hadn't enough hours of flying but still she persisted and told the ATA she'd heard there might be opportunities in Ireland to train with the ATA. Finally, in July 1941 she was told to report to Hatfield as 'some vacancies for pilots had arisen in the women's section'. On 9 August that year she took her flying test and, having passed, by 6 September reported for duty as Second Officer Dora Lang, being later promoted to First Officer.

Her ATA record reads thus: 'S/O Lang flew seventeen hours on Moths, two on Harts, eight on Magisters and a Swordfish, and was posted to training pool in March 1942. Her instructors' reports were consistently positive: "This pupil came to ATA at practically *ab initio* stage, but very satisfactory progress made in school has been furthered during stay with T.P. and she should make an excellent ferry pilot. Keen and quietly confident … very active and attentive".'

When Dora was killed I didn't really talk to anyone about it. It was so very, very sad. Every day we knew what danger we may be in but you couldn't dwell on it. Concentration on the job in hand was the main priority so you didn't put yourself in any danger.

On 3 May 1944, Dora's mother said: 'I know my daughter was very happy in her work and with her many kind friends in the ATA and I wish to thank them for all their sympathy in our great loss.'

After Dora's death I knew that life had to go on, and although I continued to fly to the best of my ability, I never ever forgot her or any of those who died doing their duty. It was my friend ATA Third Officer Margaret Frost who replied 'What feelings?' when she was asked about the tragic events of the war. She was right of course – we weren't encouraged to spend time indulging in feelings. It just wasn't the done thing as we had a war to win and work to do.

So life in the ATA really wasn't very pleasant at times. Tragedy was going on around us and when it struck someone we knew and loved, most of us, although touched deeply, would in true British style adopt a stiff upper lip and march on with our duty.

In 1943 I transferred briefly to No.1 Ferry Pool at White Waltham where a course of advanced training had started to prepare us for the task of flying not only the faster aircraft of the fighter type like Mustangs, but the heavier bombers with two or more engines. I enjoyed the school-like discipline and appreciated the patience of the engineering instructors who knew all too well the consequences of us not knowing what would happen if we were unable to interpret the readings of the various dials in the cockpit.

We were introduced to a fantastic assortment of fuel systems, oil systems, carburettors, variable speed and constant speed propellers, boost gauges, flaps, retractable undercarriages, etc. and other notable essentials. For me the flying came first when I began my training arrangement with the ATA, but for the *ab initio* pilots like Joy Gough (Lofthouse) who joined us in 1943, they had to pass the technical exams first of all before they were allowed to fly.

Joy is on record in the Imperial War Museum sound archive recalling the time she left her job at Lloyds Bank in her home town of Cirencester, Gloucestershire, to join the ATA: 'I had to report to White Waltham on

30 December 1943. We were taken to Thame IFTS – Initial Flying Training School and we had to take the Technical Training Course which lasted two or three weeks and it was the thing I found most difficult. They had only just switched it around as I learned that some girls had been allowed to learn to fly first. We did technical training before we saw an aeroplane and we had to get a certain percentage, and I just scraped through. I didn't mind the Met, it was what was going on beneath the cowling of the aircraft which foxed me most.

'My general impression of the instructors was they were helpful. My logbook shows my first flight as 20 January 1944. For this we went on a bus to Barton-in-the-Clay (Barton in the Mud, as it was known!) and each day this little airfield was used for our initial flying and there we'd sit in our Sidcot flying suit and wait for our instructors. It was all very basic, no air traffic control. We relied on one of the cadets in the corner with a Very pistol for that! It was that basic.

'I trained on the Miles Magister, monoplane and then I did a certain amount in the Tiger Moth to practice spinning, and then one day my instructor would tell Captain 'Daddy' Woods and he would give you a test prior to going solo. I had thirteen hours before I went solo and went back to tell my sister I had flown solo. I was told if you get into bad weather, land – "we want the aircraft to be safe". I was exhilarated and felt a great sense of achievement with my first flight and then telling everyone. It was great relief.'

Captain H. Woods had flown the old Maurice Farman biplanes in 1917 and had continued to pilot aircraft until 1933. He was 50-years-old when he took over as CO or 'Father Confessor' and Instructor at the Elementary Flying School at Barton-in-the-Clay. 'Daddy' Woods was known as a helpful and supportive CO who was happy to counsel ATA cadets/trainee pilots if they were experiencing problems of any kind.

People often ask how we managed to climb out of a Tiger Moth, get into a Wellington, vacate that for a Spitfire and maybe finish up with a Walrus, all in one day. The answer was of course our basic training, and then the wonderful Ferry Pilots Notes which were contained between two blue hard covers and the big spring binder which allowed for easy access to each set of information. The pages of specific information were really comprehensive and without them it would have been almost impossible to get into an aircraft which one, a) hadn't seen before and b) fly it away to its RAF or Fleet Air Arm destination.

We also used the library to help us study what we needed to know about a particular type of aircraft. The British makes were usually more manual to operate. Some of the American aircraft used electrical systems and they could be complicated, as the switches wouldn't be exactly where you would expect them.

We all knew pilots must be constantly on their guard and strict cockpit drill must to be carried out at all times. Checks really must be made. It was essential to do this during the war as there was always opportunity for distraction that led to things going wrong. For example, a mechanic working on your aircraft could be called away suddenly and so a spanner is left in the cockpit and is too close to a rudder pedal. It's always best to check the cockpit thoroughly before take-off.

During my eventful and life-changing years with the ATA there was little escape from the knowledge that ferrying aircraft could be a dangerous business.

On 6 July 1943, for example, I was sent to pick up a pilot at Yeovilton and return to Hamble. While flying over the New Forest on that gloriously fine sunny day at the controls of Fairchild Argus EV803, I suddenly heard the engine stop, silence. My biggest concern was to look for somewhere to land and this was not easy in a state of shock. However, I managed to spot a small space and preparation was made for a landing.

I was going down. It was terrifying and I was flying solo at the time and I had no radio either to call for help. However, the final effort was made successfully, and miraculously there was no damage to myself or the aircraft.

I had managed to put down in a field near the Balmer Lawn Hotel in Brockenhurst, Hampshire and after the ATA enquiry it was rightly recorded as 'pilot held not responsible'. What was going through my mind during the landing? Well, I remained calm and in control (even though I was praying hard and frightened) and the training helped of course, but it all seemed to happen in slow motion so maybe I had more control than I thought I did.

I have to admit we all had our fair share of excitement. What did frighten me that day though, me, a farmer's daughter, was the herd of cows which ran over towards me as I sat in the cockpit gathering my thoughts and thanking my lucky stars. Those cattle were obviously intrigued by the great bird that had fallen from the sky and I was more frightened of them than the actual forced-landing! I was soon cheered along though by a bunch of Marines who were stationed nearby at the hotel.

They approached me and helped me out of the aircraft and took me off for tea. They also shooed the cows away from me. What heroes! The Marines loved taking out ATA girls and if the weather was bad they'd offer to buy us lunch or dinner. That lovely group of young men had seen my aircraft in trouble and ran towards it, and then of course they simply couldn't believe a girl was flying it. From that day, however, a great friendship grew up between the ATA and the Royal Marines – and one of those friendships I made lasts to this very day, believe it or not, and we still exchange the loveliest of letters, even after all this time.

I obviously impressed one of ATA elders as I am mentioned in Captain Rosemary Rees' memoir *ATA Girl*. She wrote: 'There was one girl, Mary Wilkins, who, in a Fairchild, brought off a very good forced landing in a clearing in the New Forest, and then had to be rescued from the aircraft afterwards in terror of the cattle which came nosing round with the curiosity they always have!'

Sometimes though accidents were fatal, and by the end of 1945 it was recorded that 174 ATA aircrew had been killed on duty with fifteen of these being women. At the All Saints' Cemetery in Maidenhead there are seventeen war graves representing men and women of six different nationalities. I had known and been friends with some of them and they all gave their lives in service to their country.

On 15 March 1942, at White Waltham a Fairchild Argus taxi aircraft flown by one of the men stalled and got out of control as it approached to land and finished up smashing through roof of a house on the edge of the aerodrome. The pilot and two of the women had been killed. One of them was my good friend Bridget Hill. Bridget was so full of charm and fun and now she was gone. Her funeral was held at a little country church in Salisbury. The other passenger to die that day was ATA cadet Betty Sayer who had been another fun person to be around, and often she called new and shy ATA recruits 'Twizetts'.

The only person to survive this terrible crash was Pam Duncan, a tall, dark-haired young woman who had been a great friend of Bridget. Pam refused to let the memory of the crash prevent her from ever flying again and she did so successfully with the ATA for almost three years until she got married and left the organisation. I heard she then joined ENSA (Entertainments National Service Association) as a welfare officer and was among the armies who crossed the Rhine to liberate Europe from the Germans.

My home ferry pool at Hamble saw tragedy again on 19 April 1943, when 31-year-old First Officer Honor Salmon (the grand-daughter of the Shorthand creator Sir Isaac Pitman) was ferrying a twin-engine Airspeed Oxford from Hamble to Colerne in the Cotswolds. Her former classmate from Wycombe Abbey had been Bridget Hill, who had died a few months previously.

For Honor, it was the elements that led her to her death. As the weather deteriorated she decided to continue on her journey, being killed when she crashed into a hillside just north of Devizes in Wiltshire. She had been married less than two years. Sadness seem to rain down on the Pitman family as the war claimed not only the life of this dedicated ATA pilot but her two soldier brothers, Peter and John, as well.

Another ATA colleague of mine to die in service was 29-year-old Third Officer Joan Esther Marshall. She was killed on 20 June 1942, when a Miles Master, serial number N7806, spun out of control and crashed on approach to White Waltham. An enquiry into the tragedy found no cause for the accident which led to the death of this dedicated pilot. I was asked by our CO to be among the pallbearers at Joan's funeral at All Saints' Church, Maidenhead. Also carrying the coffin that summer's day were Senior Commander Pauline Gower, and Third Officers Winnie Pearce, Louise Schurman, Katie Williams, Benedetta Willis and Irene Arckless.

Joan had achieved a lot in her short life and in the 1930s she worked for Susan Slade – another ATA pilot of note who was also to die while flying with the ATA. Flight Captain Slade was 40 at the time of her death in July 1944. She is buried at St Peter and St Paul's Churchyard in Stokenchurch, near High Wycombe.

Of dear Joan, ATA Senior Commander Gower wrote: 'Joan's general character and behavior were excellent in every respect.' Her sister, Brenda, added: 'We know that Joan was very happy in her work at White Waltham and that, if it had to happen, she would most certainly have wished to die as she did, flying.'

Six months after Joan's funeral, one of her pallbearers, the recently-promoted Second Officer Irene Arckless, was killed when the engines cut out on an Airspeed Oxford she was flying on 3 January 1943. The aircraft crashed into a house on the outskirts of Cambridge. Second Officer Arckless was one day short of her 28th birthday.

My great ATA friend Freydis Sharland was perfectly accurate when she said of those times: 'I was often frightened, especially in bad weather. On many occasions I wondered if I would ever see the aerodrome again. We lost so many friends, you see. The next morning their name would be scrubbed off the chalkboard in the office, and the place would be horribly quiet. At the end of the war we were obviously very relieved. Yet I also remember feeling sad it was over.' (After the war my friend Freydis, from Benson, Oxfordshire, became a commercial pilot and once single-handedly delivered a plane to Pakistan – where she was barred from the men-only officers' mess).

Deaths among the RAF aircrew also hit hard among the ranks of the ATA. If we weren't careful, our emotions could be on the edge and during those times it was best not to fly if possible. First Officer Diana Barnato (1918-2008) was heartbroken when, in May 1942, her fiancé, Flying Officer Humphrey Trench Gilbert DFC, a Battle of Britain hero and Spitfire pilot, was killed. By the time of his death, aged 22, Gilbert had shot down several Luftwaffe aircraft and had survived baling out over the Thames Estuary. Ironically, he was killed after taking off from Great Sampford, Essex, in his familiar blue-nosed Spitfire with his airfield controller, a heavy man named Bill Ross, sitting on his lap. Both men were on their way to a party.

In her memoir, *Spreading My Wings*, Diana, the debutante and daughter of wealthy racing car driver Woolf Barnato, described the day she discovered her fiancé had died.

'Reaching Debden in a Tiger Moth,' she wrote, 'I circled but I couldn't see Humphrey's blue-nosed Spitfire anywhere. When I got back to White Waltham later, I rang again from the call-box outside the Mess. I was then passed from one person to another until, after some long time, I was put on to the Station Commander, Group Captain Johnnie Peel. It was he who had the unenviable task of telling me that Humphrey had been killed the previous day.

'This was the first time that someone who really meant something to me was no longer around. I couldn't stop crying, but I didn't want other people to see me, so I stayed in that phone box. Finally, a one-armed ATA pilot we called "Corrie" (F/O Robert Corrie) who was banging around outside waiting to use the phone, rapped on the glass, which brought me to my senses. Then he saw I was crying so he put his one arm around my shoulders and tried to comfort me'

The next day Diana attended her fiancé's funeral, still not knowing the truth of his death. Later she discovered a friend of Gilbert's was Squadron Leader Tony Bartley DFC, who had helped defend the pilot Gordon Brettell who once faced a court martial for flying a Spitfire to a dance with a WAAF on his lap.

By 6 May 1944, First Officer Barnato had met and married Wing Commander Derek Walker DFC and made the headlines when, quite unauthorised, they took two Spitfires and flew them to Brussels for a brief honeymoon. She wrote how the trip caused a 'furore' and news of it had been reported in *The Daily Mail* in November of that year. Wing Commander Walker was docked three months' pay.

First Officer Barnato Walker's marital happiness was not to last. Derek Walker was killed in November 1945 flying a Mustang in bad weather. She wrote: 'My shock at the loss of my wonderful Derek was tremendous. I would never hug him again, never love him again except in my heart'.

One day I was nearly killed by a flying bomb. These buzz bombs, as they were nicknamed, would go so fast and then they would stop and drop and there was a great explosion. Hitler sent these out to the south of England all the time after D-Day. It was terrifying because you never, never knew when they'd drop. These bombs had so much fuel and then they just stopped and did their damage. Buzz bombs made a terrible noise, but would suddenly stop and you waited for the big bang.

It so happened I was delivering an aircraft along the South Coast and one of these buzz bombs came in front of me; I was frightened to death. I recognised it immediately. It came at me at an angle and thank heavens didn't hit me.

I have been asked if I ever think about the RAF and Fleet Air Arm aircrews who went on to fly the aircraft I delivered – the fighter aeroplanes, the noble bombers? Of course I did. I admired their courage enormously. It was so understandable when these RAF boys expressed fear about making friends, as they were all too aware of the dangers of aerial combat and it could so often be a case of here today, possibly gone tomorrow.

All emotion was poured into the business of flying and surviving. Facing combat each day left little time for them, and us, to recognise loneliness, and there really wasn't any time to worry about 'feelings'. Every one of those aircrew knew the idea of love may cause weakness and therefore exacerbate fear. There was no escape from one's duty and it wasn't the done thing to go AWOL (Absent With Out Leave) and have LMF (Lack of Moral Fibre) written on your report.

Chapter 15

All in a Day's Work

My days were full and seriously busy, and they soon all seemed to merge into one long flight, but I didn't mind as I enjoyed the challenge as much as anything. Every day in the ATA was so different. I found it exciting apart from the fickle and maddening British weather. It could prove so hazardous. Imagine flying when the grey and the mist descends and you're looking for an airfield covered in camouflage!

Ferrying was exacting work carried out by skilled pilots of impeccable judgement and considerable physical stamina with a sense of responsibility for their aircraft and other pilots. In fact, the notorious weather in the UK sometimes prevented me from carrying out the intended daily programme and quite often I had to land at an RAF airfield which was not my destination; and generally speaking these were not terribly comfortable occasions, unaccustomed as service pilots were to having women pilots around.

Some of our people were involved in skirmishes with German aircraft and one chap was actually shot at by our own people, but it was an attendant risk and all part of the job. I think this was an Irish pilot who joked how the British seemed determined to bring him into the war. Most of us though were more concerned about the weather and the balloon barrages than being shot at in the skies. I was shot at once by anti-aircraft guns while flying over Bournemouth one day, it was not an experience I wanted to ever repeat.

One morning there were quite a few of us girls gathered together at Hamble, which was somewhat unusual, though exactly why I can't remember. I do recall that the day's work chitties weren't quite ready, so some of us marched off to the Met Office, where we discovered all was well and there was no low cloud anywhere. Ten minutes later, with the chitties put on the table, we made an orderly queue to step in and collect ours that were named.

There were little squeals of joy coming from most of us if there was an aircraft we loved on the list. In store for 'First Officer Mary Wilkins' was:

Ventura V FN957 from Eastleigh to Cosford.
Hudson VI FW895 from High Ercall to Eastleigh.
Taxi Anson 9596 with four passengers from Cosford to High Ercall.
There was an overnight stay for me at the second all-women's pool which was Cosford.

A day in my life in the ATA might also turn out that I should take the taxi Anson aircraft to St Athan in Wales, collect a Spitfire and fly it to Heaton Park at Liverpool, and then perhaps pick up a Whitley there and take it to Thruxton airfield, where a taxi aircraft would return me to Hamble. This would be an average day's flying, unless there was a flap on for priority aircraft when we would just go on as long as there was daylight.

All it takes to fly is know-how, determination, an independent spirit and a great amount of good judgement and common sense. In return there is usually pleasure, excitement and satisfaction.

The ATA had marvellous and busy Operations Room crews who organised the taxi aircraft which was supposed to be the most exasperating of jobs. It was from the Ops crew too that each pilot's work schedule for the day was decided upon, with each aircraft to be moved having different priorities attached to them.

RAF fighter pilot and Battle of Britain Ace Wing Commander Tom Neil DFC and Bar, AFC, AE recalled: 'After a tough day of fighting we'd be down to five aircraft out of sixteen and then by the early morning all these new aircraft would be waiting for us so we'd be back up to strength within hours! It rarely gets mentioned but the organisation of the RAF and the ATA was superb and helped to win the war.'

Wing Commander Neil's comment about the ATA's delivery service is right, although of course I am biased. It really was a wonderful piece of daily planning and administration and it worked extremely well. Suffice to say we always hoped for decent weather which would make our lives easier, and during the summer months we started at 06.00 hours if possible, and most of those long days were taken up flying several different types of aircraft during the course of that shift.

Without the excellent Met people, it would have been impossible to carry out our job as well as it was managed, as they were all remarkable at coping with the wartime limitations of observation reporting stations. Our weather in the UK is particularly difficult to forecast, situated as we are with the conflux of the Gulf Stream and the open Western

Approaches, even with all the computer technology available today the forecasters sometimes get it horribly wrong.

For me, as a ferry pilot keen to do her work well, one day seemed to roll into another. I did so love what I was doing and always enjoyed jumping in, say, the taxi Anson to Eastleigh then flying a Spitfire to the Maintenance Unit at Brize Norton. Then I'd take the taxi aircraft to Little Rissington where a Wellington was waiting in all its glory for me to fly her to St Athan, Wales. There I might pick up a feisty Mustang and fly it on to Bognor Regis in West Sussex. If I was lucky, there'd be a car waiting there, at what was only a grass Advanced Landing Ground (more commonly referred to as an ALG) to take me back to Hamble.

The next day I might get a Mitchell B-25 Bomber to fly from Hamble to Kirkbride in Scotland. Then a Vultee A-31 Vengeance to pilot to Cardiff. We never had any prior notice of ferry flights. We had to be ready to take what was on our chitties at 09.00 hours every morning and deliver them safely and promptly at the first opportunity.

Sometimes I flew as many as fifteen aircraft in a single day – and all of them are noted down in my logbook. In April 1943 I was a taxi pilot for a whole month and was based at Luton.

We mostly flew alone, except when it was impossible for the pilot to operate the emergency gear. We then carried a Flight Engineer and ATC cadets were always willing to come on a flight and help pump down the undercarriage. On two occasions my flight engineer was Kent-born Freddie Laker (1922–2006) who had begun his aviation career with Short Brothers at Rochester. He, of course, later went on to become Sir Freddie – the travel airline entrepreneur. In 1948/49 he flew aircraft in the famous Berlin Airlift when his airline company helped deliver essential supplies to the German population during the time of the Soviet Blockade of West Berlin.

The taxi Anson always needed the undercarriage manually wound down. But there was a war on so we couldn't have the luxury of automatic under-carriage all the time. The factories were spewing out Spitfires at an alarming rate and we needed to get to them fast and deliver them all – you couldn't worry about the small task of manual operation in the Anson, which did a wonderful job taking us from A to B or B to A. It was a wonderful workhorse. It was fantastic and very reliable.

Of course, there was always weather to contend with, so we would make a quick visit to our own Met office to get the latest situation report. Likewise to the Signals room to find out where the barrage balloons were likely to be flying that day. More often than not, if there was a 'wash out' (unable to fly) we'd sit in the Mess room playing cards, sewing clothes, knitting, reading, writing letters or chatting. Some girls, especially Jackie Sorour, liked to stand on their heads leaning against the wall. She reckoned it was good for the posture. No one batted an eyelid at her gymnastics, except for a young newspaper reporter who arrived looking for a story about us.

Our CO, Margot, dealt with the press and on this occasion she told the young man to hurry up with his photographs. Jackie continued with her headstand so Margot asked Molly to pose for the camera. Molly objected, but Margot insisted.

The gentleman of the press got very excited about discovering that a few of the ATA women had red silk linings inside their tunics – in fact, it was the blonde-haired Audrey 'Wendy' Sale-Barker who revealed her penchant for an exotic lining. She had hit the headlines before the war when she crashed her de Havilland Gypsy Moth near Nairobi, Africa, in 1932.

Wendy, a national ski champion, was flying with a woman called Joan Page. According to Wendy they were both rescued by a Maasai warrior who ran to get help carrying a note from Wendy. This had been written in lipstick and read: 'Please come and fetch us. We've had an air crash AND ARE HURT.'

In November 1945, when there was a special ceremony at ATA headquarters at White Waltham to mark the end of the war, it was 'Wendy' who is famously photographed lowering our flag.

But a few years before this momentous occasion took place, I still had my work to concentrate on, remembering always the potential dangers out there. From Eastleigh, Southampton, where Spitfires and Hurricanes were flown from every day, there were special corridors to fly through, which had names, if I remember, like Charlie or Donald. I was not too fond of doing this, especially in poor visibility, when no-one wanted to fly, but sometimes it was all a case of instinct, experience and knowledge of the landscape below that kept one safe. This was hardly satisfactory, but there you have it. Pilots need to have a desire to succeed and they must take their responsibility to land the aircraft safely very seriously.

The stately Alison King, the Ops Manager at Hamble, used to get jumpy on the days when she knew several of us had taken a chance that morning and headed off in grim weather. I got the nick-name 'The Fog Flyer' because on the occasions when several of us had taken off at around the same time and hit mist while heading for the same airfield, I always seemed to get through before them. When they would ask me how I did it, I probably mentioned something about my in-built sense of navigation.

I had got to know the UK from the air very well, of course, and yet Hamble was always such a welcoming sight. Ironically the ATA call sign was 'Lost Child' – maybe I was determined to be precisely the opposite? I was often called upon to fly P1 (Priority 1) aircraft and so quite often my skills with a new type of aircraft and poor weather were sorely taxed.

You might ask why I was flying in those poor visibilities; the reason, quite apart from sudden weather deterioration, was because of the need to frequently deliver P1 aircraft. Sadly, several ATA pilots were killed carrying out this exercise.

I recall hearing about one Saturday when Hamble was attacked by a Dornier Do 17 which had loomed out of the clouds and headed straight for the airfield. It was a winter's day and the cold air was biting as this Luftwaffe raider fired at the ATA personnel on the ground. Our CO, Margot, dived down by a privet hedge as the bomber crew flew over and then attacked the hangars with a sizeable bomb drop.

A few people were hurt that day and one hangar was hit and badly damaged. Once again we had been reminded we were sitting in the middle of a combat zone with the famous Spitfire factory at Eastleigh just along the way. But I couldn't dwell on the fact we were targets for the Luftwaffe as we were also well aware and re-assured that the RAF boys were out there working hard to defend our skies against the invaders. Knowing this helped me on.

Something else that got me through the tough days was the idea of returning home to my family and spending time with my sister, Dora. I often dreamed of just sitting idly in our friendly family kitchen with her and chatting about all the things we'd like to do. After the war my plan was to share a small cottage with my sister and we'd spend lots of time together having fun. (As it turned out Dora got married not long after the war and then started a family, whilst I was on course to continue my career in aviation).

Another of the problems we had to contend with was the sudden raising of barrage balloons, which occurred when an air raid was imminent. Having no radio, we could not be forewarned and, all of a sudden, they could start popping up all over the sky.

One of the delights, or fears, of the ferry pilot was that we never knew what we were going to fly or to where until the morning of any particular day. We might have any type, from a tiny Puss Moth to a twin-engine Wellington or four-engine Halifax. From the information on our delivery chits, we would make our preparations and we always carried an overnight bag, which had to be small, because in the fighter aircraft there was not much spare room.

We also wore a parachute when making delivery flights. However, I do wonder what the point was, especially when we had been told not

Above: When this picture was taken I was taking part in a local music festival with a few classmates. I am sitting in the front row on the right of the photograph which was taken around the time I took my first flight at Witney Airfield. (All images Mary Ellis Private Collection unless stated otherwise)

Below: A de Havilland Moth at Witney Airfield in 1936. This one has 'Witney and Oxford Aero Club' written just below the cockpit and is likely to be G-EBZP. There were two Moths at Witney Airfield at this time – the other was G-AAKO. Witney Airfield changed ownership on 14 November 1939 when it was requisitioned for the war effort. (Courtesy of Rosemary Warner (Black Dwarf Lightmoor)).

Above left: This picture of me was taken in 1938 when I was the young aviator filling her days at Witney Airfield. It was the photograph I sent to the Air Transport Auxiliary when I joined the service.

Above right: Eager for the Air! Here I am seeming very baby-faced in my new ATA uniform.

Below left: A proud day for me in uniform sporting my new ATA wings.

Below right: ATA First Officer Mary Wilkins.

Left: ATA Senior Commander of the women's section Pauline Gower MBE. This image by Bassano Ltd is now on show at the National Portrait Gallery.

Below: The first eight women of the ATA recruited by Senior Commander Pauline Gower. From the left are Pauline, Winnie Crossley (Fair), Margaret Cunnison, Margaret Fairweather, Mona Friedlander, Joan Hughes, Gabrielle Patterson, Rosemary Rees and Marion Wilberforce.

Above: ATA women pilots at No.15 Ferry Pool, Hamble, in 1943. Here I am with my friends, standing second right of the picture. In the front row, left to right, are: Rita Baines, Rosemary Bannister, Faith Bennett, Rosemary Rees, Margot Gore, Veronica Volkersz, Jackie Sorour, Mary Wilkins, Margaret Frost. In the back row, again left to right, are: Pam Tulk-Hart, Joy Gough (Lofthouse), Sylvia Edwards, Monique Agazarian and Helen Kerly.

Below: The Hamble women ATA pilots around a Spitfire. I am standing far left of the picture.

Top: In the cockpit of a wonderful Spitfire. This picture was taken towards the end of the war as the aircraft has a five-bladed propeller associated with the later Marks.

Above: A treasured picture of my friend 'Chile' (Margot Duhalde) and I. We are in the 'Taxi Anson' on our way to an airfield. As you can see we have both signed the photograph.

Above: I am standing directly beneath the Polish emblem on this lovely Spitfire. My friends around me that day include 'Chile', who is seated on the wing with her hand on the exhausts.

Below: I am on the left in this picture taken in the Hamble mess whilst I was enjoying a break and reading a newspaper. My friend First Officer Mary Fuller-Hall has joined me.

Above: My friend Dora Lang and I in the sitting room of our billet we shared in Burlesdon.

Above left: The ATA bridesmaids! Posing in our smart uniforms, Betty Grant (Hayman) and I were in Wales in August 1944 for the wedding of our ATA friend First Officer Doreen Williams, who became Mrs Illsley that day.

Above right: First Officer Mary Wilkins minus forage cap so that my hair could breathe!

Above: The morning collection of our aircraft delivery chitties at Hamble.

Below: Hamble Ferry Pool. I am seated in the middle row, third from right of the picture. Our CO, Margot Gore, is sixth from the left of the picture, middle row. Seated to her right is Flight Captain Philippa Bennett (Booth). Seated to Margot's left is deputy CO, Flight Captain Rosemary Rees (later Lady du Cros). Third Officer Joy Gough (Lofthouse) is seated front row, second left of the picture.

Right: My friend Maureen Dunlop who appeared on the front cover of Picture Post in 1944.

Below: ATA colleagues and friends at Hatfield. From the left are First Officer Lettice Curtis, First Officer Jennie Broad, Audrey 'Wendy' Sale-Barker (later Countess Selkirk), Gabrielle Patterson and Senior Commander Pauline Gower.

PICTURE POST

THE STORY OF THE A.T.A.

HULTONS NATIONAL WEEKLY CHURCHILL IN ITALY 4D

Above: A few of my friends in the ATA restroom. Dora Lang, Chile, Maureen Dunlop and Lettice Curtis are among those in the photograph.

Below: Here I am with three brave men of Bomber Command. We are standing next to a Wellington.

Above: Flight Captain Joan Hughes and me on a summer's day with a Spitfire in the background.

Above: November 1945 – the ATA flag is lowered for the last time at White Waltham Church, Berkshire. From left to right are: Ron Elliot, Eric 'John' Crowder, Ann Wood (USA), Diana Barnato Walker, Faith Bennett, Jim Qualfe, Dick Martens.

Above left: My friend ATA First Officer Jackie Sorour (Moggridge).

Above right: The late Molly Rose pictured in her ATA uniform in 1942.

Below: Myself with the glorious black Allard, CUD 818, which won many races – hence the two tophies on the bonnet.

Above left: Hard at work in the control tower at Sandown Airport.

Below: Another one of my jobs at Sandown included waving in the aircraft.

Above: Spitfire MT719, which I flew during the war, today resides in a museum in Dallas.

Below: In 1994 I was first re-united with Spitfire MV154, which still had my signature that I had written on the inside of the cockpit in 1944. Here I am in my ATA tunic as they re-fuel MV154 behind me at Sandown in the autumn of 2016.

Above: In the 1990s the ATA girls met again at the Royal Air Force Yacht Club at Hamble. Among those together again that day were Lettice Curtis, Freydis Sharland, myself (second on the right of the picture), and Molly Rose (on my right), with Jackie Moggridge kneeling in front of us. Diana Barnato Walker and Margot Gore are in the front row and Joy Lofthouse is standing back row, fourth right.

Above left: Here I am in a Spitfire ... and rarely wearing a helmet! This was the day I first flew with Carolyn Grace in Spitfire ML407. Right: Mr and Mrs Ellis.

Above: The unveiling of the ATA Memorial at Hamble, Hampshire, on 10 July 2010. From left to right are Margaret Frost, Joy Lofthouse, Annette Hill, myself, Peter George, and Peter Garrod.

Below: Mary Ellis with Spitfire Mk.Vb BM597 in 2013. (Melody Foreman)

to fly above 1,000 feet, so if we'd baled out at that height the parachute wouldn't have been much use.

With overnight bags, and maps, plus armed with the various information regarding balloon barrages and weather conditions, we awaited the Tannoy call which said, 'The Anson is now waiting on the tarmac for …' The senior pilots, of which I was one, took it in turns to fly the taxi aircraft.

One day when it was my duty, I flew the Anson over to the Isle of Man twice to pick up pilots and bring them back to Hamble. At one time it was considered necessary to carry a rear gunner in the taxi Anson; it would indeed have been a tragic loss to the ATA if a load of pilots returning from a day's duty had been shot down. 'Imagine those people down there,' said one of the taxi pilots one day. 'They're probably thinking as they look up "brave Bomber boys off to do their stuff", and all the time it's only us tired women pilots flying home.'

However, there was one occasion when the ATA did get it wrong; that was the day in June 1943 that I learned my friend Second Officer Jennie Broad had been kicked out for 'medical reasons'. We'd all been required to take some stupid breathing test to check out the health of our lungs. Well, apparently Jennie's score didn't come out too high and the doctor failed her, so she was forced to leave the service.

Apparently, she also had three 'at fault' marks on her record. But, in reality, we all knew it wasn't unusual for us to take the rap when it wasn't our fault at all, so it was ridiculous the ATA just let Jennie go like that. She was perfectly fit and a few weeks later she was called back to re-join the ATA after Pauline Gower objected to losing so many pilots to the ridiculous breathing test. But it was too late. By then Jennie had got another job.

Jennie was one of the most experienced pilots I knew. She had achieved her A licence to fly solo in 1934 when she was just 22. During her twenties she also qualified as a ground engineer and did all sorts of piloting jobs in Europe. What is not well known is the fact she became the UK's first ever woman test pilot.

By the start of the war she had joined the WAAF as a driver and then became an officer working in the cypher and codes unit. When she heard the appeal for women pilots she was snapped up by the ATA in July 1940, so in fact was one of the very first 'few'.

Jennie was born in Cape Town, South Africa, in 1912, though grew up in Sussex and attended school in Bournemouth. I remember her in the ATA as a feisty young woman who believed in saying what she thought. She always had a view on something and if that view happened to offend any politicians among the high ups then who knows, perhaps she wasn't ever going to pass the breathing tests? Outspokenness could come at a cost.

Jennie's career after the ATA continued to flourish. In fact, she joined a welfare organisation for the Royal Air Force and was eventually posted from Germany to the Middle East working at RAF desert bases in Iraq and Egypt.

She decided to move to Australia, as 'a refugee from British bureaucracy', telling a local newspaper that Australia was the only country in which to live in these days. By 1951 she had joined the Women's Royal Australian Air Force as an administrative officer.

Jennie's political views had been hardened against socialism following a visit to England in 1948. She told an Australian newspaper: 'When I had left England the people had a tremendous hope for the future and were proud of the part their country had played in the war. When I returned I spent two of the unhappiest months of my life there, as gone was the spring in the step of the people. They were tired and content to accept the rules that had been laid down for them.

'The queues were longer than ever. The people were living mainly on whale meat and fish. We got one egg every six weeks and the Labour prime minister, Clement Atlee had nationalised everything he could lay hands on. Taxes were on such a scale that the worker found it paid him better to stay away from work at regular intervals. A large number of girls in the Post Office admitted that they had deliberately lost a day a fortnight because it paid them better to do so. In 1947, we introduced the "Engagement Order". In 1935 compulsory labour was abolished in England but it rested with a Labour Party to re-introduce it.

'We had won the war but lost our freedom. Nobody is allowed to follow his own will. If he works overtime, he is summoned and fined. In Australia they had been in danger of going along the same path but they had recovered in time and realised what it meant.'

I did hear that Jennie had married a Frank Roche of Bush Pilot Airways in Cairns, Australia and that in 1954 they both flew a Dragon Rapide from England to Australia. The aircraft was to be fitted out as a special flying ambulance to help those in need in the rural parts of South Australia. Frank Roche was killed the following year in a crop-spraying accident and Jennie, then a widow, moved away. She was living in Norfolk Island, between Australia and New Zealand, when she died in 2005.

Three years later, when the remaining ATA women received recognition for our war work with the presentation of a special medal, I wondered if Jennie would have accepted hers from the Prime Minister of the time, Gordon Brown?

Chapter 16

Close Calls

The largest aircraft I flew by myself was the Vickers Warwick. This four-engine design, initially conceived as a bomber but which serve in a variety of roles, was operated by Coastal Command. I am reminded me of a little story of the first one I was to fly.

two (handwritten correction above "four")

One day I was sitting at Kemble airfield in Wiltshire waiting for the taxi aircraft to arrive to take me back to Hamble. I had just delivered a Hurricane into Kemble and thought the day's work done.

A phone call from base said, 'Mary, you must fly Warwick WS647 to Gosport'. My goodness, I thought, and so I wandered around, asking members of the airfield's ground crew or personnel if they would take me to this particular aircraft. I had to fly it to Gosport – and I don't even know what a Warwick looked like!

This was going to be the first time at the controls of such a big aircraft, and I knew that Gosport was only a small airfield. I thought 'woe is me', before the resourceful side of my nature took over and I fished out of my bag my Ferry Pilots Notes. On a page the size of a postcard was printed in terse, concise terms, with no frills, the information necessary to remind one of the flying characteristics of the aircraft one was called upon to fly, in this case the Warwick. But you can't fly by a book, the RAF would say, to which we replied 'well you can by our book'.

Eventually, we found Warwick WS647 tucked away in a corner of the airfield. I signed the necessary papers, and with my parachute I climbed aboard. My feelings were, to say the least, very mixed.

This aircraft weighed about twenty tons. I sat in the seat of this aircraft and looked around. It was an awfully long way to the tail end.

However, I summoned the courage. I started the engines; now I was happy, as I loved the roar of large powerful engines. In due course I took off straight down the runway. The weather was good and navigation was not a problem but it was a very windy day and because of this it was not a particularly pleasant flight.

I arrived at Gosport and wondered how on earth I would be able to land this great hulking thing at such a small airfield, which was smaller than Sandown on the Isle of Wight. I circled the airfield and struggling with the controls, battling against the wind, I made, thank heaven, a decent landing and parked the aircraft outside the control tower.

There I climbed out – to be met by a somewhat startled CO. He explained that his squadron was grounded due to the strength of the wind, and yet not only was an aircraft flying, but the pilot turned out to be, as he called me, 'a ruddy schoolgirl'. He didn't seem to appreciate my efforts at all.

It was before this, on 14 May 1943, that I had started a two-week conversion course at Thame, the intention being for me to be authorised to fly twin-engine types like Oxfords and Blenheims. Within weeks I was heading for promotion to a Class IV licence which would authorise me to fly bombers including Wellingtons, Mosquitoes, Hudsons, Beaufighters, Albermarles, Whitleys, Beauforts, and, of course, the 'taxi' Ansons.

This was an intensive experience and took a lot of concentration. But I wasn't afraid of hard work and was always delighted when I passed the test at the end of the course. As I explained, the training was first class and we learned from the very best.

On 21 May my logbook shows that I flew an Oxford from Portsmouth to Little Rissington, then after a ride in a taxi aircraft back to Portsmouth, that same day I climbed in another Oxford and delivered it to Andover. On 27 May, I flew another Oxford from Portsmouth to St Athan, and the following day I was in the cockpit of another Oxford making my way again from Portsmouth to Wroughton. I found the Oxford easy to fly – an aircraft without any particular vices.

In the August of 1943 I was posted to White Waltham for training on heavy twins, like Wellingtons and Blenheims. This all went well as I was always happy to learn and progress, and of course add to my growing list of aircraft.

On a fine October day that year I delivered a Spitfire Mk.VIII from Ibsley in Hampshire to Brize Norton MU. When I got there I was handed a message stating that the taxi aircraft due to pick me up would be forty-five minutes late.

The MU crew at Brize Norton, all of whom were very proud of villager Mary Wilkins, said I could borrow one of their bicycles. So, without further ado, I pedalled like mad to The Manor (home) and popped in to see my dear mother. She was alarmed at first and said:

'Where did you come from?' So I replied: 'I just flew a Spitfire to the airfield.'

We enjoyed a cup of tea together while the rest of the family were out working in the fields, though my sister, Dora, was out playing tennis. It was heavenly to see my mother and we said cheerio with much love and affection. Then I jumped on the MU bicycle and pedalled like mad back to the airfield. Five minutes or so later, I was heading back to Hamble after lovely day never to be forgotten.

In the ATA we mostly worked thirteen days on and had two days off every fortnight. I usually went home to Brize Norton and while my parents were pleased to see me they didn't ask too many questions.

Once at home I soon slipped into a different and more peaceful world and, as we had tennis courts at the house, I'd often play a match or two with my mother. It was strange to think I'd been up over the skies a few hours before flying a Spitfire and then I was in this world where I could hit a tennis ball at my opponent and win a point. If only they'd known about my life? Of course I didn't let on about what I did as an ATA pilot.

My logbook for 1943 reveals I did 181 deliveries. This included 115 Spitfires and seven Wellingtons.

Whilst it was a joy to fly Spitfires of most types, I did essentially love any aircraft which was fast and furious. I was young, I was free and had absolutely no fear of great speed. In fact, I welcomed the exhilaration which raced through my veins on most occasions I took off. Tempests and Typhoons (also known affectionately as 'Tiffys') were a delight – providing one didn't run out of cartridges trying to get them started. Mosquito bombers of course were among my favourites – they were just twin-engine Spitfires!

On 14 September 1943, it was a misty day, so probably there would be no flying, and we all did what we wanted. Some of us wrote letters, others got out their knitting, one or two did a few exercises. My nails needed painting but then, without warning, came the all clear for flying to proceed. There was a stampede to the locker room to get ready. My chitty read:

Hampden AE372 from Thorney Island to Tollerton
Fairchild EV748 from Loughborough to Ratcliffe
Dominie HG662 from Ratcliffe to Wroughton

I needed some new maps as I'd not been to Tollerton, near Nottingham, before, so needed to draw out a few straight lines, mark the balloon barrages on them and oh, I mustn't forget the overnight bag.

Quick! Quick! We were never quite sure if we would be back at Hamble for the evening.

In 1943 I was given my first Mustang – a Mk.Ia, serial FD563 – to deliver. So on 7 September I was in the cockpit of this super-fast fighter aircraft on my way from Silloth to Odiham.

By the time I had begun to make a difference as an effective and skilful pilot, the women's section of the ATA had grown considerably and was at last being taken seriously by the high-ups in the RAF, the Fleet Air Arm and the Air Ministry. I like to think ATA Air Commodore Gerard d'Erlanger was proud of our achievements and I hope he felt relieved how his idea for an aircraft ferrying service was making an important contribution to the war effort. The Prime Minister Winston Churchill also pointed out that 'without the hard-working, diligent men and women of the ATA we wouldn't have won the Battle of Britain and also beaten off aerial attacks from the Luftwaffe' which continued until the end of the war.

The only aircraft I really disliked intensely was the Supermarine Walrus. A single-engine amphibious biplane reconnaissance aircraft, the Walrus flapped about all over the sky, and at times seemed almost uncontrollable. On land it was like a penguin, but apparently it was good on the sea and during its history it had saved many lives. It is extraordinary to think the same designer had created the beautiful Supermarine Spitfire in all its beauty. Yes, Reginald J. Mitchell must have had a bad day when he drew up his plan for the Walrus.

I can't think of one ATA pilot who liked this aeroplane. It was like flying a deadly-heavy elephant. It wobbled about in the air like a crazy thing. In fact, the Walrus had a mind of its own. Even the ATA's most high-achieving woman pilots loathed it, including the indomitable Lettice Curtis. Indeed, it was the cumbersome, irrational, uncontrollable and rattling old Walrus that nearly killed my friend First Officer Anne Walker and made me think twice about ever flying again.

Anne and I had been sent to Somerton Airport at Cowes on the Isle of Wight in June 1945. Our chitties informed us we were to collect a Walrus each, but Anne's flight was doomed after take-off.

ATA pilot Veronica Volkersz, based at Hamble with Anne and myself, described Somerton airfield as, 'the size of a postage stamp and this made take-off difficult'. Due to a gusty 40 mph crosswind, Anne took off in the Walrus heading uphill.

Several people watched Anne get into the air and then gasped as the aeroplane swung about horribly dangerously. Anne battled hard to regain control of the unstable Walrus, but it veered across the field, hit a hut, ploughed through a hedge and went into a bungalow. Anne was lucky and was saved from the inferno because she hadn't strapped herself in. If she had she would never have escaped from the carnage. The impact of the crash threw her almost out of the cockpit.

A baker passing the field saw the crash and without a second's thought he stopped and ran over to Anne and bravely pulled her clear off the flames. He found Anne was unconscious with a bad head wound. She had also suffered three broken ribs.

I was talking to some of the chaps on the airfield and was waiting to take-off when someone bounded over and told me about Anne's accident. So I switched off the Walrus' engine and ran to help. I accompanied Anne in the ambulance which made its way to The Frank James Cottage Hospital in East Cowes where she stayed for a week. I greatly admire her tenacity as within six weeks of the crash, Anne was back on duty. She was an experienced pilot and had flown many varieties of aircraft including the Spitfire and even a Douglas DC3 Dakota.

In her own words Anne described what happened on the day of the crash:

'The Walrus was a very unattractive aeroplane to fly, it was like several sacks of coal. It was terribly unstable and wallowed, and it made the most dreadful noise. The airfield had a nasty up-hill slope, and you usually had to take off up-hill, and as a Walrus was a very lumbering kind of aeroplane I took off this day very much across wind, but couldn't get an angle into the wind.

'As soon as I had opened up, and we'd left the ground it felt to me as though it wanted to turn over on its back. I simply couldn't hold it I concluded that the controls must have been crossed, something which could happen, so I throttled back. But the minute I throttled back, it righted itself so then I quickly realized that it wasn't the controls, it must be able to take off, but by this time, since I had left the ground, the aircraft had swung even further across wind.

'It was a silly thing in retrospect to have opened up again but I did. I thought I could make it, but it was clearly not to be so. I did not want to crash into the hangar and managed to keep clear. I had throttled back by this time and could see I was going to crash, we hit a shed at the side of the airfield. That's the last thing I remember, the aeroplane tipping forwards, I apparently landed alongside the aircraft straggled across a road near a bungalow which was opposite. I think one of the wings hit the bungalow.

'Luckily for me I was not strapped in. In this particular aeroplane you could not reach the pedals properly, so that if you were strapped in you were even less able to lean forward and reach the pedals properly. I had rather short legs so I left myself unstrapped. When the aeroplane came to rest, it burst into flames immediately but I was half thrown out of the cockpit. The baker was just delivering his bread at that particular moment, and had to dive out of the way but when he saw what had happened he came rushing over and pulled me away from the flames. I was burnt along with my clothes and was quite unconscious – but he managed to pull me clear.'

Anne became Mrs Anne Duncan in 1948 when she married Alexander Duncan who worked for the aviation division of R.K. Dundas.

Meanwhile, for me soon back at Somerton, I still had a Walrus to deliver. It was the first time throughout the whole war I doubted myself. I never saw my flying as something courageous as it had always been an instinctive action to me. But I really did worry at that moment if my luck might have run out. Until then I had always just got on with it but I did think then, if I fly a Walrus and land safely, could it mark the last time I ever fly again?

You can imagine how I thanked my lucky stars when I did land it safely. In fact, I continued to fly with the ATA for another six months.

Thoughts of my family and home got me through any tough day during the war and I was always pleased when I had a delivery which led me towards Brize Norton. Often I would land the aeroplane and note there was waiting time for my taxi aircraft so I'd borrow a bicycle and pedal home to see my family and have tea. Everyone laughs when I tell this story and I suppose it just shows how, despite my life flying fast aircraft at wartime, there were some normal things like riding a bike that just had to go on. Normality was refreshing for me then.

My mother would be so, so, so pleased to see me and we'd not really think or talk about the fact I'd parked a Spitfire just along the road and I could just drop in during my work delivering aircraft! Things were all very matter of fact in those days and I don't think we thought that much at all about it.

After my home visit, I'd pedal back to the airfield and take off in another aircraft or get picked up by the taxi Anson flown by one of the other ATA pilots. I usually only had half an hour or so to cram in a secret visit home. On my full days off I'd arrive home and play tennis with the farmers' wives and my mother who loved the game but I don't recall these women talking to me much about my flying, and of course in those days everything had to remain hush, hush, so the ATA and the war wasn't really mentioned. (This feeling of being mindful about speaking out about my war has remained with me for most of my life. Indeed, I still find it difficult to live in such a pampered world where everyone talks about everything and nothing. These days if people catch a cold they ramble on about it endlessly. During the war if one experienced a chill or two it wasn't turned into a major occasion.)

As the war progressed, Brize Norton was firmly established as a training base and the Oxford was the mainstay, with visits from its twin-engine cousin, the Bristol Blenheim – now based at nearby Bicester airfield.

Sadly, Brize Norton was to witness the death of an ATA pilot called Captain Harald Julius Hansen. He was killed in Avro Anson R9761 after colliding with a Blenheim making an emergency landing. Captain Hansen, a Dane, died two days after this terrible accident at Oxford's Radcliffe Hospital.

The Brize Norton airfield buildings were painted green and black to act as camouflage, whilst the landing strip itself was made to look like several different fields from the air so as to deter Luftwaffe attacks. Small satellite landing grounds sprang up at Witney and Southrop, Weston-on-the-Green and Akeman Street.

It was at the busy airfield at Brize Norton that I had an unfortunate experience in a Spitfire. It was usual for a Spitfire to have one or two people weighting down the tail before take-off. I can confirm from my logbook how, on 5 December 1942, I arrived to pick up a Spitfire Mk.IX, that with the serial number BR651, from the Maintenance Unit at Brize on an extremely windy day. It was irritating to realise the ground crew weren't being very co-operative when I asked them to sit on the tail to steady the aircraft. This request was not uncommon and the RAF ground crews were used to carrying out such a task. So I asked them repeatedly and pleasantly if they would help me to steady the Spitfire on this particularly blustery day, but they refused. It was a case of them just saying 'no'. They were terribly dismissive of me, so I thought, 'Well blow you lot, I've got a delivery to make'. So I started up the aircraft and attempted to taxi out. However, the strong wind meant the Spitfire tipped on its nose.

It seemed like an age before anyone came over to help me out of the cockpit. I was horrified about the accident as I knew it was a dreadful thing to bend a valuable aircraft and felt so guilty about it all. The worst thing was having to write out the accident report. 'Dear Sir, I have to inform you …'

When I was summoned to see my Commanding Officer, Margot Gore, I explained about the weather and the high winds and no-one would sit on the tail – but I didn't see the point in mentioning the unhelpfulness of the RAF ground crew. I tried to see the big picture and I knew there was every likelihood us ATA girls would have to work with these difficult men again and it was best to just try and forget. I took the rap for the accident and it was recorded and put on my file that I was at fault, although it was written down and acknowledged just how incredibly strong the gusts were that day.

A special committee was formed in the ATA to interview pilots who had experienced a mishap or an accident. It wasn't a great feeling to know I had to go and face its members, but I took it in my stride and I knew a lot of my colleagues loathed it as much as me.

Usually our reasons for any incident were down to problems with the aircraft or the weather and therefore not our fault. The British climate could play havoc with us when we were taking off, or there was engine failure or mechanical problems which could leave us pilots with no option but to force-land.

There was one occasion when I was sitting in a Spitfire waiting to taxi out to the runway and saw another Spitfire on the other side. Suddenly it taxied straight into mine with a loud bang. It was quite a crash and I thought my end had come. I quickly got out of the cockpit and stood there shaking.

Second Officer Dorothy Bragg then appeared. 'I'm sorry,' she said. My reply was, 'Look, you have damaged two lovely Spitfires.' She said she just hadn't seen me or the Spitfire sitting there.

We travelled back to Southampton together by train and then got a lift in a car to Hamble. Needless to say, I wasn't to blame for that collision. (On 7 February 1946, Dorothy married and became the second wife of David Beatty, 2nd Earl Beatty, until they divorced in 1950.

One day I was heading to Little Rissington for the second time in a Spitfire. It was from there the RAF was operating Airspeed Oxfords and, of course, they were all on radio, but as an ATA pilot, I was not. After flying around for a while I decided to make an approach to land but, heavens above, an Oxford flew in front of me as I touched down. It was a death-defying moment I can tell you, as I watched him miss me by a whisker.

The incident was seen by both RAF and Maintenance Unit crews and I was pretty shaken up by the whole experience. I still have the letter of apology from the pilot who said his CO had criticised him for 'bad airmanship' and told him to write to me. But of course in those days you didn't take much notice if people did this.

Of course the near-miss was not an event I wished to ever happen to me again. On the subject of 'no radio' for the ATA pilots, I must emphasise it was absolutely true. As Wing Commander Tom Neil pointed out, the RAF had four channels on a VHF radio – one local, one operational, one group, and a fourth one, 'D', which was the mayday channel. Many RAF pilots couldn't believe we had no radio working at all.

Another time when I was starting to truly love the Spitfire more and more, I was asked to deliver a Mk.VIII, MD342, and so I thought if I happen to chance upon a lovely white fluffy cloud I would have a little game with it. The aircraft was so wonderful and I adored flying such a beautiful machine. This particular flight was from Chattis Hill to Cosford and then oh no – my happiness wasn't to last as this time there was a problem with the tail-wheel. But I was not of course responsible for this and was exonerated.

Chapter 17

'I *AM* the Pilot'

I can't exactly recall the time I first saw and adored the twin-engine Vickers Wellington, but I do know I wasn't frightened to fly one. This may sound surprising coming from someone of diminutive stature, but I'd had a lot of training in a Wellington as a co-pilot and it was the natural next step to go solo in such a friendly giant which had a wingspan of eighty-six feet and two inches, a length of sixty-four feet and seven inches and a height of seventeen feet and five inches. The weight of an empty 'Wimpey' (named after the cute character created by Walt Disney) was 18,556lbs. Its maximum take-off weight was 28,500lbs.

As I mentioned before, by the August of 1943 I had been posted to White Waltham for training on heavy twins, including the Wellington. I had passed my Class III conversion course and this had led me into the cockpit of the Wellington where I had to do a lot of single-engine operations. This was vitally important and necessary, as if one engine went off I had to know what to do about it.

I may well have received some instruction on the Wellington from the wonderful Joan Hughes who, early on in her ATA career, had progressed to all types of bomber aircraft, including Short Stirlings and Avro Lancasters.

The Wellington was my favourite bomber and, to be honest, I wanted to fly one from the moment I saw it. It so happened I delivered forty-seven of these lovely aircraft and this was personally very satisfying. Today, on the wall in my dining room, I have a wonderful painting of a Wellington in the clouds just to remind me of my time in the ATA when I enjoyed many a happy flight at the controls of these lovely old war-birds.

I was never overwhelmed about flying a Wellington at all and of course there was no comparison with the Spitfire. It was a case of just one aeroplane and another. However, it was very different climbing into a Spitfire of course, which took just two steps. To get into the Wellington I had to go up a ladder to a door and then get inside the cockpit.

My first heavy twin-engine aircraft delivery took place exactly four years after the start of the war on 3 September 1943. I was to fly a Wellington, Mk.X HE808, solo from Llandow in Wales to RAF Kemble. I had collected my chitty as usual that day from the Ops Room at Hamble and there it had two Wellingtons noted down for my attention. It seemed there was every confidence in me from the CO to make a success of the first delivery, as the second was Wellington Mk.VIII HZ888, this time to be delivered from Little Rissington to Llandow.

Oh joy! I had always wanted to get behind the controls of the lovely Wellington solo and now here I was about to be alone in this big bomber doing just that. Remember I had no radio and just a map to keep me on track.

So, after I had arrived at Llandow in the Vale of Glamorgan, courtesy of the taxi aircraft, I made my way to the special room to sign all the paperwork and be shown to my first Wellington. Of course I took a good look around this beautiful aircraft and everything seemed to be in order from the ground, so I made my way towards the ladder which led to the main hatch which was located in the lower surface of the nose of the aircraft.

I climbed up, keen to study the instrument panel – but remembered that the catch on the door could be opened in two ways. The Ferry Pilots Notes told me how, from inside the aircraft, this hatch can either be opened in the normal way or by a quick release catch operated by a red painted pedal outboard of the starboard walk-way. To open the hatch, this red-painted pedal is pushed outwards. It must be reset before the hatch can be closed again, or the catch will not work.

It is important, we were advised, that the hatch is correctly shut before take-off, particularly when a passenger is carried beside the pilot. If this hatch opens during flight the passenger is apt to disappear into space on getting down from his/her seat. I mention the 'hatch-catch procedure' because during a Wellington flight I had a tricky incident to deal with involving a hatch which I will explain further on.

So there I am all closed in, and the cockpit is the size of a small room. I made sure the ladder was pulled back into the aircraft as it is part of the equipment. Then from my seat I went through my check lists, as well as the starting and testing routines. Cockpit checks are dealt with separately for each Mark and I knew the air pressure should be at least 100 pounds per square inch before the chocks were cleared away.

I carried out my test routine:

Check for dead magneto at warming up speed.

At 0 boost operate propellers. In cold weather do this several times in order to circulate warm oil in the propeller hub. Do not allow engine speed to drop more than 400 rpm before returning the pitch lever to Fine Pitch.

Make a power test at full throttle. This should give 2,600 rpm, at +6 ¾ boost. (+ 5½ with 87 octane).

Throttle back to + 2½ boost and check ignition.

Check slow running.

After completing the testing, turn on the nacelle tanks if filled.

Preparation for Take Off:

H. Hydraulics. Turn on hydraulic power valve. Pre-set U/C lever safety catch

T. Elevator trim neutral. Rudder trim neutral.

T. Throttle friction as required.

M. Mixture RICH

P. Pitch. FULLY FINE

P. Petrol. All three pilot fuel cocks pushed down. Nacelle tanks should have been turned on.

F. Flaps UP. Selector level Neutral.

G. Gills. Set at No.2 on indicator. Carburettor air intake COLD.

G. Gauges. Check pressures and temperatures.

F. Fuel boosters, no check.

U. Unlock controls. Check freedom.

S. Supercharger, medium.

T. Tail wheel lock. No check.

The ignition switches were mounted on the left-hand side of the cockpit and were interconnected with the undercarriage and flap indicator switches. The throttles were to my left and were the two longest levers in the control unit.

Soon the enormous Bristol Pegasus engines roared into life. I checked my straps again and was soon ready to taxi off towards the runway. I felt the springy undercarriage propel me along quite smoothly over the rough surface of the lumpy grass and I was ever mindful not to go too fast and take advantage of such a forgiving aircraft.

I checked again to ensure the brake control did not stick in the 'On' position and then made ready to accept the swing on take-off as I engaged the flaps. I had left the ground at 80 mph and was glad the tail had risen early which meant everything was in order before I reached climbing speed at a safe height of 600-800 feet. I raised the flaps and continued to climb and watch the instrumental panel checking the cylinder head and coolant temperatures.

I had glanced again at my Ferry Pilots Notes before taking off and knew the cruising speed of the Wellington ranged between 160 and 180 mph, depending on the Mark. So once I was happy everything was directionally stable and my visibility was good, I set about employing my navigational skills to head for Kemble which is in Gloucestershire, just a few miles south west of Cirencester.

I looked out at the scenery below me and saw acres of the Welsh countryside wreathed in the deep, lush green that comes only with the last gasp of summer. When I saw such views it was hard to imagine there was a dark and brutal war tearing apart the life and soul of Europe just over the Channel.

Then I checked the instrument panel and looked out and it wasn't long before I spied the little airfield of RAF Kemble. We'd crossed a couple of counties by now and it was time to think about slow flying to come into land so I increase the revs to climbing figures and adjusted the boost to maintain height at 110 to 120 mph. The flaps were up and I knew if I let them down then my speed would drop to 95 mph. I approached my destination and did the usual drill for this lovely comfortable aircraft which had been so well behaved all through the journey. I had enjoyed a wonderful flight and always felt secure in the Wellington.

I had another look at the boost gauges and RPM indicators and adjusted the throttles to ensure equal power. I was now at 80 mph and knew it was important to reduce the flap in proportion to the wind strength on landing. Ahead of me I saw the landing strip coming in closer and I made sure the nose of the Wellington was turned up-wind sufficiently to make a straight approach along the centre line of the runway, keeping the wings level. I closed the throttles and applied down-wing rudder to get the aircraft into position for landing. Such a procedure introduced a skid into wind to expel any chance of the Wellington drifting.

As I felt the soft bounce of the wheels on the ground I breathed deeply. I felt relieved I had made my first successful delivery of a glorious Wellington.

Out of all the airfields I flew out from, there was one which I recall as quite worrisome. That was dear old Brooklands near Weighbridge in Surrey. It was there that Vickers had a factory which built the Wellington.

My logbook shows how, on 4 April 1944, I was to fly Wellington XI MP547 from Brooklands to Christchurch, near Bournemouth. In fact, I had two Wellingtons to deliver that day; the other was a Mk.Ia which was to be flown from Cosford to Kemble. However, I remember Brooklands well as I'd flown to and from this airfield on several occasions before I took off from there in a Wellington. By way of an example, I flew Hurricane HV703 from Brooklands on 11 September 1942.

Returning to the occasion when it was my turn to take-off from Brooklands in a Wellington, I had to concentrate tremendously hard as I knew there wasn't very much room, especially for an aircraft of this size. I can only describe the area as cramped because, as we all know, cars used to race around it! I had to take off within the perimeter of this big saucer and it wasn't a very pleasant experience as you had to be very exacting and get it just right. It was either a successful take-off or a disaster.

There was no real runway there at all. It was just like a field, and I tried to take-off into wind, but there wasn't much wind about in this saucer-like environment. I can't recall many of the other ATA women pilots complaining about Brooklands, but there again I don't think many of them flew Wellingtons because the weight and size of these aircraft was heavier than that which most women pilots liked, i.e. the Spitfire.

What I do remember was looking out for 'Wellington Bridge'. I obviously made it over okay as I am here to tell this tale. Indeed, I was one of the few women who happily took a Wellington into the skies. I liked all Marks of this aircraft.

Sometimes I was flying a Spitfire just before a Wellington so I was full of fire and happy to handle the Wellington too. The great variety of aircraft helped me appreciate flying large bombers. I'd rather not discuss the speeds of aircraft as it was either in mph or knots. However, I understand the Wellington had a speed of 235 mph at 15,000 feet. But it depended on the aeroplane engine and maybe I included Warwicks in my recall of Wellingtons as they were essentially outsize versions of the latter. I remember that I flew two Warwicks to the Coastal Command airfield at Thorney Island on the South Coast.

Out of all the forty-seven Wellington deliveries I made between September 1943 and January 1946, one especially remains in my memory. This is the time I had to stay over at a Bomber Command airfield one night and I enjoyed a fine meal in the Mess with all these lovely air crew. The place was full of laughter and they were all such decent chaps.

The next morning, I went down to breakfast and there were only two or three men in there, solemnly drinking tea. I asked, 'Where are all the pilots?' The stark reply was, 'They didn't come back from their missions last night'. I felt sad, very sad to hear this and remember writing down my feelings that day.

Earlier on in this chapter I pointed out the detail when it came to the Wellington hatch. Well, once I was flying along quite happily until, horror of horrors, after being airborne for about fifteen minutes, the entry hatch in the floor blew open.

I was petrified. This hatch is approximately the length and width of an average-size table and suddenly, without warning, there was this great hole beside me. Mulling over the predicament I now found myself in, I thought 'What can I do other than go down and shut the lid?'

As I looked down from my seat, there was the earth whistling past, and the draught was almost blowing me through the roof. It was also suddenly very cold. I decided to trim the aircraft so that it would fly on an even keel, then undo all of my straps and climb down and close the door, being extremely careful of course not to fall out – which would have been very easy to do.

So, I undid the straps of the seat, and having released my parachute straps, I climbed out, being frightfully careful not to fall through the hole. By this time, I had trimmed the aeroplane as I thought best to fly straight and low, hoping no one else was in the same stretch of sky at the same time. I did all the necessary things with the catch on the lid to be safe, and within seconds I'd returned to my seat and strapped on my parachute again. I can see myself doing it now and I can't help but laugh at the memory.

Well the hatch stayed shut for a time, only to again fall open after a while. As I was getting near to my destination, according to my own navigational skills, I opted to leave the blessed thing open. I was so sure I'd checked it before take-off, but obviously this particular hatch had a mind of its own.

I probably mentioned this on my report sheet about this particular Wellington, so I hope it was fixed before any RAF crews took it out on a bombing raid. When the RAF flew them they always had a crew of at least five. Always. Did I worry about flying this huge bomber all on my own? No, you don't worry when you know what you are doing.

What else can I say? The word 'worry' never came into it because I knew sufficiently what I had to do and I also was confident in my navigational skills. Remember, we had no aids to assist us. You had to know how to get a new aeroplane which you'd never flown before from A to B. When you're up in the skies navigation is easier and I think I took that particular Wellington with the dodgy hatch-catch to one of those big aerodromes on the East Coast. After that flight, as you can imagine, a good strong cup of tea was in order.

One particular day I was flown to somewhere to collect a Wellington and as usual I made my way to the office, signed the papers, and proceeded to take out my appropriate maps for the flight. It was a serious business collecting an aircraft and on occasion the men seemed to find it very difficult to believe that a mere slip of a girl should be allowed in their aircraft, let alone fly them.

So I climbed up the ladder into the aircraft as usual and took-off gracefully into the clear blue skies, making ready to enjoy my flight. All went very well and I was able to land successfully thirty minutes or so later at my destination, which was of course an RAF base where Bomber Command personnel were waiting patiently for their Wellington.

I taxied the aircraft to the stop-off point and switched off the engines and did a few more checks. Then I undid my straps and took off my parachute and opened the catch on the door. I put the ladder in place and by the time I reached the ground I noticed that some of the ground crew had gathered around me. To them I announced, 'There you are, a lovely new aircraft for you.' To my bitter disappointment they simply replied, 'Where's the pilot!' I replied 'I *am* the pilot!' Well they didn't believe me. I might have repeated the phrase, but one or two of them still decided to clamber on up the ladder and check the aeroplane for the 'missing' pilot.

To their amazement they obviously discovered that I had been telling the truth. They just could not believe women could fly these aeroplanes and it was a surprise for them to see me – a slim blonde female of five feet, two inches tall flying such a giant aircraft. This story is legendary now and I know this kind of reaction from the men often happened to the other ATA women pilots too. I remember I first told the 'I *am* the pilot' story at a party in the 1960s. People always seem to find it most amusing and the phrase 'I *am* the pilot' has become legendary in aviation circles.

An ATA pilot who later became Commanding Officer at No.9 Ferry Pool at Aston Down, near Stroud, was Hugh Bergel, author of two books about flying wartime aircraft. He shared my love for the Wellington and once wrote:

'The Wellington was one of the most likeable aeroplanes ever built. It used to rattle along like an airborne tram, easy to drive, utterly reliable and with beautiful manners. From time to time as you cruised along the controls used to twitch slightly, as though there was someone else in the back helping you to keep it on course. Also the flap mechanism was inter-connected with the elevator trim control, so that at times the trim control wheel would turn without being touched by the pilot. And it was on a Wimpey that I achieved, by luck, the only perfect landing I have ever done – so perfect that I had been running along the grass for 100 yards before I knew I had touched down. No wonder I liked the Wimpey.

'Wellingtons came with a variety of engines. The Bristol Pegasus was the most usual but they also came with American Twin Wasps, with Rolls-Royce Merlins, and with Bristol Hercules. Then there was the very rare Wellington Mk.VI, which I once flew and once was enough! This must have been the RAF's first pressure-cabin aeroplane. The normal Wellington front fuselage was replaced with what seemed to be a cylindrical steel boiler, approached from the rear through something like the door of a strong-room. The pilot could see out, more or less, by putting his head up inside a small glass goldfish bowl. Two very special high-altitude Merlins were fitted, driving very large four-bladed airscrews. It was the only unlikeable Wimpey. The pilot's view was so bad that taxiing along a perimeter track was misery. In the air she felt un-wieldy, and the familiar Wimpey control-twitch had become a St. Vitus' dance.

'An ATA pilot once successfully force-landed a Wimpey Mk.VI on an aerodrome without scratching anybody or anything, after partial failure of both engines, which I reckon is the cleverest piece of airmanship I ever heard of. My short flight ended with the second worst landing I have ever made, so perhaps I'm prejudiced.'

Today it is well worth visiting Brooklands Museum where the rare Wellington on display gives one a good sense of the size of these magnificent aircraft which played a key role in the war effort.

Chapter 18

D-Day Spitfires

It was always understood by everyone in the ATA that ferrying aircraft was a great responsibility and it was our duty to do our best at all times to make sure the RAF and Fleet Air Arm pilots had the aircraft they needed with which to fight the war.

The philosophy of the ATA was that a good ferry pilot should be able to get into any type of aircraft, often unseen, and fly, and deliver it safely, to any airfield.

I always flew alone and was completely free to decide my course of action. I liked the freedom of being in the air as it was liberating in all sorts of ways. I never wore a leather helmet while I was flying and couldn't see the point as there was no radio. Of course it would never happen like that now.

The notorious weather in the UK sometimes prevented one from carrying out the intended daily programme and quite often one was stranded an RAF airfield, and generally speaking these were not terribly comfortable occasions, unaccustomed as service pilots were to having a woman pilot at the airfield. I remember the loos at the airfield were usually for men only and visiting women pilots had to make their own arrangements. Sometimes I would have to land and just spend a penny in a convenient bush or visit the gents at the airfield and hope one of them didn't come in!

One of the Polish ATA women, Anna Leska, once said she had no choice but to squat behind a wooden hut because she was so desperate to pee. She exclaimed how she wouldn't have stopped even if the King had walked by! We soon learned the penalties of drinking too much tea before taking off. For us ATA women needing to visit the convenience, we could sometimes find a WAAF unit nearby.

It was in the all-women accommodation blocks that the ATA girls had to find a bed if they needed to stay overnight. Occasionally the billet was full of WAAF which meant the stranded ATA pilots would have to wait to jump into a warm bed left by a WAAF going on her night shift duty.

There was the time when I landed an aircraft at an RAF airfield and, owing to bad weather, I had to stay overnight. It was snowing hard and bitterly cold that afternoon, and I explained to an RAF officer I would need somewhere to sleep as there were no female quarters at the station. So I was taken to an empty officer's room where a small stove smouldered ineffectively in the middle of the room. These tiny so-called heat providers were dreadful and rarely filled a room with much warmth at all. When they did ever expel a serious blast of heat it got so hot the window had to be flung open. I might as well have lit a match and warmed my hands around it. Also the food was in the men-only Officers Mess.

That night I remember I kept most of my clothes on as I was so cold and I curled up on that hard bed waiting desperately for the morning. I don't think I slept much, and it was never much fun being stranded away from your own bed at night without friends around. Not long after dawn the following morning an orderly came in and said 'Your tea Sir'! I think he had forgotten I was a woman or maybe hadn't really acknowledged the fact in the first place. Remember, the idea of women flying military aircraft was still an alien concept to many men.

There was another time I had to spend three nights in a Nissen Hut at Millum airfield on the Scottish Border, and I have never been so cold in my life. It was because of bad weather that I had landed a Hurricane there and made ready to sit out the snow and the sleet.

There were numerous ATA ferry pools which refused to allow women pilots to join them. Whitchurch near Bristol was one of them. When Hamble ATA was wound down in the August of 1945 they had to accept a few of us. I understand it took a few rounds of cards and some friendly banter to break the ice in that ferry pool. Apparently when the Whitchurch pilots first heard there were women on the way they said 'those girls needn't think we're here just to carry their parachutes'.

I often wonder what they thought of the idea we were receiving equal pay to them. This coup for female ferry pilots was achieved by Senior Commander Pauline Gower and the Conservative MP (later Dame) Irene Ward in 1943. It was a significant and important step in the campaign for equality and the ATA women's section had quite rightly broken through the barrier. At the time of course I didn't realise the magnitude of what Pauline had achieved, for not just us ATA women but the impact her actions would have on the prosperity of future generations of professional women trying to make it in a tough man's world.

My incident at Brize Norton with the toppled Spitfire, although unwanted, shows something of my determination to deliver all of the aircraft on my daily chit. Some days I was flying four or five different aircraft from 09.00 hours until I'd finished. The decision whether or not to fly was always the sole responsibility of the ATA pilots. Sadly, four out of five fatalities in the ATA occurred during bad weather.

Some ATA records claim we were ordered to continue to deliver aircraft in inclement conditions, and yet the pilots always maintained the decision was ours to make as we were civilian air crew. We did not take 'orders' from the military. We picked up our chits in the morning and did our very best to uphold the supply and demand of aircraft.

I am a rather reserved person and with that comes quietude. I have a calm but determined nature which always led to me to focus on whatever I set my mind to – for much of my life it was flying. This helped me through the intensive ATA schedule and in making decisions about flying in adverse weather.

At Hamble we often received our weather reports from Jackie 'Met', who would always let us know what conditions we could expect for our journey. She was very good at her job and her reports were usually accurate. Of course, one had to be prepared for all eventualities and use good judgement if one flew into sudden inclement weather. I studied a lot of maps and needed to know the hills, or as the American women pilots called them 'canyons', to avoid at all costs.

My ATA colleague First Officer Naomi Allen summed up how many of us dealt with the weather issue. She wrote the following in her diary, a quote which was later published in the book, *Naomi The Aviatrix*:

'Wednesday, 1 September 1943. When I am safely on the ground picturing myself flying blind, lost, frightened to death, I say, No, of course I don't fly in bad weather. It's a mug's game. But directly I am given a job, particularly if it is Priority 1, I can't bear to sit on the ground without even trying to get through. Even in the air I find myself saying what a fool I am not to have turned back sooner, and I swear to myself I'll never do it again. And so the vicious circle goes on. What is it that makes a pilot want to get through if he (or she) possibly can? Certainly not fear that others may laugh at him if he doesn't. That is rarely – if ever – the driving force behind him. More often I think it is one's inborn pride in doing a job well that makes one hate to throw in the sponge until one knows there is no alternative.'

It is true there was pressure on the ATA women to succeed in a male-orientated world. The ultimate sin was to 'break an aeroplane' and give the RAF something to complain about. We tried our best to uphold standards and for those of us who might have experienced an occasion when damage was caused to an aircraft in our care, then the guilt lasted for a while, even if it wasn't our fault.

One or two women even asked to be transferred to other ferry pools in case the mud stuck to their name and reputation. However, most pilots learned quickly that it was important to brush away comments and behaviour deemed in today's world as sexist and chauvinistic, and to keep their confidence high.

I did have to chuckle when my ATA colleague and friend Joy Lofthouse (nee Gough) appeared on a recent television documentary about wartime flying when they asked her about gender-bias. She said in those days nobody had ever heard of sexism let alone what it actually was. Joy said she felt glad if anyone pinched her bottom as at least she'd been noticed!

My friend Jackie Sorour (Moggridge), who I first met at Witney in 1938, didn't hesitate to record her own experiences of discrimination. Always ready to jump in with her viewpoint, I wonder if her strong-willed behaviour almost landed her a posting to Cosford, which in 1943 was to become the second all-women's ferry pool. All of us at Hamble wondered who would be chosen to go to Cosford and there was a suggestion the tough girls would be sent there as Hamble was just for the glamour girls! One day Jackie was in tears because she was perceived as a 'toughie' and Cosford seemed to beckon. But it didn't and she remained with me at Hamble. Were we glamorous? Who knows? I know I didn't have much time to worry about the latest fashions and the joys of choosing lipsticks when there were aircraft waiting to be delivered.

Jackie had been posted to a radar station with the WAAF at the early outset of the war and then finally, after a lot of determination, managed to get a transfer to the Air Transport Auxiliary. By 1944, at least 500 WAAFs had applied to join the ATA. Many had been encouraged to think about training to be a pilot when the *ab initio* scheme was introduced in 1943, but eventually only a handful of WAAFs were able to join us. Sometimes we bumped into some of those girls who had applied to join the ATA but had been turned down and went back to their WAAF duties. I think they were a little envious of us, but generally we all got on well.

On the day war broke out Jackie recalls she'd taken off from Witney in peacetime as an instructor with a trainee pilot and they had flown quite respectfully over Oxford and Reading glorying in a bright blue sky. When they landed a couple of hours later solemn faces at the airfield told them Britain was now at war with Germany. Well, she thought her life was over. No more dreaming about working as a professional pilot. This was serious, she was a woman and she was grounded.

Before the war she had already found it hard enough convincing her anxious mother and doubting family, that she was going to gain an 'A' pilot's licence whether they liked it or not so she left her home in South Africa and headed to England in 1938.

Surviving records from 1939 reveal there were 100 women pilots in the UK, but it was perceived by many subscribers to the patriarchy, that, writes Jackie, 'it was not in the national interest to trust vital aircraft to the whims and fancies of feminine pulchritude'. Despite this attitude at the time, her story turns out to be one of hope, of ambition and a lesson in fortitude and reserve. She never gave up on her dream.

We were to work together again after the war and had both learned that despite everything women had achieved in aviation before and during the war, they still weren't completely trusted to be at the controls of an aircraft. Jackie felt strongly about this kind of prejudice and has talked about the treatment she received from some men on the airfield who made stupid jokes about the 'time of the month' and how it made women crazy so they shouldn't be allowed near an aircraft.

I remember there was a particular day which brought her face to face with discrimination. Her diminutive figure made her look about 12-years-old. Anyway she went to pick up a de Havilland Mosquito and went along with her permission chit to the engineering officer who was about six feet four inches tall.

Jackie said this man came right up to her and asked if she was 'supposed to be the pilot taking his aircraft'. He told her he'd been working on the aircraft for two weeks and he wasn't going to have any schoolgirl flying it. 'It's made of wood,' he said and told Jackie that if she flew it she would 'smash it up'.

So she showed him her permission chit and authorisation, but he still refused to believe her. He had to ring up Home Command and get the clearance for her to fly off.

It was the forthright Jackie who also raised the subject of continuing to carry out ferrying duties despite the gnawing pain caused by the monthly menstrual cycle. One day Jackie flew a heavy bomber with a hot water bottle on her stomach as she was in agony, but there was no way she was not going to fly.

She wrote: 'I had this clumsy old aircraft to fly and suddenly the engineer asked "What's this, is it a hot water bottle?" and I told him it was mine. He then told me I couldn't fly with a hot water bottle as it was too hot and it was summer time. Of course I couldn't tell him why I had it with me. You just didn't bother to say anything back to them then.'

In 1945 Jackie married a British Army officer, Reg Moggridge. At the end of the war she received the King's Commendation for Valuable Service in the Air. Like me, Jackie was lucky and continued her career in aviation long after the war. She gained her RAF wings in 1952 in readiness to fly a Meteor jet. I was one of just two women seconded to the RAF from the ATA in 1946 to pilot the Meteor. After the war Jackie flew Spitfires to Burma, and transported twin-engine aircraft around the Middle East.

Jackie's favourite aircraft was the Mosquito. I also loved to fly this swift and capable twin-engine bomber. That said, however, the wooden-framed 'Mossie' could prove a challenge to land. Evidence of my friend's much-missed mirth includes a story about the day she flew a Spitfire towards an RAF airfield and, just to tease the men on the ground, she had the flaps down quite early. When she'd done a couple of circuits and landed they ran over to her and told her she'd been flying with her flaps down. 'What flaps?' she replied. Their faces were a picture. Sometimes she liked to play into their hands!

When she died in 2004 I knew instantly how I would greatly miss her sense of fun and that ready laugh that always cheered everyone up. She had joined the ATA as number fifteen out of 166. She was an extraordinarily brave young women who in desperate need 'to get on with the job of flying' learned to laugh off morale-crushing socio-political taboos in a bid to help a country in its hour of need.

In April 1944, I was posted to AFTS No.1 White Waltham Ferry Pool for a refresher course and Hudson aircraft training for ten days. White Waltham airfield was often overcrowded with many types of aircraft being operated at the same time. I returned to Hamble authorised to fly Class IV+. This was wonderful and it meant I was now qualified to fly all types of military aircraft.

I was in the Ops Room at Hamble at 09.00 hours on 18 May 1944, when the chitties were already out on the table, so I had no time to call my friend to say 'thanks for a wonderful evening'. But duty comes first and mine was to be taxi pilot after I'd delivered:

Spitfire Mk.VIII MT675 from Eastleigh to Brize Norton.
Taxi Fairchild 804 from Brize Norton to South Cerney (Cotswolds) with one passenger, T/O Ratcliffe.
South Cerney to Babdown with Second Officer Freydis Leaf.
Babdown to Hamble with Second Officer Williams on board.

Taxi Fairchild 776 from Hamble to Thorney, Cambridgeshire with Second Officer Williams as passenger, again to Christchurch (New Forest).
Christchurch to Hamble.

In fact, I did seven landings in one day. Thank heavens it had been clear conditions and navigation was not a problem, but it was undoubtedly a full day's operation and was one carried out with great care – a typical ATA girl's flying day really.

By June 1944, with the Normandy landings looming, the pressure was on. It was a period during which I piloted a number of Spitfires, all of different Marks, from Hamble to airfields like Seighford (Staffordshire), Aston Down, Cosford, Cowley Factory, Brize Norton, Lyneham. We knew something was building up, as suddenly all these American ships started arriving at the docks on the South Coast.

Just before D-Day the invasion fleets were drawn up in the Solent, (ships are difficult to hide), so flying from our base at Hamble we could see daily the enormous build up. The Solent was an astonishing sight – there were so many ships it would have been possible to walk across this stretch of water to the mainland by striding across the decks of these great floating vessels of war.

There were hundreds and hundreds of them stretching as far as the eye could see. It was an image I will remember forever. It really did seem as if the Isle of Wight and the mainland had been joined together. We, of course, were never to talk about what we'd seen. As would be expected, we had very little knowledge of any sort of military plans.

Flying from Hamble on that fateful day of 6 June 1944, gave us a jolly good view of the Solent and it had been possible to glimpse so much extraordinary activity and ship movements. My ATA friend Mary Fuller Hall and I decided that if we made little parachutes from handkerchiefs and attached them to little bottles with a message inside we could drop them from the Fairchild taxi aircraft and someone might pick them up and visit the ATA!

We were very careful not to reveal our names while carrying out this activity. Whether or not any soldier, airman or sailor did find our little bottles containing those notes remains a mystery. As far as I know there were no particular visitors who arrived at Hamble after D-Day looking for the authors of those messages.

On D-Day itself I flew three Spitfires. I felt I was playing my role too on this great day, which was of course to prove a great surge forward towards victory in Europe.

My first D-Day Spitfire was a Mk.IX, serial number BS242, and I flew it from Hamble to the Cowley factory. Then I piloted the taxi Fairchild from Brize Norton to Hamble. Not long after this flight I was in the cockpit of Spitfire Mk.IX, ML314, to deliver it to RAF Aston Down, which is six miles west of Cirencester. For me D-Day had begun to feel like a relay race as I knew the clock was ticking on the invasion plans every time I started up the engine and taxied on to the runway to take-off.

By the afternoon of 6 June I was in the cockpit of another Mk.IX Spitfire, this one with the serial number ML323. Once again I was to land at Aston Down, which in 1944 had been designated as an invasion pool. All of us in the ATA were tremendously busy as the RAF air crews desperately needed every aircraft possible to join the mass formations preparing to make their way over the Channel or supporting the Operation *Overlord* itself.

June 1944 was to prove a seriously busy time for all of us in the ATA. We were on constant alert for the RAF and Fleet Air Arm calls for more and more aircraft. The winds of victory were blowing in our direction and we all felt urged on by the prospect that Europe was on the verge of liberation.

What was strange, though, was when I flew over the same places the next day. On 7 June every ship, aircraft, tank, lorry and line of troops had disappeared. It was as if they'd never been there – it was an amazing, almost eerie, sensation.

It took me a few seconds to tell myself I hadn't imagined any of it. In just twenty-four hours that unforgettable vision, sight and sound amassed for D-Day had been swallowed up into the vacuum of fate and its determination of a world's history.

The rest of the month proved just as active as I successfully delivered a dozen more Spitfires, including, by way of an illustration, a Seafire, NM365, on 25 June. The Spitfires were flown in between my piloting other aircraft too, including twin-engine bombers and hefty seaplanes like my least favourite aircraft, the Walrus.

By the time October had introduced us to the balm of autumn I had ferried thirty aircraft in a month, the total made up from twelve different types.

During the winter months of 1944 the amount of ATA flying was somewhat reduced. This was mostly because of the weather, but also because of the state of the landing areas which were reduced to little more than strips in a field. Nevertheless, my Logbook tells me that during January, February and March 1945 my actual time airborne was achieved with dexterity and airmanship. The type of aircraft I flew that winter included Spitfires, Barracudas, Hurricanes, Albacores, Wellingtons, Oxfords, Ansons, Swordfish and Skuas, landing at no less than thirty-five airfields.

A few months later, in 1945, RAF Brize Norton played host to the Luftwaffe, but by then the war in Europe was over and, ironically, the Maintenance Unit crew worked on and studied captured German aircraft. A Junkers Ju 88, a Focke-Wulf Fw 190 and a Henschel He 219 could all be seen in and around the hangars at various times.

Chapter 19

Shared Memories

Obviously I cannot think about my ATA days without mentioning my numerous adventures. There was a time I was flying in mist close to Bournemouth when an anti-aircraft gun starting firing at me as I passed by the coast. Quickly I turned the aircraft around and headed inland. I believe that the local Home Guard thought I was an enemy aircraft.

Fortunately, they missed and no damage was done but I remember seeing small, black puffs of smoke appearing to the side of my aircraft. It took me a few seconds to realise what was happening. I was not amused. When other ATA pilots mentioned a similar and frightening experience a report was filed and sent to the authorities and a reprimand was in order for the unit commander. Aircraft identification information needed to be vastly improved, although in their defence I did point out my aircraft wasn't flying the 'colour of the day' which would have helped them identify a British aircraft more clearly.

Another remarkable, and deeply memorable event, was the time I was stalked by a Luftwaffe pilot. I happened to be flying near Pershore, Evesham, when out of the corner of my eye I spotted this aeroplane with black swastikas right beside me. I thought this was most unusual and I certainly didn't want another aircraft flying so close to me in that way. I knew I was exactly on course and I was not keen on losing my way, also the weather wasn't too good or clear either, so with one hand I waved at this pilot to move away and get out of my sight.

He didn't disappear as I'd asked him to, so I waved again and again, because by now he was making me go off course. I can picture his grinning face now. Then he cheekily waved back again and again – and then suddenly he was gone.

I had no idea what type of aircraft it was but it had black swastikas on the tail and the fuselage. I was alarmed to think it might have been an enemy pilot and yet he'd seemed quite determined to gain my attention. To this day I have no idea who he was. I was very frightened at the time, especially as it was not an aircraft I thought I knew.

Perhaps he flew next to me for those few minutes staring in disbelief because it was a woman at the controls. I wondered if it was my blonde curls that caused him to stare as I never ever wore a helmet during my whole career with the ATA. What was the point of a helmet when we couldn't speak to anyone? It didn't do much for the hairstyle either.

I wonder as well if it might have been a British pilot flying a captured Luftwaffe aircraft and he was out for a test flight? I am afraid I shall never know either way. If it was a German pilot I am jolly lucky he didn't decide to attack my Spitfire.

Perhaps the mystery pilot thought I was an angel? I can still picture that aircraft and the pilot now. His face was really quite distinctive, almost bemused, and he was desperate to gain my full attention. I had to try so hard to get away from him and in doing so I went right off course. We weren't told by the ATA how to cope if we were fired upon, which when I think about it, that's quite an alarming hole in our training, especially when we were often flying about in Spitfires or Hurricanes or bombers – natural targets for the deadly Luftwaffe looking to pitch their Me109s against a British military aircraft.

Some years after the war I learned how No.1426 Flight was also known as the 'Rafwaffe'. This unit was set up to test captured enemy aircraft and make comparative notes on them against the effectiveness of our own aircraft. I understand there were a dozen or so enemy aircraft on charge with the RAE Farnborough section which were undergoing tests.

The 'Rafwaffe' with its mission to 'evaluate and demonstrate' Luftwaffe aircraft, also operated out of RAF Duxford in Cambridgeshire and RAF Collyweston in Northamptonshire. No.1426 Flight had been set up originally at RAF Duxford in 1940 and by the end of the war all sorts of Luftwaffe aircraft, including Heinkel He IIIs, Junkers Ju 88s and Messerschmitt Me 110s had been captured and flown by the RAF.

If it was an RAF test pilot I saw that day flying a German aircraft, then I'd like to know why they hadn't replaced the black crosses with an RAF roundel. I would have felt much less frightened.

Some of the ATA pilots were involved in skirmishes with German aircraft and we got shot at by our own people on the ground, but it was an attendant risk and all part of the job. I think most of us were more concerned about the weather and the balloon barrages than being shot at.

All the aircraft that were ferried in the ATA were by no means new and we would often have to collect obsolete aircraft and fly them to the breakers' yard. These included shot-up aircraft that were just flyable, those that had to go to certain places for armament, or those in need of certain repair and checks which had to be flown to the Maintenance Units (MUs) as they were called.

One of my favourite stories includes the day the Commanding Officer of an RAF airfield was in the Control Tower and had been told a female pilot was about to take off in her first Mosquito delivery flight. He barked: 'Who passes these girl pilots out?' and was told 'Er – nobody Sir, they are just trained to fly strange aircraft from their little Blue Book!' (Ferry Pilots Notes).

As a stoic young woman with a deep commitment to the job, I batted off discrimination in my own quiet way. I was aware how irritating the attitude of some men could be and had indeed experienced it first-hand. I found out very early on what a mountain there was to climb if a woman pilot was ever to be taken seriously.

In an interview with a national newspaper in 2009, my friend ATA female pilot Freydis Leaf (Sharland) spoke forthrightly about encounters with discrimination. She recalled: 'I had one man who refused to fly with me because he said he wasn't going to be flown by a woman. I was absolutely furious and had to sit in the aircraft while he took charge!'

I remember Freydis very well. She was a warm and nurturing type of woman and was always there for us if we needed support of any kind. She was like a lovely mother hen who I could imagine would one day be surrounded by happy children. I was terribly sad to hear of her death in 2014.

Another ATA colleague who encountered male chauvinism was Third Officer Eirene Bannister (Seccombe) who recalled how she had to fly her first Barracuda from Worthy Down.

In a recording for the Imperial War Museum's Department of Sound in 1987, she recalled: 'I was nervous and remarked to the chap in Flying Control it was my first Barracuda, but instead of being supportive and talking politely to me about the aircraft he started ringing people up saying things like "there's some girl here wanting to take one of our Barracudas and she's never flown one before". I think he was a failed pilot as he was behaving quite nastily. He thought it was disgraceful [that] I should be flying the Barracuda but he was told I had permission to do it and I did but it didn't help my confidence. I left my logbooks behind so he was even more pleased, I am sure, but that was male chauvinism because he was so annoyed.'

Despite such attitudes espoused by some men, British woman Sheila Roche made headway and in the ATA became the first female instructor in aircraft engineering; and former schoolteacher, my friend Pat Parker, was the first ATA female flight engineer. Pat's skills meant that four-engine bombers like the Halifax and the Lancaster could be flown by an all-women crew. Other highly valued women flight engineers included Mrs Phyllis Pierce and Mrs Barbara Thomas. (Janice Harrington was the fourth woman flight engineer but she was killed in a Mosquito accident along with my friend Dora Lang on 3 March 1944, as mentioned earlier).

One of the most detailed accounts of a particular kind of male attitude to woman at the controls of a four-engine aircraft is recounted by a wry Captain Henderson, an RAF officer based at Pocklington, Yorkshire. He recalled the day ATA First Officer Lettice Curtis went solo in a Handley Page Halifax. (Curtis was the first British woman of the ATA to fly a four-engine bomber). This was a seminal moment in the history of aviation and it indicated once again that heavy aircraft could be flown just as well with a woman at the controls.

Captain Henderson's vivid account reads like a scene from a cartoon. He wrote in his diary:

> The Halifax had barely taken off when the Control Room was invaded by no less a person than the Group Captain commanding the Station, accompanied by an Army Staff General. Everyone snapped to attention, momentarily overpowered by the weight of red tabs and 'scrambled eggs' (gold braids).
>
> 'Oh hello Henderson! No work this morning?' asked the Station-master in a fatherly manner.
>
> 'Just watching a first solo, Sir', I replied.
>
> The Control Officer could contain himself no longer.
>
> 'It's a woman pilot, Sir.'
>
> 'It's a WHAT?!' gasped the SM and turning to the General said, 'Come on Fred we must watch this'.
>
> He led the way hastily out onto the balcony. Arriving there he discovered the runway in use was the one adjacent to the Control Tower and passing it within about thirty yards. He thereupon returned to the Control Tower as hastily as he'd left it.
>
> 'Which way will the Halifax swing when it lands?' He sounded urgent.
>
> 'Away from the Control Tower with this wind, Sir,' replied the Control Officer.

The SM was relieved and returned to the Control Tower with Fred. I said nothing. Suddenly the loudspeaker began to buzz and Lettice's voice came through: 'May I come into land? Over.' The Control Officer nodded. 'You may land,' returned the operator. 'Over.' I watched confidently, the others excitedly.

The great undercarriage appeared and slowly extended itself. The Halifax slowed perceptibly, made its final turn toward the aerodrome and descended steadily towards the runway. It crossed the runway, checked its descent and held off just above the ground. Then the wheels kissed the surface gently and the thirty-ton aircraft rolled steadily down the runway in the smooth manner which seldom characterises a first solo and came to a dignified halt.'

'It didn't swing,' said the SM in a musing tone. 'It didn't even bounce. And my lads have always kidded me how difficult Halifaxes are. Why damn it, they must be easy if a little girl can fly them like that!'

I said Lettice wasn't so little. He snorted. I told him Lettice had 2,000 flying hours and a lot of variegated types of aircraft in her logbook.

'Has she by Gad!' he said.

He thought for a moment, then 'Come on, Fred. Let's drink a half-can before lunch.'

I am a great admirer of Lettice Curtis' numerous books about aviation, including *The Forgotten Pilots* which was published in 1971. Lettice was totally committed to her ATA career. I met her often at various aviation events after the war and I know she was in demand as a speaker. She was a forthright person who did not suffer fools, but those who knew her would say she was a soft woman at heart. During her time in the ATA she was quite fearless and determined. There's a famous photograph of her sitting in a bomber aircraft with Pauline Gower beside her as co-pilot. Pauline's grin looks somewhat strained. It was known the two women didn't really get on too well and some believed Lettice's headstrong attitude prevented her from being promoted to the position of CO at her own ferry pool.

It was a big day for the ATA when Eleanor Roosevelt, wife of the US President, arrived at White Waltham. During her visit she spotted Lettice sheltering from the rain beneath the wing of a four-engine Halifax bomber. They got talking and America's First Lady was most impressed when she heard Lettice had been chosen as the first woman to fly aircraft as large as the Halifax. At this time Lettice had already flown up to ninety types of aircraft and that was not to be sniffed at.

I was busy flying RAF aircraft to and from ATA and RAF stations that day so I missed out on Mrs Roosevelt's visit, but I understand everything went to plan and the First Lady was happy to hear that Lettice and the rest of us were helping to promote the cause of women at work in wartime. Mrs Clementine Churchill was also in the VIP party who toured our No.1 Ferry Pool and headquarters at White Waltham that wet autumn day, and I can only suppose those who met her were glad she had some idea of what we were all contributing to the nation in its time of great need.

I later had the opportunity to train for the relevant Class V licence and became a co-pilot on aircraft like the mighty four-engine Avro Lancaster, Handley Page Halifax and Short Stirling. When the war came to an end so did my four-engine training. This was a shame as I enjoyed my time in the cockpit of these large aircraft. I have been asked if I would like to have flown a Short Sunderland flying boat but during the war they were not allowed to have mixed crews so women were forbidden to go near the cockpit. Quite frankly, the Sunderland is far too big and I wasn't upset never to have flown one. I must say I have visited the one at Duxford, though, and have seen inside it. It's really very beautiful and luxurious inside.

Whilst I had a mostly happy time at Hamble there were other women ATA pilots who found it too 'schoolgirlish'. I do remember meeting a shy young woman in spectacles called Mary de Bunsen (1910-1982) who had overcome the effects of childhood polio and defective eyesight to finally be allowed to join the ATA. She was always a little aloof with the rest of us but now I can put that down to shyness. Most of her friends were outside the ATA and she had many hobbies in those days to keep her busy on her days off, including sailing her small yacht on the Solent.

She wrote: 'At Hamble I found myself in another "girls" school but these girls, being daily at grips with the elements, were a good deal more mature. They were reputed to be very tough and very feminine, and this I found to be true. Women are not necessarily tough because they fly, but this war-time flying required a certain amount of backbone. It was not, however, good form to be assertive, though some of my weather-beaten seniors were a little alarming at first.'

Despite being happy in her local digs Mary de Bunsen described how she found Hamble 'a rather harassing place because it was in a fighter-control zone and you had to do everything on time and be routed in and out of it in case you got shot at.' She also regarded Hamble as 'all short flights and taxi journeys'. She wrote:

'I always found it hard to get ready in a hurry. We never saw the enemy, but there were constant air-raid warnings and we took no notice of them as they interfered with our work. One day four of us took off in a Fairchild Argus four-seater taxi during an alert, and the guns opened up as we turned on course. We could see shell-splinters splashing in the mud and were rather frightened so we came down low and skedaddled up the Hamble River at nought feet.

'The Hamble was lined with troops who knew perfectly well who we were and cheered loudly because they could see the enemy aircraft and ours was the only defending aeroplane in sight, beating it as fast as possible with four frightened female faces flattened against the window panes.'

When she was at Hatfield, and like many ATA newbies including myself, Mary de Bunsen was placed under the watchful eye of one of the first eight ATA women, the 23-year-old Joan Hughes. I remember Joan – a diminutive, pretty woman, who helped us polish up our flying and instil confidence. This was very important for us to know we were equally as capable as the men when it came to flying aircraft. Joan was such a natural pilot and taught us all so much in her calm and friendly manner.

My ATA friend the late Molly Rose also recalled what a pleasant person Joan always was and how the famous photograph of tiny Joan standing beside the huge wheel of a Short Stirling four-engine bomber is a legendary marker of women's aviation achievements during the Second World War.

After the war Joan Hughes MBE, who could 'fly anything', was lucky to continue her aviation career. By the 1960s she was based at the ATA's former headquarters at White Waltham, Berkshire, as an instructor with Airways Aero Association.

In 1964 I watched her fly a replica Santos-Dumont Demoiselle monoplane from 1909 in the film *Those Magnificent Men in Their Flying Machines* and then in 1966 she was hired by a film company to fly a replica aircraft in a First World War epic *The Blue Max*. Two years later and Joan was impressing her former ATA colleagues again with her aerobatics in a Tiger Moth for the *Thunderbirds 6* film!

Joan, who never married, moved to Devon in later life and spent her days looking after her horse. Molly believed Joan had a fiancé and was left heartbroken when he was killed during the war. Many of us were sad to hear of Joan's death in 1993. She was 75-years-old. When a service was held for Joan in Maidenhead the church was crowded. Joan was a wonderful person and a delight to know. Unsurprisingly, she is fondly remembered today by those many, many people still piloting aircraft thanks to her exceptional flying instruction courses.

When Molly was asked what sort of young woman I was during my days in the ATA, she said I was always quiet, reserved and diligent. I don't think I've changed that much.

Molly said: 'Mary Wilkins was and is a shy girl but she always, always had time to stop and chat if you want to share your experiences with her. Of course Mary had flown more types of aircraft than me and was more experienced. She is one of the best.'

Molly was very kind to think so highly of me, although I couldn't be 'shy' when I was managing commandant of Sandown Airport in the 1950s and 1960s. The local boys who used to run about on the airfield when it was active got short shrift from me, I can tell you. They probably called me names but I had to be stern with them then. I was responsible for safety at the airport and I couldn't have children scampering about when there were aircraft and machinery about the place.

What I liked about Molly was her forthright attitude. She would always let you know what she was thinking and her in later years as a Justice of the Peace, she was introduced to all sorts of opinions and people. She was also a Deputy Lieutenant of Oxfordshire and had an OBE. I don't think she was frightened of anyone. Later I will write about a situation with some television people which made Molly furious.

I think Molly was the only person I knew now who has, like me, seen almost a century of flight in their lifetime. She lived in the lovely Oxfordshire village of Bampton, not far from my old homestead of Brize Norton, and Molly's son Graham Rose is the chairman of the Air Transport Auxiliary Association which organises our veteran ATA get-togethers and numerous events. I saw Molly as much as is possible at ATA Association meetings at White Waltham or television filming opportunities. Our lives were intertwined in many ways. For a start we both had very supportive and enlightened fathers who believed women could be equal to men. Molly was one of the first women to ever become an aircraft engineer.

In an interview especially for this book she explained how her father, David Marshall, formed Marshall of Cambridge in 1909. This company is still operating in the fields of aerospace, military vehicles, car dealerships and the ownership of Cambridge Airport.

Molly was born in 1920. She once remarked: 'My father was unusual in the fact he encouraged me to be an engineer and fly. Daddy wanted his girls to have skills and know how to be independent. That was his absolute aim in life. The next sister from me was five years older ... I thought I would come home and housekeep for daddy, but he thought differently and I started the engineering lark.

'My father was very keen on education and I was the fifth of six sisters. We had an elder brother too. His name was Arthur. Our second brother, Ronald, died as a toddler of meningitis. Sadly, my mother Maud died when she was just fifty-two.

'My brother Arthur was seventeen years older than me and I thought he was pretty special. When I was growing up he went up to Cambridge University and he learned to fly. My father and brother bought a Tiger Moth and it was tethered in a field at the edge of our home in Cambridge.

'If as a little girl I was hanging about as little girls do, he would sometimes say he didn't mind taking this little person with him for a flight. He'd say, "Do you want to jump in" and so of course I leapt into the seat of the Tiger Moth and had some very, very cold flights because I wasn't going to run in and get a cardigan as he might have left without me!

'But despite the fact I was shivering it didn't deter me from my love of flying so when I went home before going off to school in Paris at the age of sixteen, my father said 'do want to learn flying?' and I said 'yes of course' and I had lessons up at the aerodrome and then I went off to school and I got my licence between school in France.

'And, when I came home I really thought I was going to quietly housekeep for my father but he thought better of it and appointed a very capable woman who I instantly disliked because he made a terrible mistake of not warning her about me before I came home. When I got home he said to me "I wonder if you want to go on flying. Have you ever thought about how they work? I said "no but it's a thought," and I asked, "may I sleep on it?". I went to bed that night and thought I don't want to be around with this Mrs Brown (the new housekeeper) all day and that will at least get me out from under her feet. So I went to see daddy that morning and said I think that will be a very good idea and I will enjoy it. He said I've got the overalls for you and you will report for work at 9am Monday morning. So I did just that, and was the only woman working on the hangar floor.

'Of course there were secretaries there and one had to guard against being the boss' daughter as one had, which meant I had to get there earlier than anyone else and stay there later than anyone else. And you don't hang about talking because the job had to be seen to be done.

'The chaps were very kind to me and if there was a bolt or a nut I could not move then one of them would come along and help me. They were much stronger of course. There was one very amusing incident when I was re-wiring a Tiger Moth and was bent double in the cockpit and suddenly I had a slap on the behind and actually I got out of the cockpit, but by that time there was no one to be seen anywhere. I roared with laughter and got back in and went on doing the work. Well they all thought that was really rather good. They thought well at least she's got a sense of humour and so they continued to help me. They were very good about it.

'I went on doing that job. I was already married to Bernard Rose at this stage. I worked on Tiger Moths because they were teaching flying there. I still could work on one now, but I don't think anyone would want me to. Yes of course I could, as you always feel you can do these things you were trained to do. The only engineering thing I did when we were married and living in Bampton was coping with a motor mower. I thought this is daft. I am not going to do this again, and I realised sharpening the blades was not my forte.

'At the beginning of 1942 my husband Bernard was in tanks and I found out he was being sent out to the Middle East. I went out to Catterick before he embarked, but just before that I found out my father had died. By the time I got to Cambridge there were a tremendous number of letters, mostly about my father, and among them was a letter for me from the Air Transport Auxiliary saying "we see you've got a pilot's licence, would you think about joining us?" So I thought, well, Bernard has gone off to the Middle East, I've no idea when I will see him again and my father's not here anymore and my life is going to change considerably.

'No, had he been alive and seen my letter from the ATA he would have been the first to say "take your chances and enjoy it". The ATA found out about me because I was number W.98 licence. The ninety-eighth English woman to have a licence, so they knew that. I replied to their letter and said 'yes I will have a go' and with three weeks I was in the ATA and ferrying aircraft.

'I didn't have that many hours in my logbook. There are more hours clocked up getting in and out of an aircraft than there are being in the air. I can't remember exactly but not very many. When you first joined ATA they obviously gave people a test flight, and one of the first eight ATA women, Joan Hughes, tested me.

'She passed me and that's when I started ferrying. By the time Bernard got to Cairo I sent him a cable telling him "have joined the ATA I hope you don't mind" so I was quite civil and he had no idea what ATA was. I went off to photographer Jonathan Wilding in London who did extremely good pictures, and of course everyone looks good in a uniform, the chaps as well, particularly the young. I went up to London in my uniform with my wings on my tunic and I had my picture taken and I sent two of them to Bernard, and he must have wondered what the Dickens he had married! He was quite pleased with it and that was good.'

Molly's memories are vast and she agreed with me just how busy our days were. Whilst the press always wanted to visit us as they saw us as 'Glamour Girls', at Hamble we really didn't like that. It was all rather embarrassing to be singled out for photographs.

'Everyone had too much to do to run about posing for cameras,' continued Molly. 'The only reason we got notoriety was in 1940 when Pauline Gower got permission to appoint twelve women pilots.

'I knew Pauline as well as you knew your CO. She was the one who interviewed me when I first arrived with the intention of being accepted. She was brilliant actually, in what she did for women, but even she had to wait three years to get women flying more than the single-engine aircraft fighters. That was just before I joined ATA when Winnie Crossley tested a Hurricane and found it wasn't difficult to handle and Pauline saw there was no reason not to move the women on to the twin-engine types. You were most useful to ATA when you could fly everything.

'By the time I joined ATA in 1942, some months after Mary, they had a very good system of training or converting and you'd fly the single-seaters for a period and you'd go on to the Hurris and Spitfires and go back to school to learn fly the Oxfords – usually at White Waltham and Luton, and that opened up the whole thing for us. You'd be silly not take every chance that's offered, and at that sort of age you do! That opened up the light between us and the tricky twins in the middle, and then you went on to a Hudson which was the heaviest aircraft, and that was the one you just had to have an engineer with you because alone the pilot couldn't put down the landing gear from the cockpit.

'Your pool introduced new types to you as often as they could, and sometimes you had chance of getting the details of it out of the library and possibly had the chance of reading it on the way. We also had the taxi aircraft which took eight passengers and the Fairchild took three.

'There wasn't really competition between us but, like Mary, I do remember asking what everyone else had to fly that day. It was good to talk about the various aircraft in case someone else had already experience of it and could pass it on.

'When I took my first Spitfire flight I was quite controlled about it all really. There was no running about shouting about it. Take off is always easy on an aircraft because you feel it's got to go up cos it's going as fast as it wants to, and in those days once you got into the air you didn't have to keep to your corridor, you didn't have to keep your height. You weren't allowed to be in touch with the ground and you could do what you jolly well liked. I greatly enjoyed the feeling of being in control of this aircraft, then I had to bring this thing in and do the circuit routine and hope I would get a green light to come in and land.

'On my first Spitfire flight I got a green light and didn't do a bad landing and Joan Hughes was watching and signed me off. "Molly can take any of them," she said. You must be able to use both sides of your brain. It was unnerving to have the freedom to fly anywhere I wanted to, but we had to go to the airfield we were designated to. It was no good diving down looking at the railway stations for signs to show me where I was, because they had all been taken down like the road signs so as to confuse the Hun when he arrived in England.

'The most wonderful thing to hang on to was the spirit level in the aircraft. We also had a compass and wonderful maps we could become addicted to. The things of most help then were railway lines because they didn't move and woods because we weren't felling enormous numbers of trees and they didn't change shape. Landmarks like churches weren't that much help to the pilot as you don't really see the height of the spire. Obviously I saw cathedrals, but small churches didn't really show you the way to an airfield.

'Whilst we got our list of aircraft on a chit I was never ordered to fulfil the deliveries. We were civilian pilots. Before take-off, all of us always went to the Met office, and the extraordinary thing was they were only getting reports from around the islands; but they jolly well got it nearer right than they do now even though the information comes in from around the world. During the war if the ATA Met spoke of a warm front coming in from the Cotswolds we could bet it jolly well did.

'I tried very hard not to get into fog. I once frightened myself over the Cotswolds when I was doing just this. I thought I was going to be over the Cotswolds before the mist hit but when I arrived it was there, so I thought OK I will go over it, and I climbed got to one thousand feet. None of us flew high because of wasting fuel and yet I still had to get through the mist. So that day I thought I'd go under it, forgetting about the town of Chipping Norton. I suddenly saw this hill in front of me and, thank goodness, I had enough power in my Spitfire to pull up and go over it! That afternoon I think the good people of Chipping Norton had the fright of their lives, fortunately I never met any of them to ask. But that absolutely cured me of trying to fly through fog. It was a lesson well learned. It has remained with me. I was much more frightened about that than the one occasion I had to do a forced landing when I was flying a Swordfish over the Wreakin.

'All the fields around there looked like pocket handkerchiefs and none of them looked particularly attractive but you don't have long to make up your mind because one thousand feet is not very high. Eventually I saw one, but it was sloping downhill and with no brakes on the Swordfish I went right through the nearest hedge! When I got to the other side of the hedge there was a boy ploughing the field with a couple of horses and so to miss him and the horses I put my left foot hard down and tipped the aircraft over. When I realised the aircraft was coming down I probably said "bloody hell". Not much use saying anything else if no one is going to hear you. The amazing thing was I wasn't more damaged and having missed the boy and horses I was very pleased with myself. That over-rode the shock but I did think the boy would be absolutely furious with me.

'There I was hanging upside down on the straps. I was fortunate I didn't break my neck. The boy was a bit surprised and I told him to take care of the aircraft while I went to the farmhouse to ring headquarters. They said they would pick me up from Cosford. It was a Saturday and there was a dance in the mess that night but two airmen couldn't go as they had to guard the aircraft because it had some G equipment on it. I thought I wasn't going to be in for a happy time if they couldn't have a night out.

'Then I remembered my brother-in-law, Mont, and so I contacted him and said I was nearby in Cosford and needed somewhere to spend the night. He arrived at the mess with two bikes and we cycled to nearest pub and had a very happy meal together. I slept the night in the WAAF mess there and really went back feeling I had been well looked after. When I got back to Hamble they accepted what had happened and no one made fuss and bother.

'The atmosphere at Hamble seemed fine to me. I didn't spend that much time in the mess. Flying is a very individual thing. I did meet Mary (Wilkins) at times and we'd have a good chat. I knew her quite well. She was always very quiet and but always happy to talk if you wanted to.

'In the ATA we had our backs to the wall and everyone was doing what they could to help Britain along. No time for photographs and any messing about. I don't think many of us bothered with make-up when we were working, but I know that Diana (Barnato Walker) like to put on her lipstick and face powder before she left the cockpit!

'The atmosphere in Britain during the war was really remarkable. You did your job and went home and thanked god for Churchill. That was an extraordinary story because he was available when we needed him. I felt terribly embarrassed about the way he was dumped when he was. There was not class question or snobbery. If anyone had a problem, regardless of what they did, if you could drop anything to help you did. I just wish we could have that feeling now, we would be very much happier.

'At the time my husband Bernard was away in North Africa, then he went up through Italy and then came home to re-equip for D-Day in 1944. By then he was adjutant of the regiment and they were based in Norfolk. It was his job to get these wretched Churchill tanks from all over the country, so when I got leave from the ATA to get up to him I thought the most useful thing to do is to find somewhere I could stay very near. We found a little farm and explained to the farmer's wife what the situation was, and I was doing what I could for the country, and I would like to come up and did they have a spare room for us? The farmer's wife said she would ask her husband and they came back to us with a "yes". They were extremely kind and sweet and we had an enormous feather bed we got lost in! They had food nobody else had and very often our breakfast was far more than either of us could eat. There was always a fire in the little sitting room and they would bring us bacon and eggs which wasn't in my usual diet and if it was more than I could manage we burnt it on the fire so as not to hurt her.

'The mealtimes went out of the window with the ATA. We had breakfast at home then that was that. We did get a 2p bar of chocolate and that makes you very popular with nephews and nieces. I seldom ate mine because when you are doing extraordinary things you seldom notice if you're hungry. Then you probably didn't eat until the evening. I went through the day with a cup of tea and that was when I learned to have no milk or sugar in tea or coffee because it was always best to have it as strong as you could find. Better to have it strong without a whole lot of milk and sugar in it to prevent too many pit-stops! Now I still have black tea and coffee. It does make life easier in these times when you get all sorts of different coffee in restaurants. I am just straight and black on the coffee front.

'The Spitfire inevitably was my favourite aircraft. I particularly liked the Boston – a tricycle undercarriage. That was also a favourite aircraft. One Boston and I were stuck out for three days going north and I got to know my aircraft jolly well after three days. I thought I'd like one of these after the war. It would suit me very well.

'Quite honestly, flying different sorts of aircraft is not that different from driving other cars, you've either got the indicators on the left or right, or the vehicle is automatic. Obviously with two engines on an aircraft it is different but I don't think it is as complicated as people like to think. An Airspeed Oxford was my first twin-engine. I liked it enough.

'Other girls in the ATA got chased but because I was rather staid and married I didn't. Diana wrote in her book *Spreading My Wings* how young men were always in hot pursuit of her, and when I asked her "what sort of a story have you made up?" she laughed and said, if you want to sell a book you have to make it fun!

'Would I have gone into combat? I don't know. You can't tell unless you've experienced it. We had a tremendous number of American girls with us and they came over with the glamorous Jackie Cochran who was a millionaire in her own right and had a cosmetics business. In America they weren't flying combat aircraft and so she recruited twenty-five women pilots who came over in a bunch.

'Jackie and Pauline didn't get on. One was British and one was American and quite vocal with her views on everything. With English women if we want something doing we persuade, we don't announce, but Jackie Cochran had this idea that because of who she was, friends with Eleanor Roosevelt and Churchill and the like, she could demand lots of things anyway.

'However she only stayed with us about six months and hastily returned to America, but a lot of her girls stayed on. We knew and liked Bobbie and Gertie very much at Hamble and on one occasion some years after the war Bernard and I went and stayed with Gertie in New York, and had an amusing night with her and Bobbie.

'Really and truly I came straight out of the ATA when Bernard got back to England. I rang the CO Margot Gore and said Bernard is home tomorrow, and I don't want to do anymore for you. It was 1945 and they had more pilots than jobs anyway and soon afterwards the ATA shut up shop as quickly as it had been formed.'

Sadly, as this book went to print we learned that Molly Rose had passed away on Sunday, 16 October 2016. The Air Transport Auxiliary Association's secretary, John Webster, said: 'Molly will certainly be remembered as one of ATA's more active post-war ambassadors and she was a determined and regular participant in ATA events. Along with her surviving colleagues, she attracted a good deal of media attention and featured in several documentaries, articles and publications. Born in Cambridge in November 1920 into a family that was to establish the aerospace company Marshalls of Cambridge, Molly joined the ATA in September 1942 and went on to fly 36 different aircraft types and deliver 486 of them before leaving in May 1945.'

Chapter 20

Last Days of the ATA

Molly's mention of the American women pilots reminded me of my first impression of the millionairess Jacqueline Cochran (1906-1980) who volunteered to visit England and study the ATA and introduce twenty-five of her US trained aviatrices to the organisation. 'Jackie' Cochran was a most confident person and was already famous for being the first woman to fly across the Atlantic in a Lockheed Hudson V Bomber.

I recall Florida-born Jackie as a supremely confident woman – just as Molly first described her. There was a story among ATA colleagues about the day in June 1942 when the film *They Flew Alone* was released. This picture produced by Herbert Wilcox and released by RKO Pictures, starred Dame Anna Neagle and Robert Newton. It was based on the life of Amy Johnson, and ATA Senior Commander Pauline was invited to the premiere in London – and so was the indomitable Jackie Cochran. In the press photographs of them together Pauline is not smiling. I wonder what was going through her mind as there had been a personality clash between them, if not a cultural one, from the first day they met just a few months earlier. Jackie was famous for 'pulling strings', and 'talking to Eleanor' (Roosevelt) and 'Winston' (Churchill) and she liked to let us all know of her queen bee status back in the US. But you know what they say, there's no room for two queen bees in the same hive (i.e. the ATA).

She had some amazing connections but grandstanding didn't sit well with us reserved Brits with our dark humour and sense of irony. Jackie would be known to arrive at Hamble or White Waltham in her fur coat and diamonds while we were all shivering next to one bar of heat from the pitifully small electric fire in the Mess. Many of La Cochran's women pilots got to stay in posh flats in Knightsbridge in London while we endured the chill of a wooden billet if stranded overnight somewhere in the depths of the countryside.

What she did achieve, though, was a victory over the ATA medical. Before she arrived at the ATA any woman who joined the organisation had to strip naked and be examined by the resident doctor. When Jackie's girls complained to her about the doctor requesting they remove all their clothes just to have their eyes tested, she rightfully challenged the rule and the doctor was given the boot. The rules of the medical examination were changed. (This story led one chap I know to tell me he had better have a word with his lady optician!)

We can be grateful to Jackie for this achievement at least. Her six months with the ATA hadn't been wasted and whilst she returned to America many of the American pilots like Ann Wood-Kelly who came over to us with her, decided to remain in England and continue their work with the ATA. There were some fine pilots in the ATA thanks to Mrs Cochran, including Virginia Farr, Grace Stevenson, Jane Plant and Edith Stearns.

Back in America the high-maintenance Mrs Jacqueline Cochran-Odlum and a fellow aviatrix named Nancy Harkness Love were put in charge of the new Women's Airforce Service Pilots organisation, also known as the WASPS. Hundreds of women were trained as ferry pilots and engineers by the WASPS and by the end of 1945 Jackie was presented with a Distinguished Service Medal.

To provide some idea of the size and scope of the ATA at its peak in 1944, there were fifteen ferry pools (which later grew to sixteen), 1,245 male pilots and 166 women pilots. We had 151 Flight Engineers, nineteen Radio Officers, twenty-seven ATC and Sea Cadets and 2,786 ground crew. Out of all these personnel there were 600 women serving in the ATA. Staff from twenty-five countries were recruited. When the ATA lowered its flag for the last time on 30 November 1945, a total of 309,011 aircraft had been ferried, consisting of 147 different types. In total 174 members of the ATA were killed in service.

Among the former WAAFs to join us as 'ab initio' pilots were, Betty Stewart-Jopp, Pat Provis, Katie Smith, Peggy Lucas and Annette Mahon.

Betty was the niece of one of the original ATA men – Keith Stewart-Jopp, formerly of the Royal Flying Corps, who I mentioned earlier. Anyway Betty was to have what can only be called a miracle escape when flying a Barracuda from her ferry pool at Prestwick to Lossiemouth. She flew into poor weather and obeying instructions not to go 'over the top' she turned back in a slow turn over the Firth of Forth.

She was unaware that slowly she had been losing height and only saw the water a brief second before she landed smack into it. According to Betty it was a good landing 'all things considered', but when the aircraft decided to sink it didn't hesitate to stop until it plumped down on the sea bed. What was going on in Betty's mind at the time is easy to imagine but she stayed calmed and collected enough to carry out the correct procedure.

When she pulled the canopy release lever a massive bubble of air was released – but she had not undone her parachute and harness straps which meant, as she recalled later, 'it took forever to get to the top.'

So she began swimming and within a few seconds her guardian angel helped her strike lucky as a little fishing boat chugged past and a fisherman reached down and dragged her out of the water. Betty says he was quite shocked to find he'd found a girl pilot. She became known as 'the ATA mermaid'.

An entry in Betty's logbook for 29 May 1944 shows the departure point of Prestwick, a flight time of one hour, but in the destination column she's just made a dash mark. During the writing of this book I was sad to find out that Betty (married name, Huggett) died on 6 July 2016, at her home in South Africa. She was aged 97.

Over the years I have collected many files of newspaper and magazine cuttings about my aviation career but some of them contain inaccuracies so I hope this book can put the record straight. Some of these articles were important at the time and go way back to the 1950s. When I think of the varieties we flew with the ATA it still astounds me. The idea that in the ATA you could fly an aircraft you'd never seen before, let alone heard of, is extraordinary. These days there are only five or six different types of military aeroplanes in the world.

During the Second World War it was a far different story of course. The Blenheim which flew in the Battle of Britain was rather like the Mosquito. It was in-between a Wellington and a Mosquito. It was lovely. When I had to fly them I never looked in the gun turret and it's enough to learn the cockpit procedure. Also you couldn't hang around on the airfield when someone somewhere was waiting for it to be delivered. You walked around the aeroplane as best you could to check if everything appear alright, and then we got straight into the cockpit.

I also flew an American Boston – a tricycle aircraft and a twin-engine. Of course to see any of the types I flew it is best to visit Duxford or Cosford as they've acres of aircraft on show there. Most of them will never fly again though.

The year which marked the end of the war in Europe saw me busy as ever with the ATA, as the RAF and Fleet Air Arm were still losing many aircraft and needed them replaced as soon as was possible. Life seemed to carry on, and in May 1945 I note I flew fourteen different varieties of military fighters and bombers which included Mosquitoes, Wildcats and Hellcats, over just sixteen days. I don't remember getting over-excited about the news the war was coming to an end because it was hard to actually believe this after so many years of living it and flying during all that time. My friend Joy Lofthouse has openly said she was disappointed when the war ended because she was having such a wonderful time in the ATA.

By August 1945 we realised Hamble Ferry Pool was winding down. At that time people were being told it was the end of the ATA, whereas a few of us were told we were going somewhere else. It was terrible really and each day someone would grimly remark, 'This is the end of your time at Hamble'. I was posted to headquarters at White Waltham temporarily and was relieved it wasn't all completely changing.

Those girls who were leaving were dreadfully upset because they didn't know if they would ever fly again. For those of us who were sent on to another ferry pool, we were so very happy. Why was I chosen to stay on and not them? Well, I was near to being promoted to Flight Captain and perhaps it was because I was an extremely good pilot and experienced on so many types of aeroplane.

When Hamble Ferry Pool was closed down I was seconded to No.1 Ferry Pool at White Waltham. An ATA colleague of mine, Veronica Volkersz (1917-2000), who wrote the memoir *The Sky and I*, said:

'Gradually, all the pools were closing down, except for White Waltham, which was to carry on for three months after Christmas. It was with a heavy heart that I packed up and said 'Goodbye' to 'Hamble where I had spent three very happy years. Whitchurch, an all-male pool, had refused adamantly to have any women posted there and consequently, the men were simply furious when they heard a few girls, including me, had been posted there.

'In fact, for the first two or three days, there was definitely a "no fratting" rule. However, we managed to gradually thaw them out, especially when they heard we played bridge. Eventually we got them quite tame.'

I was sorry to never hear from some friends again. One case in point was that of dear Betty Grant (Hayman), with whom I'd had fun with and so many laughs, including the time we were bridesmaids together at our ATA friend Doreen Williams' wedding. Doreen, who was Welsh, had an RAF boyfriend, the relationship with whom was forever on and off. Even when finally, they decided to get married there was still some 'umming' and 'ahhing' from Doreen. Eventually she agreed to bite the bullet and marry this chap and so in August 1944 Betty and I were asked to drive to the ceremony which was being held at Newport, Wales. First of all, we had to get permission from our CO Margot to take the day off. 'What shall we wear as bridesmaids?' we asked Doreen, half fearing she might want us in tangerine trifle-frocks. 'Oh,' she replied, 'please wear your ATA uniforms'.

Well, on the journey to Wales I remember Betty and I were giggling and laughing a lot and we may well have been the ATA's first ever bridesmaids to wear their uniform at the wedding. The marriage went off fine and a good day was had by all including Doreen who became Mrs Illsley that day. She lived to the grand age of eighty-six.

My friend Betty who had married Norman Hayman in 1943, was a good ferry pilot and stayed until the end of the ATA in November 1945. When I was searching through my photographs the other day I found a picture of me with Betty at Doreen's wedding, our arms are linked up, and we're wearing skirts which was very rare. I think it's the only picture there is of me in a skirt in the ATA. After the war Betty seemed to disappear off the radar and none of us former ATA women knew what happened to her.

The ATA Association's reunion organisers tried hard to track her down over the decades, but with no luck. She just disappeared from my life as quickly as she'd flown into it – which was such a shame as we'd got on so well and I'd loved to have stayed in touch.

During the writing of this book, my co-author, Melody, managed to discover that Betty's first husband, Norman L. Hayman, had died in Surrey in 1951. A Betty Hayman is recorded as living in the same area in 1964 when she married a John Edward D'Aguilar. Mr D'Aguilar died in 1981 and the death of a Beatrice (Betty) his wife is recorded as taking place in 1990. It's difficult to be completely sure this is Betty, but it's pretty likely and if so I'd like to pay tribute to her amazing work as a ferry pilot. Thank you Betty and blue skies to you forever.

On 30 November 1945, and with the war at an end, the Air Transport Auxiliary held a pageant at White Waltham. By this time many of the ferry pools had already closed and now it was the turn of our headquarters to lower its flag for the last time. Our pilot colleague from the women's section Audrey Sale-Barker had this honour and the pageant, which attracted hundreds of people, was held to mark the considerable achievements of the ATA.

Lord Beaverbrook (Minister of Aircraft Production from May 1940 to May 1941) had funded the events to mark the closing ceremony of the ATA, and in a speech he told the crowds assembled among the aircraft at White Waltham: 'Without the ATA the days and nights of the Battle of Britain would have been conducted under conditions quite different from the actual events. They carried out the delivery from factories to the RAF thus relieving countless RAF pilots for duty in the battle. Just as the Battle of Britain is the accomplishment of the RAF, likewise it can be declared the ATA supported and sustained them throughout the battle. They were solders fighting in the struggle just as completely as if they had been engaged on the battlefield.'

Was I sad that the ATA was about to disappear as quickly as it had begun? Well, I was thankful the war was over, but of course I was happy that the flying of these wonderful aircraft had been my allotted task and pleasure between 1941 and 1946.

On 15 May 1945, Gerard d'Erlanger CBE – founder of the ATA – released the following message: 'In these great days of the magnificent victory of our fighting forces in Europe, I send to you and all your members of the Air Transport Auxiliary my congratulations and my most sincere thanks for a great job well carried through. The ATA has formed an essential link between the factories and the Royal Air Force and the Fleet Air Arm. The unfailing regularity with which they have cleared aircraft from the factories in all weathers and under all conditions has enabled us to maintain our programmed flow of production. Since D-Day the ATA has made a valuable contribution to the victory by supplementing the facilities for air transport to and from the Continent of Europe. In the course of these onerous duties there have been many casualties in the ranks of the ATA and today we remember with pride those who thus gave their lives in the service of the country. This great service faithfully, unobtrusively and constantly performed has earned for every member of the ATA the gratitude of the country. The Air Council wish to associate themselves with me in this expression of admiration and gratitude to all ranks of the ATA.'

So it marked a time when so many of us went off to find our lives again in a variety of directions. On 31 December 1945, only six ATA women pilots were still delivering aircraft – there was me, First Officer Mary Wilkins, First Officers Joan Naylor and Ann Blackwell, Captain Rosemary Rees, and Flight Captains Lucy Faulkner and Joan Hughes.

When the powers that be decided in early 1946 it would a good idea for a few select ATA pilots to be seconded to the Royal Air Force, two men and two women were chosen for this work including me. We were to teach the RAF a few techniques peculiar to the ATA – an interesting position, as remember we'd flown many more varieties than the RAF and Fleet Air Arm boys who stuck with the same fighters or bombers throughout their war service.

In the January of that year I received a signed certificate from the ATA and Senior Commander Pauline Gower and Air Commodore d'Erlanger thanking me for my work and commitment during the war effort. I found out too I had been chosen by the CO to go to No.41 Training Unit which was based at RAF Old Sarum in Wiltshire. In March I was delighted to pick up my chitties which indicated I was to fly a Gloster Meteor III – the Meteor was the RAF's first jet-powered fighter. This was another enormous achievement for me to record in my logbook. I'd never flown a jet before and I can't remember if I'd ever seen one at that stage.

Unfortunately, these gorgeous, high-powered little aircraft came along a little too late to really play a major part in the war which, by the time I got into the cockpit of one, was at an end. The Meteor did go on to play a key role in the Cold War and were flown by the RAF for thirty-eight years. I think they were as important a landmark to military aviation as the Spitfire or the Hurricane.

Anyway, the Meteor was still very much in development stage and I was one of two women chosen to test them. My ATA colleague Veronica Volkersz was the first woman to take one of these jets into the air and I was the second. The RAF affectionately called these aircraft the 'Meatboxes' which was a little unfair as they were of lovely design and were super-fast. Their turbo-engines had been designed by Sir Frank Whittle's company 'Power Jets Ltd'. They were produced from 1943 to1955 and 3,947 were built in total.

The Meteor was the next best thing after the Spitfire but without the propeller of course. In March 1946 when I found my name written next to 'Meteor Mk.III' on my chitty I was flown in the taxi aircraft from White Waltham to pick up this aircraft.

I find it extraordinary now that I got into the cockpit of an aircraft I'd never seen before, and this one had no propellers and I flew it. I remember thinking when I saw it – 'I can't fly this it hasn't got any propellers'. I hadn't seen a photograph of it either. I had glanced over my Ferry Pilots Notes, but obviously an aeroplane takes-off, goes into the sky and it lands.

I had already asked one of the test pilots if the aircraft had any particular characteristics. His only reply was: 'Yes, watch the fuel gauges. They go from full to empty in thirty minutes so make sure you are on the ground by then. The Meteor also drops like a brick when you take the power off when coming into land.' He then stalked off. A girl pilot, indeed.

160

He was right about all of it. Those early Meteors could reach up to 600 mph and more at full speed and they were very thirsty. The test pilot was right about watching the fuel gauges as in the Meteor they go from full to empty in thirty-five minutes. The other thing was when you take the power off the aeroplane sinks very fast whereas any other aircraft, like a Spitfire, it wouldn't drop dramatically, it would go down at a manageable speed.

So I climbed into the Meteor's cockpit at RAF Morton Valence, just south-west of Gloucester, and taxied out. Remember I had no help with the radio because we weren't allowed to have that; so in consequence I didn't wear a helmet. Everyone was used to seeing me in the Spitfire or a Wellington without a helmet which is not normal these days.

I took off in the Meteor and looked at all the gauges and then I realised when I peered out of the window that I didn't know where I was, as I had been staring intently at the instruments to see what they were saying. It's hard to understand, but that's what happened. It took me thirty minutes to reach my destination. (Remember the fuel ran out after thirty-five minutes).

These Meteors were the first jet aircraft made for military action and so for the time they were very advanced. The fact they ran out of fuel quickly can't be regarded as a technical fault as really they were still being developed and no doubt the fuel capacity was improved as they went on. You can't grumble about them as the first British jets. It was strange to look at it without propellers but the feeling of flying it wasn't any different.

I was asked to deliver that Meteor Mk.III to RAF Exeter – to the great excitement of the friendly chaps of 222 Squadron. It turned out that they were changing over from Spitfires and this was the first Meteor to arrive at the base. The whole squadron turned out to welcome its arrival and I made a good landing. I was delighted with the flight, and I had to chuckle as those RAF chaps seemed very surprised and could hardly believe their eyes to see it had been flown and landed by a little ATA girl pilot.

The CO was most courteous. He said they were having a party that night and he asked if I might like to join them. He told me he was keeping the Meteor I'd flown all to himself. But the taxi aircraft was waiting for me, so I flew off again back to White Waltham. I kept in touch with the CO after that but it was all harmless fun and more of an aviation friendship – but wonderful.

I wasn't the only one to recall my first flight in a Meteor. My friend Veronica described her experience of it well:

'When Hamble closed in August 1945 I was posted to Whitchurch near Bristol which covered the Gloster factory at Morton Vallence. Apparently Whitchurch was the first pool to ferry jets. After I had been there a week or two, I asked if I might ferry one and Flight Captain Cuthbert, one of the flight leaders, said he would try and arrange it. I felt rather dubious as to whether anything would come of the idea, as I knew the powers that be were rather anti-female. Also, I was a very new addition to the pool. However, on 15 September, the CO and second-in-command were away and Bill Cuthbert was doing the programme. You could have knocked me down with a feather when somebody handed me a chit to deliver Meteor III EE386 to 124 Squadron at Molesworth.

'Three of us set off for Morton Vallence in the Anson, flown by George Dutton. The weather was poor with cloud on the hills, which probably meant about a two-hour delay before we could get away. One of the other pilots showed me around the cockpit, which seemed much the same as that of any other aircraft, except for the extra O on the rpm counter. I was now dealing in thousands of rpms instead of hundreds. The big snag with the Meteor was the fuel consumption and I had just enough that day to get to my destination, with a reserve for an overshoot if necessary. Having no R/T I should have to fly below cloud at a low altitude, consequently eating up more juice. I find it difficult to remember anything special about it. The flight was no different from any other delivery except that as I was the first woman to have the opportunity to ferry a jet I wanted everything to go without a hitch. And it did.

'The only difference I found from the usual drill was in the take-off, where I had to open up to full throttle on the brakes. As I released them, the aircraft seemed to hurtle away like a shot from a gun, and I was back again flying the Audax and the Hurricane. But what a kick in the pants this time! On getting airborne I turned straight on to course to avoid wasting time and fuel. The landing was straightforward and easy, and as I taxied to dispersal I felt very pleased with life. It was a good note on which to end my ATA career and helped to soften the thought that there might be no more flying. The taxi Anson was waiting for us, engines ticking over, and after getting signed up, we bundled in to return to base.'

Just before my first experience at the controls of a Meteor, I flew and delivered my last Spitfire for the ATA on 3 March 1946. I took off at precisely 12.20 hours, having jumped into the cockpit of Spitfire Mk.XVIII PS327, on a journey that saw me fly from Eastleigh to Culham in Oxfordshire.

Swiftly and assuredly, and as slick as a dart, the Spitfire soared high into the chilly air of early spring for a fifty-mile journey into my home county. By 13.00 hours I had landed and taxied this lovely aircraft to her designated parking place. I can't recall lingering in the cockpit for too long, but who could blame me if I did sit still for a few seconds to savour yet another special time of flight?

The Mk.XVIII with its dramatic five-bladed propeller and re-enforced wing structure, had a Rolls-Royce Griffon engine and it could carry more fuel than the other earlier types. In general, the Mk.XVIII did not see much combat action, although a handful were destined for RAF Seletar in Singapore. (There's every chance that last Spitfire I flew was bought by the Royal Indian Air Force which had twenty ex-RAF Mk.XVIIIs on its airfields in 1947).

However, when I took off that day in March I didn't realise it would be my last ever solo Spitfire flight. Obviously I knew the time was fast approaching for such a farewell to my favourite little fighter aircraft, but I had no idea exactly when. I do recall thinking around this time that I'd better enjoy every chance to fly even more than ever. The ATA was almost wound-up and the clock was ticking on my extraordinary airborne experiences. I knew in my heart that never, ever again would young women like me have the opportunity to fly such a beautiful aircraft so often and so freely.

It wasn't only the Spitfire but all the other 147 types which we'd had the opportunity to pilot during the six-year history of such an unusual and yet essential wartime organisation. Looking back on all the different marks of Spitfire in my logbook I have to claim the Mk.Vb as my favourite. This Merlin-engine war-bird had been supercharged to climb faster than the other Marks and was created as a worthy opponent in combat against the German's new Focke Wulf Fw 190. Sometimes the Mk.Vb had clipped wings which was meant to help it reach great heights even quicker and make it versatile to carry bombs too. Whether this new-style wing really helped the aerodynamic or not I don't know but for me the elliptical and original wing-shape makes for a more beautiful looking Spitfire.

I discovered the power of the Spitfire Mk.Vb soon enough during the war, and there were many times I was tempted to carry out the occasional aerobatic – something which was definitely forbidden in the ATA rulebook which demanded pilots keep aircraft steady and straight to ensure safe delivery at all times. When I was flying the Mk.Vb though I really did feel as if I was wearing the aircraft, as it was so essentially part of me. Other pilots have said the same. This Spitfire gave me those beautiful aerodynamic wings I had longed for as a child and had so pestered my Pa about twenty years previously.

I can't remember every type of aircraft I flew – there were seventy-six different varieties so I must be sure to point that out. Some of them are now obsolete of course and there are lots and lots that have disappeared and nobody knows anything about them anymore, including several of the 210 airfields mentioned in my logbook. I know I clocked up more than 1,100 hours flying with the ATA and with that came a lot of experience.

Chapter 21

Rally Driver

It didn't take me too long to get used to the idea of leaving the ATA once the reality of the war's end had kicked in. I remember thinking how wonderful it would be to just go home and stay home and help on the farm. I also wanted to see my family and spend a lot of time with my sister as we were always close. (I was terribly upset when she died in January 2016. Dora was ninety-one, eight years younger than me and we had enjoyed such happy times and shared wonderful memories together).

Although many of the girls in the ATA were saying we would have trouble finding other jobs after the war, to be honest I was quite happy to get back to the family farm and do nothing. We had domestic staff, so the thought of just taking it easy was rather a nice one.

When I got home in 1946 I did write off for a few flying jobs, but of course there was nothing much for me out there, and two years later I wrote to *Flight* magazine which had recommended women should be allowed to take part in speed flying to beat a current record of 292 mph. I wrote and informed the editor of how, in the ATA, I had qualified to fly a Gloster Meteor heaps faster than that!

Then, to cheer myself up, I bought a fast car off of my brothers. It was a gorgeous black Allard K1 and I loved driving it so much. Within a few years the Allard and I would become members of the Isle of Wight Car Club and we'd be taking part in and winning a raft of rally events; but more on that later.

In 1948 my Pa happened to meet a wealthy friend on a pheasant shooting trip. His name was John Stephenson Clarke (whose ancestors had built up Britain's oldest shipping company) and he told my Pa he was looking for a pilot, so I went to see him and I was offered the job. It seems my new-found life of leisure was about to end sooner than I thought.

Of course I was delighted about this and to be honest I had missed flying, but the only thing was I did not want to do was return to the Isle of Wight. I'd been there with the ATA flying Walruses and Sea Otters and I was there at Cowes when Anne Walker had her serious accident. I had bad memories of the Isle of Wight and I really didn't like the water. But Mr Stephenson Clarke owned Sandown Airfield – plus he knew nothing about aircraft and so he trusted me to find a good one. First of all, we had a Percival Proctor which wasn't really suitable for what he wanted, so I got rid of that and we acquired a lovely Gemini. My new boss seemed happy and on our business trips he liked to sit up at the front in the co-pilot's seat and watch the world go by.

By 1950 I found myself at Sandown and had been flying over the Solent to get to and from the airfield for a few months. At this time there were all sorts of bigwigs running the site, including the person in charge who was a naval officer. It soon became clear Mr Stephenson Clarke had decided this chap wasn't really the person he wanted to run the airfield so I was parachuted in to save the day.

Sandown Airfield really got going in 1935 but like many small landing strips it was closed during the war to help prevent invasion.

I must admit that I did think long and very hard about taking on the challenge of running it. There were already some staff there like engineers and it was ticking over but not working as well as it could. It needed building up and I saw it would be a terrific opportunity for me. I loved flying and I kept asking myself shall I accept this job or not? I debated it in my mind for some time and then I decided I like a challenge – but what a big challenge. And I am going to do it? Although I wasn't happy about being stuck out on the Isle of Wight.

I had to recreate the whole site and turn it into a good business, and in order to do that I had to get the licence from the Air Ministry and that took a lot of paperwork and diplomacy. (Sadly, the airport today does not have such a licence).

There was also a need to obtain CRDF (Cathode-Ray Direction Finding) and VHF radio apparatus in order to encourage the airlines to come in, and if I hadn't had a friendly, good natured boss he wouldn't have allowed me to spend so much money. It was such hard work for a whole year to get the CRDF. Then I had to learn how to operate all the new equipment so I could talk to the aircraft, after which I then I had to employ someone to do all this. When the airlines came in to Sandown I discovered just how much all that paperwork eventually paid off, but it was an ongoing job and there was always something else to do. Sandown was able to offer full night-flying facilities too.

At one time I had seven different licences to be able to operate and no one would believe I was doing all this. One newspaper cutting of the time reported: 'A new weekend air service between Manchester and the Isle of Wight is to be operated by Overseas Air Transport Ltd from May 20 to September 29 using a four-engine Heron aircraft at a return fare of £10/10shillings. This trip takes 90 minutes and is one of several new services to the island. Regular flights are planned from Gatwick, Birmingham and Leeds now that Sandown has been upgraded with many improvements carried out. So far the airport carried 6,000 passengers in one year.'

The airport was to receive a visit in November 1951 from Lord Ogmore, who was then Minister of Civil Aviation, and Sir Arnold Overton, the ministry's permanent secretary. I welcomed them, of course, in my position as airport manager and knew they had landed at Sandown on their way to look over the new Princess Flying Boat at Saunders-Rowe at nearby Cowes.

When people would ask me who was running the airfield I would say I was and they'd just poo-poo that story and walk away! (Strangely reminiscent of my ATA experience of flying a Wellington bomber to an RAF airfield and the ground crew refusing to accept the fact I was the pilot.)

It was always rewarding when I met up again with my ATA friend Jackie Moggridge as she was one of the lucky few women pilots who managed to get a job in commercial aviation after a busy time with the post-war RAF delivering Spitfires to the Far East. By the 1950s she was flying passengers from Portsmouth to Jersey, but often she wasn't allowed to let anyone know she was at the controls because there was still this fear about women flying aircraft.

Sometimes Jackie flew in to Sandown during her commercial flights and we'd catch up on old times. She'd come through on the radio and tell me to put the kettle on as she was about to land. If we had to make sure any passengers never found out their pilot was a woman, she covered her head with a scarf or a newspaper as she made her way to my office. It was ludicrous that discrimination against women in aviation was still as rife as ever and yet ironically the dangerous work we'd done in the ATA kicked all sorts of feminist rhetoric in to touch.

One of the highlights of the late 1950s was the arrival of the largest aircraft to ever land at Sandown. This was a four-engine Blackburn B101 Beverley, which, as an RAF Transport Command aeroplane, had arrived to pick up a rocket made by the special aerospace factory on the Isle of Wight. The aircraft then took off again to deliver its special cargo to

Australia. The Beverley had a wingspan of forty-nine metres and was thirty metres long. It was powered by four tough Bristol Centaurus engines and had a top speed of 383 km/h.

During my years at Sandown I got used to people not believing I was the one in charge and it was deemed incredible by some people I was doing so much. Of course, I did indeed wonder at the time what else there was in life. It couldn't be all work and no play. I gave so much of my life to aviation and the airport that there was not much time for romance at all, but that said, I always, always missed my days flying a Spitfire. I just had a passion for speed and wondered what I could do to fulfil it.

The answer to my question soon arrived. I would become a part-time rally driver. To be honest, getting behind the wheel of my Allard sports car was a relief for me and acted as a sort of release from the work pressures. I still had the speed of the Spitfire roaring through my veins of course, and once you've experienced this particular rush of excitement and adrenaline inspired by the power of those powerful Merlin engines, it will never leave your blood. Just ask my friend Carolyn Grace who pilots her own Spitfire today. I just love speed, and in the 1950s, as a young, vibrant, all-achieving young woman, I knew my speedy and handsome black Allard was out to feed my need.

The car itself was a rare one indeed. Sydney Allard's factory made just 1,900 cars from 1945 to 1958 when it stopped trading. My treasured K1 had a large American Ford V8 engine built into a fairly light frame built by Thomsons of Wolverton. Side-rails and cross-members helped the Ford suspension. My Pa was always a fan of American cars and I am sure he would have helped my brothers when they were thinking about which sports car to buy. My Pa always knew best when it came to transport and with the Allard's big, powerful and trusty engine, he was certain it was a good addition to the family car collection.

Early in the 1950s I was thrilled to be invited to join the Isle of Wight Car Club and I took part in race events with everyone else. It was all such a breath of fresh air and an amazing change of scene from flying and all its anxieties. During my time with the club I won six of those races and I've got the cups and trophies to prove it sitting well dusted and cared for on a shelf in my house. I did all my races on the mainland, but mind you there were always two of us – me and a navigator. The last run was Abingdon so we stayed the night and then went off at 18.00 hours which meant we were driving around the Welsh mountains all night long trying to find out where we should be.

The navigator that time was my friend Marie Crinage (of Crinage Transport), and once I recall we landed up in a farmyard with the chickens running about everywhere. It was just getting daylight then and the hens started clucking and fussing about at the sight of these two women and the car. We soon reversed out of there and I hope the farmer wasn't too cross. A lot of people didn't finish the course that day but we did.

In 1953 I won the Isle of Wight rally with Regatta Queen Caroline Humphreys as co-driver, and the Ladies Challenge Cup now sits proudly on my trophy shelf.

That was the year I was working as Traffic Manager at Sandown and my Bees Flight Company added pleasure flights to the programme. The Sandown aircraft fleet comprised of a Dragon Rapide (G-AKMH), two Gemini, an Autocrat, and one Auster. We flew the Rapide for pleasure flights to take passengers to Daedalus airfield to see the RNAS Coronation Review Air Day at Lee-on-the-Solent – the same airfield where I had ferried Seafires during the war.

In the evening of 29 April 1954, I had the chance to defend my title in the Isle of Wight Car Rally, so I drove the Allard to Cowes Parade with Miss Caroline Humphreys as co-driver. We were watched by large crowds; thirty-six competitors left at one minute intervals. I was the first driver away and Caroline and I took turns to navigate and drive. Most competitors finished the 322-mile course at Sandown the next morning, after thirteen solid hours of gruelling driving.

I recall the course was kept secret until a few minutes before the start and all of the cars had to pass route controls and time checks. Drivers covered three figure-8 routes around the island, mostly over second and third class roads. This left some drivers so exhausted after the night competition they took the chance to get a few moments to sleep in their cars.

Crowds of spectators lined Sandown Esplanade in the morning to watch the conclusion of the elimination tests, with open sports cars, like my Allard, having a serious speed advantage over the others.

I love fast cars, always have and always will. Night rallying is very exacting, as get it wrong and you've lost your way in the dark. But I didn't often lose and have the trophies to prove it.

Chapter 22

'Miss Wilkins Runs an Airport'

Each day at Sandown Airport was smooth-running because of the hard work that went into it. As Mr Stephenson Clarke's personal pilot I'd got to know him as a good friend and he appreciated my knowledge of aircraft and often talked to me about the ATA as he was so interested in aviation. He also had land at what is now Gatwick Airport and he was also interested in shipping, so we'd often fly to the east coast and stop for a lunch.

The Gemini was kept in a hangar at Sandown and I organised all the maintenance and servicing there. When I dived in head first and accepted the managing director's job I knew I wanted to build up Sandown from being a little place for pleasure flights into an airport which welcomed the airlines in. We had pleasure flying there and a restaurant serving teas – the same as these days, but I had a lot to think about and it was a very intense job and could become all-absorbing if I let it.

I have a cutting from the Evening Standard dated 4 August 1951 with the headline 'Miss Wilkins Runs an Airport!' The article about me was written by the newspaper's air reporter, James Stuart, who came to Sandown to interview me as I was obviously a great novelty idea to him – whatever next a girl running an airport! Even the headline reads like something Enid Blyton might have dreamt up.

I can quote from the article which ran alongside a photograph of me and my chief instructor and former ATA colleague, Vera Strodl, and my pet dog, Perky Mignon. The report says:

> Holidaymakers coming to the Isle of Wight by air will be met by a blonde haired young woman in a cotton-print dress. She will collect their tickets and arrange their road transport. If their aeroplane needs help in finding the grass runway she will give radio

instructions to the pilot. And if some of the passengers come back to the airfield during their holiday for a round-the-island joyride or a 10shilling 'flip' the pilot will be another fair haired girl.

These two young women are out to prove that money can be made out of flying. Their names – Mary Wilkins and Vera Strodl – are in the records of the Air Transport Auxiliary, the wartime civilians who ferried the RAF's airplanes from the factories to the squadrons. Miss Wilkins is manager of Sandown Airport (the only woman airport manager in Britain) and manager of the Isle of Wight Aero Club. Miss Strodl is the chief flying instructor.

Mary Wilkins is also the managing director of a private air charter company operating from the airfield, and she's also boss of a local chalkpit.

'Ours is the island's largest airport,' says Miss Wilkins. 'All the services from Croydon, Bournemouth and Manchester come in and out here at weekends, and on busy days we ourselves take up about 200 people on pleasure flights.'

Vera Strodl learned to fly in 1935. When she left the ATA she took a flying boat course in the USA then joined a Swedish charter company piloting flying boats off the lakes. Her trips took her beyond the Arctic Circle. She says: I carried mail, went looking for people lost in the mountains and did power-line laying from the air in Lapland.

As I left the airfield the little cream Auster aircraft buzzed along the runway and climbed into the sky. The blonde girl in the slacks was off with more joyriders. Next week flying the seven-seater, twin-engine Dragon Rapide, she will be giving people an aerial view of Cowes Regatta.

People I knew from my Sandown days sometimes visit my home and say they enjoyed working with me but I was so very, very strict. Well, I had to be! I have letters from pilots who said they remembered me as a terrible person. They say, 'You gave me a lecture' about this or that, but then they admit that information from this lecture had saved their life many times and they are always grateful. So all that turns out to be fine really. If they did something they shouldn't, or they forgot to do their reading before they flew, I let them know it was and always was up to them to do the right thing.

At this point I must mention that my love of farming was not quashed by the thrills and spills of my awesome aviation career. Far from it! I kept sheep when I moved to Sandown on the Isle of Wight and one of my first, and favourites, was called 'Sarah'. People say sheep aren't very intelligent, but I can tell you they are actually extremely bright.

At the clubhouse in Sandown we had tables and chairs and people were always smoking in those days, and Sarah would come in and go around the tables and find the ashtrays and eat all the cigarette ends. Then she'd walk out again, quite content she'd done her job as cleaner! The only problem was when she blew the ash out of her mouth – and, by the way, I thought that was a most intelligent thing to do, though one just didn't want to be too close to her when she did it! Sarah was a wonderful sheep and lived with a dozen or so woolly friends. Once I even shipped a ram over to bring new blood into the flock.

Sarah and the other sheep always got to know when an aeroplane was coming around as, if they were eating grass on the runway, they would move off sharpish out of harm's way and starting scoffing again! They are frightfully intelligent. It's just that people don't have the patience to realise this. I'd argue sheep are more intelligent that lots of dogs. Sarah was an Oxfordshire ewe with black legs and a black face. I was very fond of her and my lovely poodle – Mignon.

I had him from a pup and he was always with me. When he grew up he was always trimmed and looked so smart. I am not sure whether he actually enjoyed flying with me as someone told me once that it affected dogs' hearing, so after that I tried not to take him flying. Now you can't take a pet flying unless it is crated in. The good old days when you could fly with your pet by your side in the cockpit are long gone.

Although I had been promoted to managing director of Sandown, after learning how to handle many demanding roles at the airport, I continued to be a personal pilot for the boss, Mr Stephenson Clarke. I wasn't flying every day though. I was never an instructor and as that job did not appeal to me I hired one to work at the airfield. That person was another former ATA girl – Vera Strodl (1918–2015) who was born in England of Danish descent.

Vera had joined the ATA at the same time as me in the autumn of 1941. As well as flying aircraft she also made broadcasts for the BBC and flew over Denmark on secret missions to drop leaflets. For this work she received the Freedom Fighters Medal. Vera had already been teaching people to fly after she left the ATA and had also served with the Women's Royal Air Force Volunteer Reserve. She joined us as Sandown after working as an instructor at Speke, near Liverpool. Years later when Vera was interviewed by her biographer (Warren Hathaway), she said:

> When I went to Sandown to work for Mary Wilkins I was back at the
> first airfield from where I'd taken my first flight as a 12 year old! My

new position offered me many opportunities to fly and take passengers on joy ride, much like I did when I was working in Sweden.

For joy-riding at Sandown we flew twin-engine aircraft around the Isle of Wight and on trips to the Channel Islands, especially Alderney. Occasionally we even made trips to Paris. One of these trips turned out to be rather amusing for me, although perhaps not my passengers. This particular flight was scheduled to take a load of senior citizens on an outing.

The day was very mild and pleasant and I chose to wear a very pretty, flowered dress instead of my drab slacks I wore for flying. Once all the passengers were in their seats, I continued down the aisle collecting their tickets. Everybody was cheerful and filled with anticipation. With the collection of the tickets completed I closed the door of the aircraft. On seeing me carry out this operation one of the women enquired anxiously, 'where's the pilot?' With a smile I took my seat in the cockpit and began to go through the necessary pre-flight checks. The looks of astonishment on their faces was priceless. How prone we are to cast people into traditional roles based only on what they wear!

Vera worked for me as Sandown's Chief Flying Instructor from 1949 until 1952. In the spring of 1952 she also continued her flying instruction courses for the RAFVR and was qualified to test pilots under official examination. Often during her time with the RAFVR she'd land at our old ATA home at Hamble and one day while she was waiting for an aircraft here she saw a copy of *Flight* magazine. Vera picked it up and was flicking through it when she spotted a job advertisement for a flying instructor based in Lethbridge, Alberta, Canada. At that moment she felt such a post would be a good move for her and off she went and applied!

They wrote back swiftly and said she'd got the job, although some of us had asked her exactly why she wanted to go so far away! It was March and we said, 'There won't be a blade of green grass to be seen and the mud will stick to your boots – great cakes of it! They call it gumbo mud.'

Many thought Vera would hate Canada – but we were wrong as she settled there to became the first woman instructor in Alberta before moving to Edmonton in 1957 and she married Stan Dowling. In the 1960s and 1970s her ever-present faith in God led her to work with a Christian mission and she often flew to various small communities in the Prairies. I met up with Vera again in 1989 when she travelled to

England to an ATA reunion event where we were all finally presented with our medals from the British government. We received the Defence Medal and the Victory Medal. In the year 2000 my former instructor and friend Vera Strodl Dowling was voted into the Canadian Aviation Hall of Fame.

I was to make headlines again on 14 August 1953 when *The Southern Evening Echo* ran a piece with a headline which marked a milestone in my career: 'Now She's Europe's First Woman Airport Manager.'

The reporter had described me as 'a slim, fair-haired farmer's daughter who ran a 100-acre grass airfield which is busier than it has ever been'. He wrote:

> Miss Wilkins' staff are on the go all the time to keep the Dragon Rapide, Tiger Moth, two Auster and two Gemini flying, the airfield grass and hedges trimmed and to keep the tidy hangar and clubhouse spick and span.
>
> Her two pilots Colin Street, 24, and Alan Tucker, 28, spend ten hours a day giving joy rides to holidaymakers and another ten hours a week flying charter trips to such places as Manchester, Paris, Brussels and the Channel Islands. When Miss Wilkins first arrived at Sandown in 1947 it was just a field. In 1941 she was one of the first women to join the Air Transport Auxiliary as a ferry pilot and during the war totalled 6,000 hours on her licence flying 76 different types of aircraft across Britain and the continent.
>
> At Sandown she not only has to run the airport but the flying club and the 'Airport Arms' clubhouse too. Then there's her air charter company and a chalk pit to manage!

This article was accompanied by a photograph of me with Mignon, my Poodle. I regularly took him flying with me until I was told altitudes can affect a dog's hearing so my pet was grounded when I took off! Mignon was a joy and followed me everywhere and when he did fly with me he clocked up more than fifty hours.

I used to get home to my parents' farm once a month and I'd borrow one of the Gemini aircraft and land it in one of my father's fields. By then the Wilkins' family farm had grown to one thousand acres so I was never short of space to park the Gemini!

Another memory from my scrapbook was created in 1960 when I am quoted in a story beneath the headline 'The Charming Commandant'. The article continued: 'Asked whether there have been any accidents at the airport and Miss Wilkins replies with a firm "No, we never mention such things" and hastily touched wood. It seems that modern aviators like medieval sailors, have a healthy respect for the uncertainties in life. And use the same charms to placate gremlins.'

However, I kept my wits about me all the time and I recall how in 1959 I had to talk down a twin-engine aircraft which had one engine on fire and the other was rapidly losing power. Thanks to the hi-tech equipment in the Control Tower I picked up the mayday signal from the pilot who was halfway over the Channel when the fire erupted. I advised him calmly to turn around and make for Sandown and as he didn't have my airport marked on his map I had to talk him through the navigation all the way right up until he landed. We had a fire engine waiting for him when he came in and the blaze in the engine was rapidly extinguished.

It was one of the times I knew I had done the right thing to have such modern radio aids installed at Sandown. Such a move meant the Ministry of Aviation upgraded the airport and we were licensed to take in aircraft weighing up to 39,000lbs. Of course we also had a meteorological service installed which made us part of the nationwide chain.

Another VIP to visit us was the wartime ace Sir (then Group Captain) Douglas Bader, who made his first flight in a glider from Sandown with the Isle of Wight MP Sir Peter Macdonald. The instructor was my husband-to-be Donald Ellis. I would have loved to know how the conversation went that day in the glider as Sir Douglas was a tremendously seasoned aviator used to the vast speed of the Spitfire. I hope he didn't find the glider too slow and silent. It was never an aircraft I wanted to fly more than once. In the late 1970s Donald encouraged me to fly gliders but I really didn't like them as I didn't feel I had any control whatsoever.

Other visitors to Sandown in the mid-1950s included the British Women Pilots Association who organised a flying weekend on Tiger Moths, the Autocraft and the Miles Magister. My resident pilot at the time was Betty McCulloch and we welcomed fourteen women pilots to the airport including the then BWPA secretary, Janet Ferguson.

If the car rallying in the 1950s and my small farm of sheep, dogs and cats were a great release from flying, then I must include my foray into fashion as another outlet from the stress! I opened a boutique in Ryde and hired a manageress to help run the business. I have always been interested in fine clothes, style and design and as I was inspired by the television personality and popular hostess Katie Boyle I decided to call the boutique 'Lady Katie'. The shop ticked along very well as another distraction from the intensity of running the airport so, as you can see, I had a very busy life and very soon it was time to find room for another important development – the day I married 36 year old Donald Ellis in the Autumn of 1961.

Donald was keen to court me and after a while we became an item but kept it all very quiet and no one suspected there was anything going on between us. We returned to my home county of Oxfordshire for the wedding which was held at the gorgeous 12th century St Mary's Church at Swinbrook near Burford. My family and close friends were invited to visit this pretty place of worship with its unusually tall 19th century tower, to watch Donald and I exchange our vows. (Today St Mary's graveyard is the final resting place of the famous and local aristocratic Mitford family whom as a child I often saw riding along the country lanes near my home).

At the time of my marriage the airport was doing very well and business was brisk. Donald had been the chief instructor at the Sandown Gliding Club when I met him. He was such a handsome chap and a popular person to have about the airfield and he had such a sense of occasion. There was always a good reason to have a glass of Champagne with Donald around or a sumptuous meal. I loved his joie de vivre and he was so interested in everything around him. I never drank alcohol until I met Donald and I soon learned how a fine wine of a certain vintage can be a real treat.

Not long after we married, we decided to make the Isle of Wight our permanent home and so we moved into the house I still live in. At first there was an old isolation hospital on the site, but we had it pulled down and we designed and built our cottage which I love and cherish with its lawns, flowers and the grassy paddock which over the years became home to many sheep and horses. You see, I never stopped being a farmer's daughter and my love of gardening continues to this very day.

While the work was taking place on the house, we newly-weds lived happily in a caravan on the site. Life was very good indeed and I was having fun. I still enjoyed running Sandown Airport of course and yet being married was a real bonus and made a big difference to my life.

Donald had been born in East Grinstead, West Sussex, in 1925. That same year, along with his parents and four older siblings, he moved to the Isle of Wight and made many friends. When he was 7-years-old the family moved to Folkestone, Kent and then as a teenager Donald joined the Air Training Corps when war broke out. It was during his time in the ATC that he was posted here and there to various airfields to assist the Air Transport Auxiliary and, who knows, our paths may well have crossed in that very different lifetime!

During the war the ATC cadets would fly with ATA pilots and wind down the undercarriage on those aircraft which needed some manual assistance, or they would help the ground crew with airfield jobs but most of them enjoyed a flight and seeing what they could learn from the pilot.

For Donald the ATC and the ATA fulfilled his dream of flying and just after the war ended he was able to join the Fleet Air Arm and was trained in Canada where he was awarded his wings. Donald returned to the Isle of Wight in 1958 to found the gliding club and soon got to know the shy but sometimes fierce commandant of the airport!

In April, 1965 the Minister of Aviation, Roy Jenkins, who was a member of Prime Minister Harold Wilson's Labour government, visited Sandown Airport and a photograph exists of me with him and a Mr E. Orman who was the promotions manager at British Westpoint Airways. The picture was taken at Sandown just before the Minister's flight back to London and he is the one who appears to be smiling. I can't think why my eyes are closed in the shot and the bespectacled Mr Orman is very down in the mouth. Perhaps Mr Orman and I were just camera shy that day but Mr Jenkins was beaming after a visit to the Westland Aircraft Factory at Cowes on the Isle of Wight.

Among my cuttings from the Sandown days and my life as Europe's first ever female Air Commandant, I have an article from a diary column which appeared in the *Portsmouth Evening News* on 7 July 1966. There is a picture of me at my desk in front of a poster promoting the airport and our pleasure flights. Open in front of me is a book where I kept a list of all the aircraft flying in and out of Sandown.

The article was written by Ray Stanhope and is entitled 'The Air is Her Oyster'. It went on to state:

> Sandown Airport is estimated to be one of the busiest holiday airports on the south coast. Pleasure flights, visiting private aeroplanes, and scheduled flights from Manchester, Birmingham, and Castle Donnington keep the staff on their toes during the summer months. Small and private though Sandown Airport may be, it is run with maximum efficiency, and in compliance with the rules and regulations laid down by the Ministry of Aviation. And in charge of administration, as airport commandant, is a woman ...
>
> Miss Mary Wilkins is not an Islander. She comes from Oxfordshire, but for twelve years she has been concerned with the commercial development of this main Isle of Wight air traffic base. As far as she knows she is the only woman airport commandant in the UK and Europe.
>
> A licensed air traffic controller and a licensed meteorological observer, Miss Wilkins has herself been a pilot since the age of 17.

Now, she is managing director of the small charter aircraft company based at Sandown (Bees Flight).

'The duties of commandant involve me in every aspect of airport administration,' she explained, sitting before a baffling mass of gadgets, instruments and dials in the control tower.

Women are in the majority at Sandown Airport, for, apart from two pilots and a second air traffic controller among her staff, Miss Wilkins is assisted by three girls. But their duties are concerned primarily with bookings, the bar, and looking after the passengers.

During World War Two, Miss Wilkins was a pilot with the ATA, flying all sorts of aircraft including jets. 'I was by no means the only woman,' she added. 'There were 166 of us.'

And it is her obvious experience as a pilot which allays any apprehension on the part of pilots now coming into Sandown Airport as to her ability to deal efficiently with air traffic even at the busiest of times. Although Sandown Airport is bustling with activity during the summer, it is quiet in the winter months. Miss Wilkins has a cottage not far away, and behind the airport, she has a small farm, and sheep graze alongside the runways. But the farm is not a profitable sideline. 'The animals are friends. I don't rear them to send them to market,' she said.

The atmosphere at Sandown Airport is friendly and comfortable – an atmosphere which Miss Wilkins and her staff strive to maintain, knowing that strict formality does not encourage visitors.

Nonetheless up to date management is combined with the informality, and achievement all to the credit of the woman in charge.

Although I had become Mrs Ellis in 1961, I kept my maiden name, Wilkins, for professional reasons and it was more convenient if anything else. Donald became a pilot with the British Parachute Club at Sandown and did a jump himself and in 1965 he joined the British Hovercraft Corporation as a pilot commander and an instructor. One of his many adventures involved piloting a Hovercraft in 1968 on a 450 mile journey along the Amazon River with the comedian Michael Bentine CBE.

That peculiar journey was a first for Hovercraft and a first for Donald and Michael. Why Michael was chosen to accompany Donald I am not sure but I do know Michael had been in the RAF and his father had worked as an aeronautical engineer with the Sopwith Aircraft Company. Both Michael and Donald had lived for some years in Folkestone as boys so they had quite a lot in common and got on extremely well.

During the war, however, a medical experiment with a typhoid inoculation went horribly wrong and Michael who would become one of the Britain's leading comedians, was left in a coma for several weeks. When he recovered he was severely myopic and unable to pilot an aircraft so the RAF drafted him into MI5.

In the 1960s Donald and I joined in the social whirl and a local newspaper diary columnist described our parties as 'legendary!' This implies there was some hair-raising debauchery going on at Sandown, but it was nothing of the kind – just lots of fun, chatter and music of course. We had some lovely times and made many friends and life really was worth celebrating. I laugh when I think our parties helped to liven up the Isle of Wight several years before the guitar legend Jimi Hendrix arrived to play at the island's famous festival in 1970!

During the early years of our marriage Donald decided to buy a BA Swallow aircraft just like the one I first owned in 1938. Well when he finally flew it into Sandown I looked in my logbook, then I looked again and thought the aeroplane was strangely recognisable in all sorts of ways and then I discovered it was indeed my first aircraft! I couldn't believe I had been re-united with it again and what a lovely feeling to know after all those years it was still in great condition. It had been much loved and cared for and now it was home with me!

In 1970 some great changes came into my life and I took the decision to leave the airport. I felt I was ready for a different sort of life, a change of pace if you like, and Donald had been offered the opportunity to work in Saudi Arabia with the British Hovercraft Corporation.

He had been working all over the world by then, and since 1965 he'd been teaching various people how to 'pilot' this wonderful new form of transport. In 1968 Mr Stephenson Clarke had sold the Bees Flight Company and the airport was purchased by Mr Nat Somers who owned Southampton Airport. Mr Somers was keen to sell off part of Sandown for housing and I wasn't happy about this at all, so in 1970 I left. Simple as that, and I walked away to embrace a new life and a new decade.

At first I was happy about staying at home in Sandown and doing the odd bit of flying when I could, but Donald wanted me with him so, we packed up a few clothes and I locked the house up, said goodbye to the farm animals, and my poodle went into kennels (but unhappily he died there while we were away). I'd already closed the boutique so that was one less job to sort out. We didn't want to rent the house out to anyone, so we had a friend keep an eye on it plus it was good to know our home was waiting there for us during our time abroad.

I soon discovered how living in Jeddah, Saudi Arabia was a serious a culture shock and I didn't always find it easy especially as in the 1970s it was a barren place with very few luxuries. The heat and sand seemed relentless and I often longed for the rain and bright spring weather of England. We were there in the heat and dust of Saudi for four and a half long years which were only made bearable by parties at the British Embassy. It was a good thing Donald's job gave him a certain position in society so we often got invited to events. One time I headed up a dinner party at the house for 100 guests. It was just one single maid and me organising the whole event and much to my relief it turned out to be a fun occasion and a great success. But still it wasn't England and I started to long for home.

One day when Donald and I were in the desert in Jeddah we were beckoned into a tent by some Bedouins. I kept very quiet because I was a woman and I knew I had to let Donald do all the talking. I was quite nervous but didn't let it show as I remembered this was their custom and I was a guest in their country. I had no idea what they wanted but they served us some tremendously strong coffee and were most courteous throughout the meeting. I think they just wanted to know what we thought of their country and I convinced myself it was important to find out about the lives of others, and so we sat cross legged on the floor in that tent for quite some time before we felt it was the right time to leave for the house.

Our property was next door to that of the Australian Air attaché although we didn't see that much of him and his family because the walls around the houses were ten feet high. To organise anything with the neighbours we had to knock on their door and arrange to meet them on the golf course in the desert. This had to take place at 5am in the morning before the heat began to kill us! It was hard to be a woman in Jeddah as I couldn't go anywhere alone, so that didn't amuse someone like me who lived to fly and drive fast cars. I just seemed to waft about looking glamorous. There wasn't much to do at all. We had no real roads either and a severe lack of telephones.

There were times when I'd sit about trying not to wilt in the heat and think about my youthful days in the ATA. I romanced about those winter days of wartime when it was dark and cold and I was stuck out somewhere in the wilds of the north-east freezing in a draughty billet for the night with only my clothes and a thick blanket for warmth!

It all seemed so strange to me somehow and I'd muse to myself just how exciting the job had been and then as the sun began to set over the desert I dreamed I was in a Spitfire again soaring beneath the clouds over green fields and the summer blossoms of that is forever England.

It all seemed like a lifetime ago and I began to wonder about the lives of all my friends, loved and lost, of the ATA.

While we were abroad in 1972 I heard my dear Pa died in the March and then not long after our return to the UK my mother followed him to the heavens in December 1976. They had both had good, healthy, happy and long lives, but knowing this still doesn't ever stop me from missing them every day. Over the years, my brothers, Lewis, Charles and Edward Wilkins, have died too, and yet I always have fond memories of them from our days growing up together on the family farms.

When we arrived back in Sandown I was, of course, relieved and felt I could really breathe and revel in the English air again. Donald was still working with the British Hovercraft Association and doing very well at sales and management. Indeed he must have been doing something right as we had a letter from Buckingham Palace to say he'd been honoured with an OBE for services to industry and transport! What an honour and what a great day in 1978 when we went to the Palace for Donald to meet HM The Queen and receive the honour. I was very proud of him and we had a wonderful party to celebrate his success.

He was very well thought of by the company as in 1977 we had a free flight from Saudi Arabia to London in Concorde! Imagine! When the crew learned I had been in the ATA I was invited to sit in the cockpit of this magnificent aircraft and I watched how the atmosphere turned completely navy blue as we passed above the earth so high the sun had disappeared. I was overwhelmed with the experience and thoroughly appreciated such a unique experience.

I loved Concorde and the idea of flying at 2,000 mph was just thrilling. With a few days training I would have had no hesitation at being a Concorde pilot. Just sitting there looking at the deck of instruments and dials during my special flight made me think I was in a rocket but it was basically flying and it was the most brilliant aviation invention that did all credit to the British and French designers who made it happen. I really hope Concorde gets to live again – she was a beautiful bird so please, someone somewhere, give this supersonic aircraft a chance to fly again. I wouldn't say no to learn to fly it! My flight in it was recorded with the presentation of a certificate which now sits proudly in my bathroom and I feel very lucky indeed to have flown in this magnificent aircraft. Today, one of the few remaining Concordes still left in one piece is on show in The Imperial War Museum at Duxford and I hear the queue to look around this iconic aircraft is often a long one.

When Donald left the British Hovercraft Corporation in 1980 he didn't want to retire so he became managing director of Sandown Airfield and with his usual energy and drive was determined to build it up again into an ongoing aviation concern. It didn't take long for him to buy a Cessna 172 for pleasure flights. My job was to promote these experiences and sell the tickets to the tourists and I happily got involved in all the administrative tasks which meant it could all actually happen.

It was a delightful day in 1988 when Donald met two Royal Flying Corps veterans, Norman Fielden and Hamish Currie. Norman was 88 and Hamish was 90 and they had a wonderful time flying in the Cessna over the countryside and Donald told me he let them take the controls more than once.

It was around this time I learned that a Spitfire I flew during the war was MT719 and it is still around today and lives at Cavanaugh's Flight Museum in Addison, Texas. This lovely aircraft is a Mk.VIIIc and I flew it to No.9 Maintenance Unit in June 1944.

It was then shipped to Bombay (Mumbai) India to join 17 Squadron and in December of 1947 joined the Indian Air Force. It became an instructional airframe and found its way to Duxford in 1977 with its hulk being recovered from Jaipur, India, that year.

In 1979 MT719 was bought by Franco Actis from Turin, Italy, and was made airworthy again with its first flight taking place in 1982. Six years later it was bought by Adrian Reynard and in 1993 changed hands again, being bought by the late Jim Cavanaugh for his Museum in Dallas, Texas. I understand this is where MT719 now remains on show to an adoring public.

Throughout the end of the 1970s and well into the 1980s and 90s life ticked along well and Donald and I attended many ATA and FAA reunion events. I was delighted to meet up many times with my friend and former ATA colleague Benedetta Willis who lived nearby at Bembridge.

Bright, engaging and a very relaxed person Benedetta and I belonged to the Isle of Wight Aircrew Association and were among the honoured members who met reguarly for dinner and social occasions. Benedetta was born in Cyprus in 1914 where her father Bert was an engineer building railways. By the age of ten she was in England at boarding school and went on to London to gain her honours degree in architecture. When she was in her twenties Benedetta (also known as 'Bennie') learned to fly and quickly joined the Civil Air Guard. When an uncle left her £100 she bought a Gypsy Moth aircraft and flew off on honeymoon from Sandown Airport in it. Benedetta married Charles Willis who was a flying instructor in the RAFVR.

She joined the ATA on 1cSeptember 1941 with her pilot's A licence (RAeC) gained in 1937. Her job before the war was to work as an architect's assistant, but as soon as she heard the ATA were looking for women pilots she applied and was accepted, became a First Officer and remained with the service until August 1943.

During the war Benedetta and I often saw each other at Hamble or talked over a cup of tea if we happened to be hanging about the Mess waiting for the weather to clear. Meeting up with her again as a fellow Islander some decades later was wonderful and she always happy to share a joke or two. In fact Donald and I saw a lot of her and we had many lovely trips out and about together.

She joined the RAFVR (Volunteer Reserve) and after instruction got her official wings at the age of 40. Benedetta and Charles had four children. They moved to Bembridge, Isle of Wight in 1972 and Charles was the local harbourmaster for many years before his death in 1990.

In June, 1994 the local paper, the *Isle of Wight County Press*, sent a reporter to interview us both and Benedetta talked about our experiences in the ATA which quashed a lot feminist rhetoric into the ground! We told the journalist how in an age that modern society would not consider to be the ideal of female emancipation, we took on responsible jobs that many men would baulk at. We did this dangerous work without fuss or any apparent awareness that we were going anywhere or doing anything beyond the normal call of duty.

I said we got around the country with just a map and the grace of God! The reporter could hardly believe we could have managed such a task. I admitted I did get lost once but in the end I found where I was so I wasn't really about to end up in the Channel.

In 2008, Benedetta and I shared a wonderful time with the remaining 'few' of the ATA when we visited Number 10 Downing Street to be presented with our ATA veterans' badge by the then Prime Minister, Gordon Brown. During her ATA career Benedetta had flown 135 Spitfires and numerous other varieties of aircraft.

A short while after our excursion to Number 10 and in December of the same year Benedetta died at the grand age of 94. She had been one of my best friends on the island and will never be forgotten.

Chapter 23

'Spitfire Mary'

In the 1980s, and as I was often invited to aviation and anniversary events, I travelled to RAF Lyneham for the ATA Association dinners. We always had a wonderful time and it was at one of these events where I first met HRH Prince Michael of Kent and we got on so well.

On one occasion I told the prince I had once met his father the Duke of Kent when he visited the ATA in 1942. It seemed I'd started my career meeting his father and had ended it talking to his son! Prince Michael enjoyed this observation of mine and I am so proud he agreed to write the foreword of this book. It means a lot to me.

In the 1990s I well recall my visit to the former RAF Marwell near Winchester in Hampshire where today there is a zoo on the outskirts of the site. During the war years with the ATA I landed at Marwell many times and for that reason I was invited to a reunion party along with other veteran pilots to mark the fiftieth anniversary of D-Day.

In 1944 Marwell had been a secret flight test base and used for aircraft coming out of the Cunliffe Owen Aircraft Factory at Swaythling because it was outside the Southampton balloon barrage. The managing director of the factory was the owner of Marwell Hall at the time. I do remember Marwell could be a devil to find from the air as the test flight area was covered in camouflage to protect it from the Luftwaffe. When I look back to those wartime days of poor weather as we flew out and landed at those small, hidden airfields it's hard to believe it all actually happened.

The reunion event was great fun and I had a wonderful day at Marwell catching up with all my chums from the war days.

My husband, Donald, decided to retire from flying in 1997 as his eyesight was failing but he took this on board like the trooper he was and we got by as best we could, and as ever I kept busy keeping the house and the grounds in order. There were often friends dropping in to see us and we all marvelled at Donald's good sense of humour and stoicism. Our friends managed to help kept his spirits up and we had some fun dinner parties and good conversation.

By the time the new century had dawned I began to notice many of my ATA colleagues were no longer with us. But there was some comfort in the knowledge the Maidenhead Heritage Centre had set up a small museum in 1993 in honour of our war work.

For so many years the men and women of the ATA had been largely forgotten until the Heritage Centre's curator, Mr Richard Poad MBE, found space for an exhibition about the organisation at Maidenhead. This, of course, is the nearest town to White Waltham – the headquarters of our wartime ferrying operation.

I have visited the Museum on several occasions and there's a photograph of me as I am now pointing to another picture of the young me in the ATA. I think it is splendid that the Museum continues to attract so many visitors each year and it is helping to keep the memory of us ATA aircrew alive.

One or two of the volunteers at the Museum actually remember some of us from our ATA flying days too. One of the first eight women in the ATA was Joan Hughes and she stayed on at White Waltham for some years after the war as an instructor. Today she is remembered with fondness by one chap who volunteers at the museum as she had taught him to fly.

Then, in 2005, I received a wonderful invitation to fly in a two-seater training Spitfire, ML407, with its pilot and owner, the lovely Carolyn Grace. The aircraft had been bought from a museum in 1979 by Carolyn's husband, Nick, who was a qualified pilot and design engineer. He then spent five years bringing ML407 back to life. By 1985 this remarkable Spitfire was airborne again and for three years Nick flew her proudly across the skies with passion and verve.

It was a tragic time for his family and friends when he was killed in a car accident in 1988. His Spitfire, ML407, had lost a highly skilled pilot and pal. His wife Carolyn, however, was determined to keep her husband's memory alive and learned to fly the Spitfire herself. She said she wanted the aircraft to firmly remain in the Grace family and this ambition has come true as her son Richard also keeps ML407 in the air in honour of his father.

It was the historian Hugh Smallwood who began looking into the background of ML407 and he discovered it had first been flown by my ATA friend Jackie Moggridge on 29 April 1944. When Carolyn heard about this she was deeply touched as she is so inspired and in awe of us ATA women and the job we carried out during the difficult days of wartime.

Carolyn soon met Jackie during the filming of *The Perfect Lady* – a documentary about ML407 – and they saw in Jackie's logbook how she'd delivered Carolyn's Spitfire to 485 (New Zealand) Squadron. It became the personal aircraft of Flying Officer Johnnie Houlton DFC, who while at the controls of ML407 shot down the first enemy aircraft of D-Day on 6 June 1944.

Fifty years later, during the making of the film in 1994, Jackie was in the cockpit once more as co-pilot with Carolyn. They flew from Land's End across the southern skies and back again. When I met Jackie at an ATA reunion event shortly afterwards she told me all about the experience and how Carolyn had coaxed her back into taking control of ML407 again.

I thought it was wonderful to hear about it all and what an extraordinary coincidence for such a rare reunion between Spitfire and pilot. I believe Jackie and I are the only two female ATA pilots who ever got to meet up with Spitfires we'd flown during the war. Jackie of course will remain the first ATA woman veteran to ever fly in one again owing to its converted two-seater status as a trainer Spitfire. On 1 August 2004, and a few weeks after Jackie's death, Carolyn was immensely honoured to scatter Jackie's ashes from ML407.

Before she died I think Jackie may have talked to Carolyn about me, and so what a delight it was to hear I would be offered a chance to fly in ML407. It had been sixty-five years since I'd flown in a Spitfire – the aircraft of my dreams. I had sat in them of course to pose for press photographs over the years, but to fly in a Spitfire again?

I was in heaven. It was a day I was to join in the wonders of internet phenomena too as my flight was filmed by a small camera in the cockpit and now it can be seen by audiences across the world on YouTube.

It was a bleak time in 2007 when my husband Donald was diagnosed with a rare form of leukaemia. He was eighty-two and yet fought so bravely to remain strong for us both. For a while he was in and out of hospital and then a nursing home and when he came home for a visit he'd sleep in a bed we'd put in the dining room so he could feel the sun on his face when he awoke.

For eighteen months he battled on against this dreadful disease and yet I watched him fade as it stifled his energy and attacked his will to live. I adored Donald and when he died in December 2009 it came as a tremendous shock even though I suspected it would happen. We'd been so lucky to have almost fifty happy years together and I always remember this fact every day now as I go about the housework and the garden. Sometimes memory is truly a wonderful thing.

Donald's niece, Rosemarie Martin, and her husband, Ted, live nearby and I see them quite often to catch up on old times and exchange news and views on all sorts of things. They were both very fond of Donald and we all miss him very much.

In 2010 as I was trying to get used to living without Donald I received an invitation to attend the unveiling of a new ATA Memorial at Hamble-le-Rice where I was stationed during the war years. It was a beautiful day on 10 July as I met up again with a few of my friends from those wartime flying days. There was cheerful Margaret 'Maggie' Frost, Tony Bray, Annette Hill, Peter George, Joy Lofthouse and Peter Garrod. The fine Memorial stone, with its small but tough metal Spitfire positioned as if in flight on the top, is situated on the corner of Aquila Way, Hamble, and after we'd all been photographed next to it with a wreath there was a reception in the local village hall.

So many people associated with the ATA, relatives and friends, had been involved in the creation of this wonderful tribute to all of us who ferried aircraft or worked as ground crew during wartime. It was a treat to watch a flypast by Joe Dible and Owen Watts in Joe's 1937 Foster's Wikner Wicko aircraft which had previously been owned by two ATA greats – Philippa Booth (nee Bennett, 1919-2007) and Lettice Curtis.

I met with Joy again in June 2011 when we were invited by a Mr Peter Jewson to his Lodge Hill Garage in Abingdon, Oxfordshire. Mr Jewson had placed a full size replica Spitfire on the roof of his premises in a bid to raise money for a new ATA Memorial. Joy gave a rousing speech and we enjoyed a 1940s-style lunch and 1940s music as Mr Jewson's guests of honour.

In recent years I have noticed an increase in my mail and am encouraged to hear from students, pilots and media from all over the world wishing to know more about my flying experiences during the war. This is, in fact, part of the reason why I wanted to see this book completed. Then it's all there in black and white to be read, hopefully learned from, and enjoyed.

When I met Melody, the co-author of this book, she was in a position to invite me on a special trip to fly in a helicopter next to a Spitfire Mk.Vb – my favourite mark of this super little aircraft. So on a sunny day in June 2013, I flew right over the White Cliffs of Dover and saw the Battle of Britain Memorial at Capel-le-Ferne in Kent, with Spitfire BM597 performing wonderfully right next to me as I looked out from my window seat in the helicopter.

All sorts of memories came flooding back. How could they not? Suddenly I would have given anything to be back in the cockpit of a Spitfire as they really are such beautiful aircraft to fly and always, always gave me the feeling I was wearing wings. It is the nearest I ever came to actually becoming a bird.

Spitfire BM597 is owned by The Historic Aircraft Collection and she is based at Duxford. When I watched her dance among the clouds on that summer's day in 2013 she was flown by Flight Lieutenant Charlie Brown – a splendid pilot with a traditional handlebar moustache and someone with whom I had a wonderful chat after we'd landed at a small grass airfield. Charlie told me I mustn't tell everyone the Spitfire is as easy as riding a bicycle in case everyone wants to try it!

I am so lucky to have a kind friend who keeps a small aircraft at Sandown and so I was able to fly back home with him after my flight experience in Kent.

In 2014 a full page photograph of me appeared in *The Lady Magazine* as part of a feature series called 'People We Love'. I felt very honoured.

That same year I visited Biggin Hill and joined my ATA friend Joy Lofthouse on a seat in the sun outside the Heritage Hangar. We talked a lot that day to cheery Fleet Air Arm veteran pilot Keith Quilter who told us how he'd flown Seafires and Corsairs during the war and had joined in the aerial bombing of the German battleship *Tirpitz*. Later that year I met with Keith again at a special wartime anniversary concert and we danced together in a marquee at Biggin Hill. The event was hosted by actor and aviator Martin Shaw who has a great interest in vintage aircraft and social history.

These days I still receive visitors to my home and was delighted to meet two pilots I once employed at the Bees Flight Company at Sandown – Victor Scrivens and Brian Turpin. They arrived at my door in 2015 and we had a catch up about old times. They told me how they appreciated the way I ran the airport so efficiently and why they always knew I had to remain stern about so many rules when it came to safety. It's always lovely to see them now and again as they've both retired with some great memories of Sandown and their more recent careers in aviation. Victor and Brian also knew my husband Donald and it's good they keep in touch with me. I like to think I was their favourite boss.

Another surprise was in store when I turned up at a friend's home on the Isle of Wight only to find myself seated near the celebrity gardener and television presenter Alan Titchmarsh. The following week he wrote all about me in his *Daily Telegraph* column.

On the anniversary calendar the year 2015 proved an important one as it marked seventy-five years since the Battle of Britain in 1940 and I was in demand by the media to talk about the war years. I was asked, as always, about the Spitfire and I am always happy to point out this aircraft is not just an effective military machine – it is the absolute symbol of freedom.

Then there was a surprise in store when a Channel 4 camera crew arrived at Sandown to film *Battle of Britain: The Last of The Few*. The producer had written to me and asked if I would take part in the documentary and mentioned I would be interviewed by television presenter Dermot O'Leary. Other veterans on the list were my ATA friends Joy Lofthouse and Molly Rose, RAF Wing Commander Tom Neil DFC and Bar, AFC, AE, Squadron Leader Geoffrey Wellum DFC, and several other notables who had served as ground crew or in the Ops rooms.

Well, when the day of filming arrived I noted Joy and Molly were sitting on a couple of chairs on the airfield at Sandown. It was a breezy day and so we waited, and waited and waited for the presenter and aircraft to show up. Molly was furious about this – and even more so when no apology was delivered. We were all getting cold from the wind blowing across the airfield and we wondered why there was such a delay.

We are all tough old birds well into our nineties, but there is a limit to our endurance when it comes to hanging about in cold weather. Anyway, suddenly in the distance I heard a Spitfire. Well, we all looked up at the sound of that throaty Merlin engine roaring towards us, and it came into land more or less at our feet.

Out jumped a pilot from the Boultbee Flight Academy at Goodwood in West Sussex and suddenly I was told I was going on a flight! This was all such a surprise and I couldn't believe Joy and Molly had kept it all a secret from me. I thought to myself, Spitfire TR9 here I come!

So it was on with the parachute and a tough white helmet was jammed firmly on my head – a helmet which didn't do a lot for my delicate ears. However, soon enough we were off soaring high and proud and I was filmed taking in the views and, at times, the controls as we roared around the skies for twenty minutes before landing at Goodwood. I loved it. I was even more delighted when I knew HRH Prince Harry was going to be part of the programme, and in September that year Joy and I had a happy day at the Battle of Britain 75th Anniversary event at Goodwood.

I wore my ATA uniform and Joy was dressed in a lovely frock patterned with Spitfires which had been given to her by Dr Margaret Clotworthy – trainee pilot, Spitfire enthusiast and also a dear friend of Battle of Britain pilot, Wing Commander Tom Neil. We met all sorts of people in the marquee that day and I was asked to pose for all manner of 'selfies'. It was a most special day and I praise the organisers for all their wonderful work.

Once again I was welcomed and made to feel like a celebrity and the national press were out in full force asking me to stand next to Spitfires for their photographs. The following morning, I visited my local garage to pick up a *Daily Telegraph* and there I was, beaming out from its pages in my ATA uniform. Then there I was in *The Times*, and I made the centre pages of *The Guardian*.

Then I thought if only Donald and my long lost friends from the ATA had been around to have enjoyed that day at Goodwood. I am sure if my ATA pal Maureen Dunlop, who had so famously appeared as the glamour girl pilot on the front of the *Picture Post* in 1944, had lived to see all this coverage about shy little First Officer Mary Wilkins in 2016, she would have been proud I was still around to wave the flag for the ferry pilots of the Second World War. Indeed 2015 was quite a year for me and all the veterans I know and I do so love meeting up with everyone whenever I can.

One really big treat arose in 2016 as I head for my centenary year. I was contacted by ITV to find out if I would like to take part in a show called *100 Year Old Drivers Re-booted*. This time it was going to be all cars and, joy of joys, I was to take part in a hill climb in an Allard – a vintage sports car from 1948 just like the one I had raced in all those rallies more than sixty years ago! How marvellous and how could I resist? It was a bright and sunny day in May when I arrived courtesy of The Allard Owners Club, for the Vallence Vintage Car Day in Sevenoaks, Kent, for the filming. There I met David Haley – the owner of a beautiful bright red Allard K1, and he was going to let me drive her. Oh, I was ecstatic, it was overpowering and David was happy too because he had a woman Spitfire pilot at the wheel. It was splendid when one of the Spitfires from the Biggin Hill Heritage Hangar flew overhead in a sort of salute. I believe the pilot that day was the owner of the aircraft, Peter Monk.

For this particular programme I was at first filmed in my grey Toyota Yaris driving along, singing a song, on the roads of the Isle of Wight. I am seen overtaking people on the road pootling about on mobility scooters – and there I am at the wheel watching out for another car at a junction, so I slow before I put my foot down again and take off.

You see, when you are 99-years-old everything is that much slower, but only a teeny, weeny bit. I was described by the narrator of the programme as 'one woman not afraid of speed or taking the odd risk'. Too true, I thought, as they described my life in the ATA flying Spitfires, Hurricanes, bombers and of course the Meteor jet. I reminded viewers my job in the ATA was very dangerous and the biggest danger was the weather. We flew alone and the more I think about it the more I wonder how on earth we coped, us girls. But we did.

The programme highlighted my 'taste for speed' and pointed out my long held passion for racing cars and one in particular – my Allard sports classic. I will never forget the Allard because it was a soulmate and it becomes part of one. It had a top speed in 1948 of 86 mph. To me it was rather like a Spitfire. All I had to do was apply just a little bit of foot on the accelerator and off I could go. When I settled on the Isle of Wight I decided to give up the Allard and it is a decision I have regretted for more than half a century. My car now lives in Australia. I have missed that car and miss it still so terribly and so wish it was here. It would mean an awful lot to have that car back because it would bring back so many lovely memories.

When I took part in the hill-climb event for the television programme I hadn't seen an Allard for fifty years. Of course when I spotted that beautiful red K1 my heart melted on the spot. I really was overjoyed about it. I told the owner his car was beautiful and so at first he took me for a spin and my scarf flew behind me like Biggles. I couldn't stop shouting with joy. I had the wind in my hair and it brought all those happy days back to me – the days when I was at the wheel racing with the Isle of Wight Car Club. To drive the Allard is just lovely, you just point it where you want to go, put on some power and there it goes – marvellous.

It meant an awful lot to me to be able to drive an Allard again. I never ever thought I'd see an Allard again. It was just so splendid, it really was.

In fact, I will never give up driving as I need my little car so much – it is all part of my independence and I require it for shopping, collecting a newspaper, seeing friends, generally getting out and about.

I used to catch the car ferry, travel over the Solent and drive on to the New Forest to see my sister Dora until I had some bad news in January 2016. I got a phone call over Christmas to say she was ill, before I then found out, on 10 January, that she had died. That was a bitter blow and I was terribly upset. I stopped everything I was doing as I needed to cope with such a loss. Then in April my sister-in-law at Brize Norton died. It's true I've had a hard time recently what with losing so many people I knew in my life. It's amazing, you know, when you see all these people in old photographs and now there's so very, very few of us left.

Do I have any regrets? Well I would have loved to have had children but it wasn't to be. My secret to a long life is keeping busy, also my housework and garden keeps me on my toes and the vitamins help too. I also have a kind friend, Bruce, who is a former Squadron Leader and he is also a member of the exclusive Royal Flying Corps and Royal Naval Air Service Association. I am proud to be the only woman pilot in this club of elite ex-service aviators and they treat me like a queen at the various dinners and social events. The rule is not to allow women pilots but for me they make an exception.

I was so delighted in 2016 to learn I had been nominated and accepted for a rare Master Air Pilot certificate. I had been nominated for this notable award by The Honourable Company of Air Pilots and the certificate itself is signed by the Duke of York who is Grand Master of the Company. A presentation event involved a trip to London. What an honour for me.

What does make me happy is to know that the Air Transport Auxiliary will never be forgotten – and that there is so much interest. People stop me in the street and say, 'It is magnificent what you did'. I think once you've been on the television you can't get away from this sort of attention. Over the decades I have had opportunity to meet again with many friends from my past – the great test pilot Neville Duke and his wife Gwen, Gordon Mitchell (son of R.J. Mitchell) and Raymond Baxter. It was a lovely day when we all met up in the 1980s for a photograph during a special aviation reunion event where another special guest was the Luftwaffe pilot and author Ulrich Steinhilper.

I do appreciate having seen Joy and Molly over the years, as always all sorts of memories came out that only we can truly share. We used to keep in touch with our old ATA friend Maggie Frost too, but she had a fall in the summer of 2014 and died in hospital on 4 August.

However, in June 2016 I saw Joy again and it cheered me up so much. Joy is always a tonic and is full of life. When I knew Joy in the ATA she was the baby at Hamble and is four or five years younger than me. Before she called by in June she had been to Leeds East Airport (formerly RAF Church Fenton) for the Project Propeller annual dinner for Second World War veterans – an event which I was unable to attend – and so she asked the personal pilot to fly her to the Isle of Wight afterwards and fill me in on the chat. Oh, I was thrilled. When there's hardly anyone left from your era it's difficult in so many ways and then when you do have a chance to see them of course all sorts of recollections are passed between us. In the ATA I had often flown into RAF Church Fenton which then was used mostly for training night-fighter aircrews and our local ATA Ferry Pool was at Sherburn-in-Elmet.

Now that I am in my 100th year I realise I have had a long and happy life – and a charmed one at that. I have tried to make the most of it giving pleasure, kindness and happiness to others. What I find of great comfort to me is the knowledge that the Spitfire will live on and on as there is so much love out there for this wonderful fighter aircraft which is arguably the best ever example of British design and technology.

The Spitfire really does mean so much to so many and will do so for generations to come. I know this because there's a little boy of 5-years-old who I've met a few times now and he always runs over to me when we meet, hugs me tight and calls me 'his Spitfire Mary'. He is very aware of what a Spitfire looks like and why it is so famous. It's always a joy for me to see him and have a chat about aeroplanes. His mother is delighted he is keen to learn all he can from me about flying.

In all my dreams the feisty little Spitfire is there, of course, waiting for me on the horizon, always welcoming and always beckoning me to fly her close and fast as if it were yesterday.

Appendix I

FIRST OFFICER MARY WILKINS
SPITFIRE DELIVERIES
1942-1946

Date	Mark	Serial	From	To	Time	Notes
October 1942						
13.10.42	V	AR513	South Marston	Lyneham	30	First Spitfire flight
13.10.42	V	AR516	South Marston	Little Rissington	35	
25.10.42	IX	BS401	Chattis Hill	North Weald	40	No.15 F/P Hamble
27.10.42	Vb	AD571	Hamble	Llandow	40	
28.10.42	Vb	BM120	Hamble	Colerne	30	
31.10.42	IX	BS507	Eastleigh	North Weald	35	
31.10.42	IX	BS405	Chattis Hill	Hornchurch	40	
November 1942						
2.11.42	V	BL583	Hamble	Lyneham	25	
2.11.42	IIc	MB197	High Post	Wroughton	20	Seafire
6.11.42	Vb	AR377	Hamble	Lyneham	35	
6.11.42	IX	EN123	Chattis Hill	Northolt	40	
7.11.42	Vb	W3380	Hamble	Llandow	45	
9.11.42	IIc	MB248	Chattis Hill	Wroughton	25	Seafire
16.11.42	Vb	BL674	Hamble	Llandow	45	
16.11.42	Vb	ER863	Llandow	Wroughton	40	
17.11.42	IX	EN181	Eastleigh	Debdon	40	
17.11.42	IIc	MB249	Chattis Hill	Wroughton	20	Seafire
18.11.42	Ic	R6769	Hamble	White Waltham	20	
20.11.42	Vb	BM493	Hamble	White Waltham	20	
21.11.42	Vb	W3759	Hamble	Brize Norton	25	
22.11.42	Vb	ES113	Lyneham	Wroughton	20	
22.11.42	IX	EN136	Chattis Hill	White Waltham	20	

22.11.42	IX	EN126	Chattis Hill	Debdon	40	
23.11.42	IX	EN186	Eastleigh	White Waltham	45	
26.11.42	V	EE744	Yeovil	Llandow	25	
29.11.42	IX	EN197	Eastleigh	White Waltham	20	
29.11.42	VI	EN189	Eastleigh	Colerne	30	Pressure cabin

December 1942

1.12.42	IX	EN204	Eastleigh	Brize Norton	25	
2.12.42	IIc	MB260	Chattis Hill	Wroughton	20	Seafire
4.12.42	II	P7742	Hamble	Lyneham	25	
5.12.42	IX	EN144	Chattis Hill	White Waltham	25	
5.12.42	IX	BR651	Brize Norton	White Waltham		Tipped on nose in strong winds
6.12.42	II	X4499	Mount Farm	Brize Norton	30	
9.12.42	IIc	MB264	Chattis Hill	Wroughton	20	Seafire
12.12.42	Vb	EP384	Hamble	Llandow	50	
12.12.42	Vc	EE747	Llandow	Westhampnett	50	
15.12.42	II	MB267	Chattis Hill	Wroughton	25	Seafire
20.12.42	IX	EN295	Eastleigh	Colerne	35	
20.12.42	IIc	EE752	Colerne	-		Struck by Spitfire V whilst waiting to T/O
22.12.42	IX	EN155	Chattis Hill	Wroughton	40	
29.12.42	Vb	EN965	Colerne	Westhampnett	35	

January 1943

2.1.43	VIII	JF286	Eastleigh	Llandow	45	
9.1.43	IIc	MB304	High Post	Wroughton	25	Seafire
17.1.43	V	X4488	Hamble	Colerne	30	
21.1.43	VIII	JF292	Eastleigh	Llandow	40	
21.1.43	V	AD320	Llandow	S. Marston	30	
23.1.43	V	AD271	Hamble	Wroughton	20	
23.1.43	XI	EN337	Chattis Hill	Mount Farm	30	PRU

February 1943

18.2.43	IX	EN478	Eastleigh	Colerne	30	
18.2.43	Vb	BM532	Colerne	Westhampnett	45	610 Squadron
19.2.43	IIc	NM924	Chattis Hill	Wroughton	30	Seafire
19.2.43	IIc	LR633	Wroughton	Lee-on-Solent	40	Seafire
24.2.43	Vb	EN966	Hamble	Colerne	25	
24.2.43	V	EF452	Colerne	Worthy Down	30	
25.2.43	V	EF528	Colerne	Wroughton	20	
25.2.43	IX	EN480	Eastleigh	Colerne	30	
26.2.43	IX	EN483	Eastleigh	Brize Norton	35	
28.2.43	II	NM966	Chattis Hill	Wroughton	20	Seafire

March 1943

1.3.43	IX	EN491	Eastleigh	Cosford	45	

2.3.43	II	NM968	Chattis Hill	Wroughton	20	
4.3.43	Vb	AB786	Hamble	Little Rissington	35	
6.3.43	Vb	AB367	Lyneham	S. Marston	15	
7.3.43	IX	EN401	Chattis Hill	Colerne	20	
7.3.43	VIII	JF346	Eastleigh	Lyneham	30	
12.3.43	Vb	AR932	Colerne	S. Marston	20	
14.3.43	VIII	JF351	Eastleigh	Cosford	45	
15.3.43	IIc	NM978	Chattis Hill	Wroughton	25	Seafire
17.3.43	VIII	JF354	Eastleigh	Llandow	40	
17.3.43	V	BL420	Llandow	Hamble	45	
18.3.43	IX	EN405	Chattis Hill	Colerne	20	
18.3.43	V	BL846	Colerne	Hamble	25	
19.3.43	IIc	BL635	Hamble	Lee-on-Solent	10	Seafire
20.3.43	XI	EN422	Chattis Hill	Benson	20	PRU
22.3.43	VIII	JF360	Eastleigh	Cosford	45	
23.3.43	XI	RN421	Chattis Hill	Benson	20	PRU
24.3.43	II	MB323	Chattis Hill	Wroughton	20	Seafire
26.3.43	VIII	JF393	Eastleigh	Llandow	45	
31.3.43	Vb	BM538	Hamble	Cosford	50	

April 1943

17.4.43	VIII	JF447	Wroughton	Hamble	50	
18.4.43	IIc	NM946	Chattis	Wroughton	20	Seafire
20.4.43	IIc	NX884	Hamble	Cosford	50	Seafire
20.4.43	IIc	NX884	Cosford	Stretton	20	Seafire
20.4.43	V	BM580	Brize Norton	Hamble	25	
21.4.43	VIII	JF453	Eastleigh	Cosford	40	
22.4.43	III	NX893	Hamble	Lee-on-Solent	10	Seafire
24.4.43	III	NX885	Hamble	Stretton	70	Seafire
29.4.43	XI	EN410	Chattis	Brize Norton	20	

May 1943

1.5.43	VIII	JF465	Eastleigh	Cosford	45	
1.5.43	Vb	BM422	Cosford	Redhill	60	
2.5.43	V	BM302	Christchurch	Kirkbride	110	Seafire
4.5.43	Ib	NX698	Hamble	Cosford	50	Seafire
4.5.43	V	BM632	Cosford	Hamble	40	
6.5.43	Vb	X4821	Hamble	Wroughton	20	
6.5.43	Vb	AB271	Wroughton	S. Marston	10	
28.5.43	XI	EN652	Chattis	Chattis	35	Wheels jammed when partially retracted; unable to move selector, so landed wheels up!
29.5.43	Ib	AD358	Hamble	Cosford	45	
30.5.43	Ib	MB149	Christchurch	Lee-on-Solent	15	Seafire
30.5.43	VIII	JF522	Eastleigh	Colerne	30	

30.5.43	VII	R7211	Brize Norton	-		Taxy accident

June 1943

4.6.43	-	LR687	Wroughton	Christchurch	30	Seafire
5.6.43	VIII	JF295	Lyneham	Yeovilton	20	
24.6.43	-	LR687	Christchurch	Lyneham	25	Seafire

July 1943

2.7.43	-	NK986	Hamble	Henstridge	30	Seafire
3.7.43	VIII	JF750	Eastleigh	Llandow	45	
4.7.43	-	EP762	Hamble	Cosford	50	Seafire
4.7.43	V	BM587	Cosford	S. Marston	35	
5.7.43	-	MA800	Cosford	Colerne	30	
12.7.43	IIc	P8475	Hamble	Colerne	25	
20.7.43	VIII	JF777	Eastleigh	Colerne	25	
22.7.43	IIc	P8373	Hamble	Lyneham	30	
23.7.43	VIII	JF695	Chattis	Llandow	45	
23.7.43	Vb	AB227	Llandow	S. Marston	35	
26.7.43	VIII	JF834	Chattis	Colerne	25	

September 1943

3.9.43	VIII	JF290	Hamble	Lyneham	25	
5.9.43	VIII	JF294	Eastleigh	Colerne	25	
9.9.43	Ia	AR219	Cosford	Colerne	35	39 Maintenance Unit
11.9.43	VIII	JF882	High Post	Brize Norton	25	
11.9.43	XI	MB904	Chattis	Benson	20	PRU
19.9.43	-	MB221	Christchurch	Cosford	45	Seafire
22.9.43	IX	MH924	Colerne	Wroughton	20	
25.9.43	VIII	JF896	High Post	Brize Norton	30	
26.9.43	VIII	JG331	Chattis	Cosford	40	

October 1943

1.10.43	II	LR735	Hamble	Lee-on-Solent	10	Seafire
1.10.43	-	MB246	Worthy Down	Christchurch	15	Seafire
3.10.43	VIII	JG255	Eastleigh	Cosford	50	
3.10.43	IX	MH822	Lyneham	Stretton	45	
7.10.43	VIII	JG263	Eastleigh	Brize Norton	30	
13.10.43	VIII	JG348	Chattis	Cosford	45	
16.10.43	V	BM113	Cosford	Ibsley	75	
16.10.43	VIII	JG699	Ibsley	Brize Norton	30	
21.10.43	Vb	W3605	Hamble	Brize Norton	35	
22.10.43	IIc	MB150	Hamble	Christchurch	15	Seafire
22.10.43	IIc	LR711	Christchurch	Lee-on-Solent	20	Seafire
24.10.43	VIII	JG376	Chattis	Brize Norton	30	
28.10.43	VIII	JG312	Keevil	Watchfield	30	
28.10.43	VIII	JG312	Watchfield	Brize Norton	1	

| 30.10.43 | VIII | JG542 | Eastleigh | Brize Norton | 25 | |

November 1943

3.11.43	VIII	JG475	Worthy Down	Brize Norton	25	
5.11.43	VIII	JG490	Eastleigh	Cosford	50	
30.11.43	I	X4936	Hamble	Cosford	50	
30.11.43	V	EE617	Colerne	Ibsley	25	

December 1943

1.12.43	-	LN635	Hamble	Lee-on-Solent	10	Seafire
2.12.43	VIII	MD231	Eastleigh	Brize Norton	30	
2.12.43	VIII	JG479	Keevil	Brize Norton	20	
4.12.43	VIII	JG610	Chattis	Brize Norton	20	
13.12.43	XI	PA866	Chattis	Benson	20	PRU
13.12.43	VIII	MD230	Keevil	Brize Norton	25	
19.12.43	IX	LV649	Hamble	Colerne	25	
20.12.43	IX	JG536	Eastleigh	Cosford	55	
20.12.43	IX	LX665	Chattis	Cosford	45	
22.12.43	VIII	JG529	Eastleigh	Cosford	50	
22.12.43	IX	LV670	Keevil	Cosford	35	
28.12.43	IX	LV672	Chattis	Brize Norton	25	
28.12.43	Vb	AA613	Colerne	Marwell	25	
29.12.43	VIII	-	Chattis	Brize Norton	20	
30.12.43	IIc	LR707	Hawarden	Christchurch	75	Seafire. Flak over coast

January 1944

1.1.44	VII	MD123	Eastleigh	Lyneham	25	
2.1.44	VIII	LV738	Chattis	Cosford	45	
6.1.44	VII	MD128	Eastleigh	Colerne	30	
8.1.44	VIII	MD215	Keevil	Cosford	40	
10.1.44	VIII	LV744	Chattis	Brize Norton	25	
20.1.44	VII	MD130	Eastleigh	Lyneham	20	
20.1.44	VIII	MD273	Chattis	Brize Norton	20	
21.1.44	VIII	JG551	Keevil	Cosford	30	
23.1.44	VIII	MD280	Keevil	Cosford	30	
24.1.44	IX	NM362	Hamble	Kidlington	25	
28.1.44	V	ER315	Hamble	Colerne	30	
28.1.44	VIII	MD279	Chattis	Cosford	40	
29.1.44	XI	PA902	Chattis	Benson	20	PRU
30.1.44	VII	MD142	Eastleigh	Lyneham	30	
30.1.44	XI	PA905	Chattis	Benson	30	PRU
30.1.44	VII	MD273	Christchurch	Lee-on-Solent	15	

February 1944

| 5.2.44 | VIII | MB341 | Keevil | Brize Norton | 20 | |
| 5.2.44 | IX | MH871 | Hamble | Yeovilton | 30 | |

6.2.44	VIII	MD374	Keevil	Brize Norton	20	
7.2.44	IX	MH630	Hamble	Cowley	30	
8.2.44	VIII	MD342	Chattis	Cosford	45	Landed with tail wheel retracted
12.2.44	VIII	MD376	Keevil	Brize Norton	30	
14.2.44	V	EN898	Hamble	Cowley	30	
15.2.44	VII	MD143	Eastleigh	Colerne	25	
15.2.44	II	LR683	Colerne	Henstridge	20	Seafire
16.2.44	III	NM936	Hamble	Lee-on-Solent	10	Seafire
28.2.44	IIc	MB269	Lee-on-Solent	Hawarden	65	Seafire

March 1944

1.3.44	VI	P8036	Hawarden	Brize Norton	40	
11.3.44	VIII	MD301	Chattis	Brize Norton	30	
12.3.44	VIII	MD402	Eastleigh	Cosford	45	
12.3.44	IX	MR614	Cosford	Redhill	45	
12.3.44	VIII	JG659	Chattis	Brize Norton	30	
14.3.44	IX	MJ684	Hamble	Cowley	30	
16.3.44	-	MB217	White Waltham	Christchurch	30	Seafire
18.3.44	XI	PA957	Keevil	Brize Norton	20	
18.3.44	III	NF520	Colerne	Lee-on-Solent	35	Seafire
20.3.44	VIII	JG670	Chattis	Cosford	45	

April 1944

4.4.44	IX	BS239	Hamble	Cowley	25	
6.4.44	VIII	MT518	Chattis	Brize Norton	30	
6.4.44	II	NF513	Colerne	Lee-on-Solent	30	Seafire
6.4.44	V	AR604	Hamble	Cosford	45	
10.4.44	IX	BS348	Hamble	Cowley	30	

May 1944

6.5.44	XI	PL827	Chattis	Farnborough	20	
6.5.44	IX	-252	Little Rissington	Redhill	30	
7.5.44	VIII	MT763	Chattis	Cosford	45	
7.5.44	IX	ML421	Cosford	Newchurch	60	
8.5.44	VIII	MT764	Chattis	Cosford	45	
8.5.44	IIc	LR732	Henstridge	Hawarden	55	Seafire
9.5.44	XII	EN609	Hamble	Lyneham	30	
9.5.44	III	NF626	Lyneham	Henstridge	25	Seafire
9.5.44	IIc	MA977	Henstridge	Hawarden	55	
10.5.44	VIII	MT660	Chattis	Brize Norton	25	
16.5.44	VIII	MT767	Chattis	Cosford	45	
16.5.44	V	EN950	Cosford	Friston	60	
18.5.44	VIII	MT675	Eastleigh	Brize Norton	25	
19.5.44	IX	ML348	Little Rissington	Lympne	45	
23.5.44	XIV	RM673	Chattis	Colerne	20	

23.5.44	II	P7832	Colerne	Hamble	25	
24.5.44	IIa	P7853	Hamble	Gosport	10	
25.5.44	VIII	MT787	Chattis	Brize Norton	25	
25.5.44	Vc	JK280	Brize Norton	Horne	35	
27.5.44	XIV	RM623	Chattis	Colerne	30	
27.5.44	VIII	MT553	Keevil	Brize Norton	25	
27.5.44	VII	MD189	Eastleigh	Lyneham	30	
28.5.44	XIV	RM676	Chattis	Lyneham	30	
29.5.44	Vb	AR515	Hamble	Cowley	30	
29.5.44	IX	ML323	Little Rissington	Hamble	30	

June 1944

2.6.44	I	X4652	Hamble	Seighford	60	
3.6.44	IX	ML273	Hamble	Aston Down	30	
4.6.44	VIII	MT708	Eastleigh	Cosford	45	
6.6.44	XI	BS242	Hamble	Cowley	25	
6.6.44	IX	ML314	Hamble	Aston Down	35	
7.6.44	IX	ML323	Hamble	Aston Down	35	
7.6.44	IX	ML141	Little Rissington	Hamble	30	
8.6.44	IX	NH471	Aston Down	Hamble	30	
10.6.44	IX	NH205	Marwell	Aston Down	30	
14.6.44	VIII	MT713	Eastleigh	Cosford	50	
15.6.44	VIII	MT933	Chattis	Brize Norton	30	
19.6.44	XIV	RM728	Chattis	Lyneham	20	
20.6.44	VIII	MT821	Eastleigh	Brize Norton	25	
21.6.44	VIII	MT719	Eastleigh	Cosford	45	
21.6.44	Vb	W3249	Cosford	Heston	50	NEA
24.6.44	XI	PT916	Lyneham	Hamble	25	
25.6.44	-	NM365	Eastleigh	Lyneham	25	Seafire
27.6.44	XIV	RM762	Chattis	Colerne	20	
27.6.44	XI	MJ571	Hamble	Little Rissington	30	

July 1944

6.7.44	IX	BS262	Hamble	Lyneham	30	
7.7.44	VIII	MT967	Eastleigh	Cosford	45	
8.7.44	IX	-220	Hamble	Bognor	20	GSU
8.7.44	XIV	RM737	Chattis	Colerne	20	
10.7.44	VIII	MT984	Chattis	Brize Norton	20	
13.7.44	II	NN380	High Post	Colerne	15	Seafire
13.7.44	IX	PL248	Colerne	Hamble	35	
13.7.44	IX	PL248	Hamble	Detling	30	
14.7.44	VIII	MT989	Chattis	Cosford	45	
14.7.44	IX	PL379	Cosford	Detling	60	
16.7.44	VII	MT994	Keevil	Cosford	45	
19.7.44	VII	BL892	Hamble	Brize Norton	40	
22.7.44	VIII	MV123	Eastleigh	Brize Norton	25	
29.7.44	VIII	MV129	Eastleigh	Brize Norton	20	

30.7.44	XIV	RM758	Chattis	Colerne	20	
30.7.44	IX	NH549	Colerne	Bognor	40	83 GSU
31.7.44	V	EN562	Hamble	Cowley	35	

August 1944

1.8.44	III	NN400	Eastleigh	Colerne	25	Seafire
4.8.44	III	NN262	Lyneham	Colerne	10	Seafire
13.8.44	Ia	X4648	Henstridge	Hamble	30	
13.8.44	XIV	RM754	Lyneham	Hawkinge	55	
16.8.44	II	NN410	Eastleigh	Colerne	30	Seafire
16.8.44	IX	NH211	Colerne	Thruxton	15	
16.8.44	VII	MV135	Eastleigh	Brize Norton	25	
16.8.44	IX	PT735	Brize Norton	Thruxton	20	
17.8.44	VIII	MT372	Keevil	Cosford	40	
17.8.44	IX	MJ299	Cosford	Bognor	60	83 GSU
20.8.44	VIII	MV141	Eastleigh	Brize Norton	20	
25.8.44	XIV	NH692	Hawkinge	Lyneham	50	
25.8.44	XI	PT754	Lyneham	Thruxton	25	
26.8.44	XIV	RM787	Chattis	Colerne	20	
28.8.44	VIII	-882	Keevil	Brize Norton	20	
31.8.44	XIV	RM792	Eastleigh	Colerne	35	

September 1944

1.9.44	VIII	MV425	Chattis	Brize Norton	20	Seafire
5.9.44	II	NN289	Colerne	Wroughton	15	Seafire
6.9.44	II	NN2-	High Post	Colerne	20	
7.9.44	VIII	MV146	Eastleigh	Brize Norton	25	
7.9.44	IX	PT827	Brize Norton	Thruxton	15	
11.9.44	V	BL892	Brize Norton	Lee-on-Solent	30	
15.9.44	VIII	MV154	Eastleigh	Brize Norton	25	

October 1944

1.10.44	XIV	RM869	Eastleigh	Colerne	30	
3.10.44	XIV	RM825	Eastleigh	Colerne	30	
3.10.44	V	EE623	Colerne	Hullavington	25	
4.10.44	I	T3932	Hullavington	Eastleigh	20	
8.10.44	XIV	RM843	Eastleigh	Lyneham	20	
14.10.44	IX	MJ561	Hamble	Colerne	30	
14.10.44	XIV	RM808	Colerne	Thorney Island	35	
15.10.44	XIV	RM879	Eastleigh	Lyneham	25	
15.10.44	IX	ML181	Lyneham	Thruxton	20	
16.10.44	XIV	RM872	Keevil	Colerne	15	
17.10.44	XIV	RM878	Eastleigh	Cosford	35	
27.10.44	IX	MJ794	Hamble	Cosford	45	
27.10.44	IX	MK323	Cosford	Thruxton	40	
27.10.44	VIII	MV197	Chattis	Brize Norton	20	
28.10.44	XIV	RM820	Sealand	Lyneham	40	
29.10.44	VIII	MV344	Chattis	Brize Norton	25	

November 1944

16.11.44	XIV	RM822	Lyneham	Westhampnett	30	
20.11.44	Vb	AA836	Middle Wallop	Brize Norton	20	
20.11.44	XVI	SM229	Brize Norton	Newbury	30	
20.11.44	XVI	SM229	Newbury	Tangmere	20	
21.11.44	XIV	RM927	Eastleigh	Sealand	60	
21.11.44	XIV	RM866	Sealand	Westhampnett	60	
23.11.44	III	PP937	Lyneham	Lee-on-Solent	30	Seafire
25.11.44	XVI	SM369	Cosford	Westhampnett	45	
26.11.44	IX	MH529	Hamble	Brize Norton	25	
29.11.44	XIV	RM920	Fairford	Sealand	35	
30.11.44	XIV	RM927	Sealand	Colerne	40	

December 1944

1.12.44	III	NN548	Eastleigh	Lyneham	30	Seafire
2.12.44	XIV	RM942	Keevil	Cosford	35	
5.12.44	IX	NH453	Hamble	Yeovilton	30	
6.12.44	III	NN562	Eastleigh	Colerne	30	Seafire
6.12.44	XVI	RK888	Odiham	Hamble	20	
9.12.44	-	NF514	Lee-on-Solent	Kirkbride	95	Seafire
10.12.44	XIV	RM974	Keevil	Brize Norton	15	
11.12.44	III	NN513	Lee-on-Solent	Cosford	45	Seafire
17.12.44	III	PP945	Lee-on-Solent	Cosford	50	Seafire
22.12.44	XIV	RM984	Keevil	Grove	30	
31.12.44	XIV	RM972	Eastleigh	Brize Norton	25	

January 1945

3.1.45	XIX	PS850	Eastleigh	Benson	20	
3.1.45	IX	PT732	Lasham	Westhampnett	15	
4.1.45	XI	MH423	Middle Wallop	Lyneham	15	
4.1.45	-	PR254	Lyneham	Hawarden	45	Seafire
7.1.45	XIX	PB857	Eastleigh	Benson	20	
13.1.45	-	RM139	Chattis	Benson	20	
14.1.45	XIV	MV269	Eastleigh	Colerne	30	
14.1.45	XIII	RM922	Colerne	Westhampnett	40	
15.1.45	XIV	RN115	Colerne	Westhampnett	30	
17.1.45	XIV	RN145	Chattis	Cosford	45	
21.1.45	XIV	RN160	Chattis	Brize Norton	25	

February 1945

1.2.45	XIV	-287	Eastleigh	Colerne	25	
1.2.45	XIV	MV915	Colerne	Westhampnett	35	
3.2.45	XIV	RN157	Keevil	High Ercall	35	
3.2.45	VI	BS453	Cosford	Hamble	50	
5.2.45	XIV	RN186	Keevil	Brize Norton	25	
9.2.45	III	NN613	Eastleigh	Colerne	20	Seafire
9.2.45	XIV	RN122	Colerne	Westhampnett	35	
9.2.45	IX	-452	Hamble	Yeovilton	30	

13.2.45	XIV	RM294	Keevil	Lyneham	15	
14.2.45	XIV	RM203	Keevil	Brize Norton	20	
20.2.45	XIV	RN201	Keevil	Cosford	30	
20.2.45	XIV	RM873	Lyneham	Dunsfold	25	
24.2.45	XIV	RN214	Keevil	Cosford	30	
24.2.45	XIV	-	Cosford	Wroughton	30	
25.2.45	XIV	RN206	Chattis	Cosford	45	Landed with tail wheel retracted
25.2.45	XIV	TB630	High Ercall	Dunsfold	60	

March 1945

1.3.45	XIX	PS8657	Eastleigh	Brize Norton	25	
5.3.45	XIV	NH792	Keevil	Lyneham	15	
7.3.45	XIV	NH640	Eastleigh	Brize Norton	30	
15.3.45	XVI	SM838	Chattis	Brize Norton	40	
16.3.45	XIV	NH642	Eastleigh	Brize Norton	25	
18.3.45	XIV	NH808	Keevil	Lyneham	25	
18.3.45	XVI	SM836	Keevil	Brize Norton	20	
20.3.45	XIV	RM616	Hamble	Brize Norton	25	
21.3.45	XIX	SM882	Eastleigh	Brize Norton	20	
23.3.45	XIII	R7308	Brize Norton	Hamble	30	
24.3.45	XIV	NH649	Eastleigh	Cosford	40	
29.3.45	XIV	NH836	Keevil	Lyneham	20	
29.3.45	XVI	TD280	Lyneham	Lasham	20	
31.3.45	XIV	MV351	Chattis	High Ercall	35	

April 1945

2.4.45	XIV	SM825	Brize Norton	Dunsfold	25	
3.4.45	XIV	NH901	Keevil	Brize Norton	15	
6.4.45	XVI	TD190	Brize Norton	Lasham	30	
8.4.45	XIV	MV532	Eastleigh	Colerne	35	
16.4.45	XIV	NH844	Eastleigh	Colerne	20	
16.4.45	XV	SR479	Colerne	Sealand	45	Seafire
16.4.45	XV	SR479	Sealand	Barrow	35	Seafire
17.4.45	XV	SR479	Barrow	Prestwick	45	
21.4.45	IX	TD299	Colerne	Lichfield	35	
22.4.45	XIV	NH912	Lyneham	Lasham	15	
23.4.45	XIV	NH696	Colerne	Dunsfold	30	
24.4.45	XIX	PS908	Eastleigh	Benson	20	
30.4.45	XIV	RM931	Warmwell	Lyneham	25	

May 1945

1.5.45	-	TE187	St Athan	Lasham	35	
2.5.45	XIV	NH921	Keevil	High Ercall	35	
3.5.45	XIV	MV290	Hamble	Brize Norton	20	
3.5.45	XIV	NH868	Brize Norton	High Ercall	35	
4.5.45	XIV	-	Lyneham	Lyneham	5	U/S

4.5.45	XIV	NH859	Lyneham	Sealand	55	
4.5.45	XIV	NH859	Sealand	Dumfries	35	
22.5.45	XIV	TP237	keevil	Brize Norton	15	
23.5.45	IIc	-	Lee-on-Solent	Cosford	45	Seafire
28.5.45	-	MA970	Lee-on-Solent	Kirkbride	105	Seafire

June 1945

| 1.6.45 | XIX | PM505 | Eastleigh | Benson | 15 | |
| 22.6.45 | XV | PS357 | Eastleigh | Culham | 25 | Seafire |

July 1945

2.7.45	XV	PR307	Eastleigh	Lyneham	30	Seafire
2.7.45	XVIII	PT404	Keevil	Lyneham	15	
6.7.45	IX	-	Hamble	Brize Norton	30	
13.7.45	IX	MJ915	Hamble	Brize Norton	30	
14.7.45	XIX	PS559	Eastleigh	Hamble	30	Bad weather
27.7.45	XVIII	TP399	Keevil	Lyneham	20	
27.7.45	XXII	PK315	Lyneham	Boscombe Down	20	

August 1945

1.8.45	XV	PR362	Colerne	Woodvale	60	Seafire
1.8.45	XV	PR362	Woodvale	Kirkbride	45	
9.8.45	XVIII	TP433	Keevil	Brize Norton	20	

December 1945

| 3.12.45 | XV | PM636 | Eastleigh | High Ercall | 60 | |
| 8.12.45 | XVIII | LP382 | Aldermaston | Colerne | 25 | |

January 1946

| 30.1.46 | XVIII | PS/SP327 | Eastleigh | Culham | 20 | |

March 1946

| 20.3.46 | - | - | Eastleigh | Culham | 60 | Last Spitfire ferried from Eastleigh |

Appendix II

Date	Serial	From	To	Time
1942				
11.9.42	HV703	Brooklands	Kemble	40
12.9.42	JS324	Langley	Shawbury-Silloth-Prestwick	150
14.9.42	JS265	Langley	Sealand-Millom	120
16.9.42	JS265	Millom	Prestwick	60
1.10.42	HW297	Langley	Hawarden	60
2.10.42	HW318	Langley	Hawarden	65
4.12.42	JS243	Hullavington	Wroughton	15
7.12.42	BX106	Hullavington	Wroughton	15
1943				
15.3.43	HV643	Middle Wallop	Hullavington	30
26.9.43	KZ604	Cosford	Detling	75
1.10.43	LD894	Kemble	High Ercall	35
1944				
15.3.44	V7133	Lee-on-Solent	Hawarden	70
1945				
5.9.45	LF377	Horsey Toll	Sherburn-in-Elmet	50

Appendix III

Date	Serial	From	To	Time
1942				
19 April	DK779	White Waltham	Hamble	40
1 October	P4131	Hawarden	White Waltham	80
18 November	HS298	White Waltham	Lee-onSolent	40
30 December	HS379	White Waltham	Worthy Down	25
30 December	HS386	White Waltham	Worthy Down	25
30 December	HS389	White Waltham	Worthy Down	25
1944				
10 February	P4206	Eastleigh	White Waltham	40
21 February	W5915	Cosford	Gosport	75
8 May	NF209	Hawarden	Worthy Down	105
17 May	DK774	Hamble	Eastleigh	15
5 June	NF304/G	Worthy Down	Hawarden	105
16 June	HS639	Eastleigh	Cosford	75
7 July	NR942/G	High Ercall	Worthy Down	90
12 July	HS399	Hamble	Eastleigh	15
17 July	NR994/G	High Ercall	Worthy Down	80
17 October	NS137/G	High Ercall	Worthy Down	100

Appendix IV

FIRST OFFICER MARY WILKINS
WELLINGTON DELIVERIES
1943-1945

Date	Mark	Serial	From	To	Notes
1943					
3.9.43	X	HE808	Llandow	Kemble	
3.9.43	XIII	HZ888	Little Rissington	Llandow	
21.9.43	X	HE851	Hawarden	Kemble	
25.9.43	XIII	HZ735	Hullavington	Thorney Island	
7.10.43	XIV	MP824	Little Rissington	Kemble	
9.10.43	XIV	MP823	Little Rissington	Kemble	
17.10.43	X	LN680	Hawarden	Little Rissington	
1944					
4.1.44	X	LN658	Hawarden	Harwell	
10.1.44	XIII	HZ651	Little Rissington	Lyneham	
11.2.44	XIII	LN841	Hawarden	Aston Down	
20.2.44	XIII	?150	Hawarden	Shawbury	
22.2.44	-	LP124	Little Rissington	Kemble	
28.2.44	X	LP312	Hawarden	Kemble	
19.3.44	VI	MP564	Hamble	Christchurch	
21.3.44	X	LP338	Hawarden	Kemble	
4.4.44	XI	MP547	Brooklands	Christchurch	
6.4.44	IA	P9231	Cosford	Kemble	
14.5.44	V	MF465	Little Rissington	Kemble	
5.6.44	X	HE461	Hawarden	Westcott	
29.6.44	X	MS368	Hawarden	Gosport	
6.7.44	XIII	MF579	Hamble	Gosport	
7.7.44	X	LP764	Hawarden	Little Rissington	
27.7.44	X	MF729	Little Rissington	Kemble	
27.8.44	X	NC351	Hawarden	Kemble	

3.9.44	XIII	HZ759	Little Rissington	St Athan	
9.10.44	X	LP726	Kemble	Llandow	
14.10.44	?	PN712	Kemble	Gosport	
26.11.44	XIII	HZ641	Little Rissington	Greenham Common	
1.12.44	XIII	MF639	Cosford	Gosport	
4.12.44	XIII	HZ641	Greenham Common	Gosport	

1945

4.1.45	XVI	R1172	Hawarden	Stoney Cross	
5.1.45	XIII	W5709	Hawarden	Broadwell	
6.1.45	XIII	W5709	Broadwell	Stoney Cross	
14.2.45	XIII	NB938	Little Rissington	St Athan	
27.2.45	XIII	NA737	Hawarden	Down Ampney	
2.3.45	VI	HZ549	Lee-on-Solent	Doncaster	
11.3.45	XIV	NC622	Little Rissington	St Athan	
16.3.45	XIV	MF127	Hawarden	St Athan	
30.3.45	III	BK456	Gamston	Little Rissington	[From] 30 OTU
25.7.45	III	RP492	Hawarden	Little Rissington	
2.8.45	?	FG384	Sherburn	Brooklands (Weybridge)	
1.9.45	XIII	JA384	Fersfield	Little Rissington	
25.9.45	III	BJ706	Sywell	Little Rissington	
10.10.45	X	?459	Sywell	Shawbury	
5.12.45	X	LP879	White Waltham	Stoney Cross	

1946

21.1.46	?	LM898	Wisley	Hawarden	

Appendix V

FIRST OFFICER MARY WILKINS
TYPHOON DELIVERIES
1945

Date	Serial	From	To	Time
7.1.45	RB377	Lasham	Westhampnett	15
3.4.45	MN261	Kemble	Lasham	-
8.4.45	EJ899	Kemble	Chilbolton	30
9.4.45	EJ899	Chilbolton	Lasham	30
21.4.45	MP117	Lichfield	Dunsfold	45
30.4.45	EJ975	Lasham	Kemble	20
12.5.45	SW630	Kemble	Lasham	20
15.5.45	MN601	Lichfield	Dunsfold	40
18.5.45	RB219	Odiham	Lichfield	35
22.5.45	MP123	Tangmere	Lichfield	40
2.6.45	MN518	Odiham	Kemble	25
24.6.45	MN187	Odiham	Ringway	50

Appendix VI

TEMPEST DELIVERIES
1945

Date	Mark	Serial	From	To	Time
25.4.45	V	NV787	Tangmere	Aston Down	30
25.4.45	V	JN755	Aston Down	Redhill	30
30.4.45	I	SN125	Aston Down	Lasham	20
12.5.45	-	SN258	Aston Down	Dunsfold	30
18.6.45	V	NV700	Warmwell	Aston Down	35
19.7.45	V	NV790	Warmwell	Aston Down	35

Appendix VII

MOSQUITO DELIVERIES
1945-1946

Date	Serial	From	To	Time
1945				
5.9.45	TE822	Ansty	Colerne	100
26.9.45	TE822	Colerne	Saint Athan	20
6.12.45	TK606	Hatfield	Silloth	90
1946				
12.1.46	PF635	Luton	Benson	30
29.1.46	PF653	Luton	Langham-Oulton	50
1.2.46	TV984	?	Shawbury	45

Appendix VIII

FIRST OFFICER MARY WILKINS
ELEVEN TYPES IN TEN DAYS
MARCH 1944

Date	Type	Mark	Serial	From	To
15.3.44	Hurricane	Ib	V7133	Lee-on-Solent	Hawarden
15.3.44	Oxford		LX117	Hawarden	Kidlington
15.3.44	Fairchild		-725	Kidlington	Hamble
16.3.44	Oxford		NM597	Portsmouth	White Waltham
16.3.44	Seafire		MB217	White Waltham	Christchurch
18.3.44	Spitfire	VIII	PA957	Keevil	Brize Norton
18.3.44	Seafire	III	NF520	Colerne	Lee-on-Solent
19.3.44	Wellington	VI	MP564	Hamble	Christchurch
19.3.44	Fairchild		-	Christchurch	Hamble
19.3.44	Oxford		NM519	Portsmouth	Sealand
19.3.44	Barracuda		MV727	Hawarden	Worthy Down
20.3.44	Spitfire	VIII	JG670	Chattis Hill	Cosford
20.3.44	Anson		T7052	Shawbury	Cosford
20.3.44	Barracuda		BV727	Worthy Down	Gosport
21.3.44	Oxford		NM684	Portsmouth	Sealand
21.3.44	Wellington	V	LP338	Hawarden	Kemble
24.3.44	Albacore		BA774	Lee-on-Solent	White Waltham

Appendix IX

Date	Type	Mark	Serial	From	To
1.8.45	Seafire	XV	PR362	Colerne	Woodvale
1.8.45	Hellcat		JV139	-	-
2.8.45	Firebrand	II	DK373	Farnborough	Sherburn-in-Elmet
2.8.45	Warwick		FG384	Sherburn-in-Elmet	Weighbridge
4.8.45	Fairchild		604	Hamble	Cowes
4.8.45	Walrus		X9467	Cowes	Wroughton
4.8.45	Reliant		FB563	Hamble	Gosport
8.8.45	Sea Otter	II	JM284	Cowes	Wroughton
8.8.45	Corsair	III	JS842	Yeovilton	Gosport
9.8.45	Spitfire	VIII	TP435	Keevil	Brize Norton
10.8.45	Mitchell	II	FW143	Boscombe Down	Hawarden
11.8.45	Anson		982	Hamble	Ratcliffe

Appendix X

TWELVE TYPES IN TWENTY DAYS
MAY 1945

Date	Type	Mark	Serial	From	To
10.5.45	Fairchild		332	Hamble	Beaulieu
10.5.45	Fairchild		332	Beaulieu	Hamble
11.5.45	Barracuda		MX844	Wroughton	Cosford
11.5.45	Corsair	III	JS657	Cosford	Gosport
12.5.45	Typhoon		SW630	Kemble	Lasham
12.5.45	Tempest		SN258	Aston Down	Dunsfold
15.5.45	Hudson		AM621	Eastleigh	High Ercall
15.5.45	Typhoon	III	MN601	Lichfield	Dunsfold
16.5.45	Fairchild		809	Hamble	Dunsfold
16.5.45	Fairchild		809	Dunsfold	Hamble
17.5.45	Sea Otter		179	Cowes	Wroughton
18.5.45	Typhoon		RB219	Odiham	Lichfield
22.5.45	Typhoon		MP123	Tangmere	Lichfield
22.5.45	Spitfire	VII	TP237	Keevil	Brize Norton
23.5.45	Seafire	IIc	-	Lee-on-Solent	Cosford
28.5.45	Seafire	IIc	MA970	Lee-on-Solent	Kirkbride
28.5.45	Boston	IV	BZ471	Kirkbride	Filton
30.5.45	Ventura	V	FN961	Eastleigh	High Ercall
30.5.45	Avenger		JZ284	High Ercall	Worthy Down

Appendix XI

FIRST OFFICER MARY WILKINS
AIRCRAFT TYPES FLOWN

SINGLE ENGINE

De Havilland DH60X Moth (G-ABBV;
    first solo flight, 13 July 1938)

Auster Autocar
Avro Tutor
Blackburn Firebrand
Blackburn Roc
Blackburn Skua
Boulton Paul Defiant
British Aircraft (Klemm) Swallow Mk.II
Cessna C170/172
Curtiss Seamew
de Havilland DH.60G Gipsy Moth
de Havilland DH.80A Puss Moth
de Havilland DH.82 Tiger Moth
Fairchild Argus
Fairey Albacore
Fairey Barracuda
Fairey Battle
Fairey Firefly
Fairey Fulmar
Fairey Swordfish
Gloster Gladiator
Grumman Avenger
Grumman Hellcat
Grumman Wildcat
Hawker Audax

Hawker Hart
Hawker Hector
Hawker Hind
Hawker Hurricane (Marks I and 2)
Hawker Tempest
Hawker Typhoon
Miles Magister
Miles Martinet
Miles Master
North American Harvard
North American Mustang
Percival Proctor
Piper Cub
Piper PA-22 Tri-Pacer
Stinson Reliant
Supermarine Seafire (Marks II, III, VIII
    and XV)
Supermarine Sea Otter
Supermarine Spitfire (various Marks)
Supermarine Walrus
Taylorcraft Auster
Vought Corsair
Westland Lysander

TWIN-ENGINE

Airspeed Oxford
Armstrong Whitworth Albemarle
Armstrong Whitworth Whitley

Avro Anson
Bristol Beaufighter
Bristol Bisley
Bristol Blenheim
de Havilland DH.89 Dominie
de Havilland DH.98 Mosquito
Douglas Boston
Gloster Meteor Mk.III
Handley Page Hampden
Lockheed Hudson
Lockheed Ventura

Miles Gemini
North American B-25 Mitchell
Vickers Warwick
Vickers Wellington

FOUR-ENGINE (As Second Pilot)

Avro Lancaster
Consolidated B-24 Liberator
Handley Page Halifax
Short Stirling

Appendix XII

FIRST OFFICER MARY WILKINS
AIRFIELDS FLOWN TO AND FROM
DURING ATA SERVICE

Abingdon
Aldergrove
Aldermaston
Andover
Ansty
Aston Down
Ayr

Babdown Farm
Balmer Lawn
Barnstaple
Barton
Beaulieu
Benson
Berrow
Biggleswade
Blackbushe
Bobbington
Bognor
Booker
Boscombe
Boscombe Down
Brenzett (My
interpretation of Mary's
writing)
Brize Norton
Broadwell
Brooklands
Broxbourne

Brussels

Cambridge
Cardiff
Cark
Castle Bromwich
Chattis Hill
Chedburgh
Chepstow
Chilbolton
Chivenor
Christchurch
Church Lawford
Church Stanton
Clyffe Pypard
Colerne
Coningsby
Cosford
Cowes
Cowley
Cranwell
Cranwell
Croughton
Croydon
Culham

Debden
Derby
Desford

Detling
Doncaster
Down Ampney
Down Farm
Droitwich
Dumfries
Dunsfold

Eastleigh
Elmdon
Exeter

Fairford
Farnborough
Fearn
Feltwell
Fersfield
Ford
Friston

Gatwick
Gosport
Gransden Lodge
Greenham Common
Grove

Halfpenny Green
Hamble
Hanworth

Hartfordbridge
Harwell
Hatfield
Hawarden
Hawkinge
Hendon
Henlow
Henstridge
Heston
High Ercall
High Post
Hinstock
Honeybourne
Honiley
Hornchurch
Horne
Hullavington
Hurn

Ibsley

Keevil
Kemble
Kidlington
Kirkbride

Langham
Langley
Larkhill
Lasham
Leamington
Leavesdon
Leconfield
Lee-on-Solent
Lichfield
Linton
Little Rissington
Llandow
Loughborough
Loveston
Luton
Lyneham

Manston
Marham
Marwell
Middle Wallop
Middleton St George

Mildenhall
Millom
Moreton Valence
Mount Farm

Netheravon
New Church
Newbury
Newmarket
Newton
North Weald
Northolt
Nutts Corner

Oakington
Odiham
Old Sarum
Ossington
Oulton

Penshurst
Pershore
Peterborough
Polebrook
Portsmouth
Prestwick

Radlett
Ratcliffe
Reading
Rearsby
Redhill
Renfrew
Ronaldsway

Sanderstead
Sealand
Seighford
Shawbury
Sherburn-in-Elmet
Shoreham
Silloth
Snailwell
Somerton
South Cerny
Speke
Squires Gate
St Athan

St Merryn
Stapleford Tawney
Stoney Cross
Stradishall
Stretton
Swindon
Sywell

Tachbrooke (Bishop's
Tachbrook)
Tangmere
Tarrant Rushton
Ternhill
Thame
Thorney Island
Thruxton

Upavon

Waddington
Warmwell
Warton
Watchfield
Watford
Westhampnett
West Kirby
Westcott
Weston Zoyland
Weybridge
Wheaton Aston
Whitchurch
White Waltham
Wing
Wisley
Witney
Wolverhampton
Woodvale
Worcester
Worthy Down
Wroughton

Yatesbury
Yeadon
Yeovil
Yeovilton

Zeals

Bibliography

Barnato Walker, Diana, *Spreading My Wings* (Grub Street, 2003).

Bergel, Hugh, *Fly and Deliver: A Ferry Pilot* (Airlife Publishing, 1982).

Bond, Steven, *Meteor: Gloster's First Jet Fighter* (Midland Counties Publications/Aerophile, 1985).

Brooks, Robin, *Oxfordshire in the Second World War* (Countryside Books, 2001).

Bruce, The Hon. Mrs Victor, *Nine Lives Plus: Record Breaking on Land, Sea and Air* (Pelham Books, 1977).

Cadogan, Mary, *Women with Wings: Female Flyers in Fact and Fiction* (Macmillan, 1992).

Cheesman, E.C., *Brief Glory: The Air Transport Auxiliary* (Maidenhead Heritage Trust/ATA Museum, 1946).

Cobham, Sir Alan, *A Time to Fly* (Shepheard Walwyn, 1978).

Curtis, Lettice, *The Forgotten Pilots* (Nelson and Saunders, 1985).

Curtis, Lettice, *Her Autobiography* (Walton on Thames, 2004).

de Bunsen, Mary, *Mount Up with Wings* (Hutchinson, 1960).

Fahie, Michael, *Harvest of Memories: The Life of Pauline Gower MBE* (GMS Enterprises, 1995).

Gillies, Midge, *Amy Johnson – Queen of The Air* (Weidenfeld & Nicolson, 2003).

Hathaway, Warren E., *Pursuit of a Dream; The Story of Pilot Vera (Strodl) Dowling* (Pagemaster, 2012).

King, Alison, *Golden Wings* (G .Arthur Pearson, 1956).

Lovell, Mary S., *The Sisters, The Saga of the Mitford Family* (W.W. Norton & Co., 2003).

Longstreet, Stephen, *The Canvas Falcons* (Barnes & Noble, 1970).

McKinstry, Leo, *Spitfire – Portrait of a Legend* (Hodder & Stoughton, 2007).

Moggridge, Jackie, *Spitfire Girl (Woman Pilot): My Life in the Sky* (Michael Joseph Ltd., 1957).

Moolman, Valerie, *Women Aloft* (Time-Life Books, 1981).

Narracott, A.H., *Unsung Heroes of the Air* (Frederick Muller Ltd., 1943).

Norris, Geoffrey, *The Royal Flying Corps* (Muller, 1965).

Rees, Rosemary (Lady du Cros), *ATA Girl* (Frederick Muller Ltd., 1983).

Timms, Kathy, and Hicks, Clare, *Old Brize Norton* (Bookmarque Publishing, 2002).

Thomas, Nick, *Naomi the Aviatrix* (Incline Village, Nevada, 2011).

Volkersz, Veronica, *The Sky and I* (W.H. Allen, 1956).

Welch, Ann, *Happy to Fly* (John Murray Ltd., 1983).

Wright, Peter, *The Royal Flying Corps in Oxfordshire 1912 – 1918* (Self-published, 2009).

Index

221

INDEX